AF606891

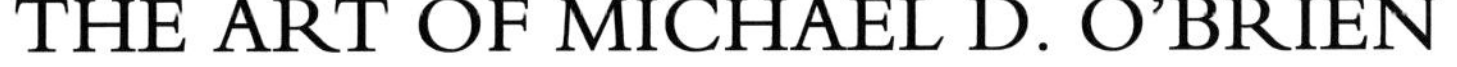

THE ART OF MICHAEL D. O'BRIEN

THE ART OF
MICHAEL D. O'BRIEN

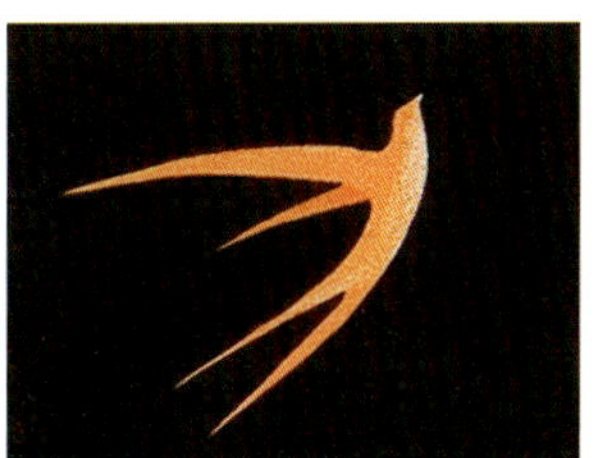

SAN FRANCISCO IGNATIUS PRESS

Cover art: *Freedom* by Michael D. O'Brien

Cover design by John Herreid

ISBN 978-1-62164-277-0
Library of Congress Control Number 2019931421
Printed in Canada ♾

CONTENTS

INTRODUCTION

Clemens Cavallin

In almost every large art museum in the Western world, the story is the same. From rows of classical Greek and Roman sculptures we enter into the medieval Christian world, dominated by sacred art; then, with the Renaissance, the gaze is once again directed to the naked human body, and a realist description of the natural world is opened up with the mathematical perfection of the central perspective. The pagan gods and goddesses return, and gradually Christian motifs diminish until we arrive at the quantum leap of modernism. Imitation of nature is left behind; and, after some decades, modern rigidity gives way to postmodern fluidity, in which the very idea of art evaporates, and we are left with an intellectual game of mirrors reflected in mirrors.

This is how the history of art is usually displayed, and it constitutes an integral part of the grand story of the Western world—an evolutionary tale hidden by the seemingly innocuous structure of chronological periods. The main principle is that you cannot retrace your steps. In fact, you are not allowed to; *il faut être dans son temps*—you must be a child of your times. The hands of the clock move inexorably forward, ever forward.

In this way, secularism is built into the way we understand ourselves, irrespective of whether we are believers. The Middle Ages is perceived as merely a one-thousand-year parenthesis in the development of Western civilization, a chivalrous but superstitious era that left us beautiful Romanesque and Gothic churches to which tourists go to marvel at the architecture, rose windows, and frescoes. But that the culture behind these art forms ought to be alive today is out of the question, the very idea almost a crime. And attempts to revive its ways of expression are deemed merely reactions to the inevitable progress of the human race—signs of fundamentalist desperation.

For Michael D. O'Brien, a young Canadian in the 1970s who wanted to be an artist and, at the same time, a serious public Christian, the secular imperative of modern art introduced a tension that led to an existential crisis. Though his first exhibition—mainly drawings of nature—was a success, it left him unsettled. In fact, wanderlust and the sheer force of the impossibility of his situation drove him from modern civilization; he left for a simple life in the mountains of British Columbia, gave up his art, and joined a Catholic apostolate on the margins of society.

If, instead, he had opted for art school, he might have found it impossible to disentangle himself from the grand narrative of Western art. Day after day, his eyes and mind would have struggled to draw the model standing in front of him: merely a specimen of flesh without symbolical meaning and dignity, a person reduced to an example of anatomy. Instead, in the wilderness, O'Brien discovered that the story Western modernity was telling itself was not the whole truth. Christian sacred art had not everywhere followed this supposedly inevitable path of modern maturity. The tradition of the Eastern Orthodox icon was unbroken; and by submitting to its regime, the young artist was formed by the principles of an unsentimental sacred art—so different from the effeminate saints on the holy cards still dominating Catholic imagination. The austere discipline of the icon and its dignified expression provided him with an alternative aesthetics and an outside perspective on the spiritual decline of Western art. The icon lacked the swirling bodies of superficially "baptized" pagan figures and the illusion of depth. Instead, it used highly formalized symbols and was surface oriented; the "third dimension" lay in the relation to its spiritual prototype. The icon maker flattened the physical world in order for another kind of depth to become palpable.

For O'Brien to take up sacred art was thus not a reaction, a turning back; on the contrary, he received a tradition and took it forward to the next generation, as the baton in a relay race. If one scrutinizes art history from such a perspective, a plurality of story lines emerges. Contemporary art, in the descriptive sense, is, then, not the expression of the core principles of late modernity; it consists, instead, of a plurality of competing stories, some of which are not allowed into the temples of modern art. Among them are traditional attempts to move Christian sacred art forward by artists who do not see themselves primarily as expressing the values of a modernist avant-garde but try to hand over an inherited treasure to the next generation.

Still, to attach oneself to a tradition without being formally initiated into it was difficult for the young O'Brien. He was, after all, living in a small village in British Columbia, with a break of three years in Ottawa. After seven years, during which he mostly studied and painted Byzantine art, he came to the point at which he could reintroduce into his art certain forms and principles from the Western tradition. It was as if he attempted to put into practice the principle formulated later by Pope John Paul II: the Church must breathe with both her lungs.

The first of these Western styles was expressionism. This came naturally to O'Brien due to his rich interior life, which, with its images, stories, and spiritual promptings, moved his imagination and emotions powerfully. Georges Rouault (1871–1958), a French painter and friend of the philosopher Jacques Maritain, greatly inspired O'Brien. In midlife, Rouault had increasingly turned to Christian motifs in his paintings, which were characterized by broad black outlines (perhaps a trace from his training as a glass painter) and a mix of muddied and strong colors. The shapes are both simplified and distorted; the overall impression is rough and raw; as in expressionism, the interior emotional life determines the shapes of things. This comes to the fore in Rouault's paintings of the crucified Christ: the lack of realist depth and the primitive, but still figurative, style conveys effectively the brutality and intensity of the Passion. This is parallel to O'Brien's depictions of the Crucifixion, which he often painted in tones of dark umber and ochre: from earthy yellow highlights through shades of burnt sienna to black. The face of Jesus hides a dramatic emotional landscape; the Passion is primarily interior, as the eyes of Jesus seem to be fixed somewhere in the distance or are closed. The background is flat, mostly dark. Symbols that the viewer can easily decode—the Cross, the crown of thorns, and the nails—signal the Christian meaning of redemption, but behind them vibrates the devastating and manifold experiences of pain.

The main principle of expressionism stands in a tense relation to the symbolism and pure beauty of the icon. In expressionism, the formal clarity and the transcendent prototype of the symbol recede as the intensity of emotion distorts the figures and the objects in the painting. The logical result is abstract expressionism, in which the hand of the artist, holding a brush loaded with paint, functions as a seismograph recording his psychological states or, when acting as a medium, those of others. In O'Brien's paintings of the Passion of Christ, this expressionist principle is mostly tempered by the obvious Christian symbols, but in, for example, *Christ in Gethsemane* (1991), the expressionist tendency is taken a step further. The background is divided by the horizontal edge of a dark rolling hill with three cypresses silhouetted against a brown night sky lit up by a full moon. In the foreground, taking up three-quarters of the space, is a bearded man with his head resting on his right arm, his neck bent at an anatomically difficult angle, his face stiffened by interior anguish. The focus of the painting is clearly the interior life of the suffering man; the exterior landscape, as in Edvard Munch's famous painting *The Scream*, merely curves around the man like ripples in water. Without the title specifying the scene as set in Gethsemane, the viewer would be at loss to decode its Christian meaning.

This expressionist tendency is even more pronounced in the two versions of *Adam Sleeping* (1985, 1986). In the same way, both images are dark, with the horizon merely indicated by a red glow or a strong light; the moment is just before sunrise or after sundown; a full moon shines in the upper right corner without illuminating the landscape, as if the darkness absorbs its rays. Still, the naked man lying on the ground is lit up by another strong light source to the left, outside the frame. As he is sleeping and there are no symbols indicating how the image is to be interpreted, the real but hidden meaning is inside the man's dreams. The paintings provide a serious, austere mood, but as the sleeping Adam is not a very frequent motif in Christian iconography, it is even harder to decode without the title than the Gethsemane scene is.

A similar painting is that of the prophet Elijah sleeping, painted in monochrome yellow ochre and black. A man is lying on the dark ground with a rolling horizon lit up by a rising sun just below the horizon; he has a stone pillow under his head and wears a long-sleeved garment. Behind him stands a bird with a small, glowing oval object in its beak. This provides a clue to decode the sleeping figure as the prophet Elijah and the bird as the raven that fed him. But, once again, the fact that the man sleeps and the landscape is dark makes us wonder about his dreams, his thoughts, and the stories played out in his mind. A typical icon of the same motif includes the black raven with a piece of bread in its beak, but the prophet does not sleep; instead, he looks at the bird, seemingly contemplating the goodness of God, feeding him in the desert, which is indicated by stylized mountains.

In these paintings, O'Brien thus stretches the symbolic connection between the image and the biblical story and refocuses it on the interiority of first Jesus, then Adam and Elijah.

This is also the case in *St. Joseph Dreaming* (2012), in which the sleeping man lies, as in the other paintings, with his head to the left, facing the viewer, and dressed in a long-sleeved red tunic, with his arms folded over his breast. The ground is dark, but in the sky are swirling light-blue shapes, like stars and nebulas dancing. Around the man's head glows an intense blue light, chromatically connected to the celestial dance. From the left side of the painting, a hand of another man stretches into the pictorial space, hanging over the head of the sleeping man; it is as if this second man, whom we cannot see, pauses before giving his blessing or bestowing an anointed dream, or perhaps it is a gesture of protection. Once more, the real, merely implied, meaning is inside the mind of the sleeping man; his closed eyes cut us off from his experiences, but the landscape bends and twists in accordance with the movements of his soul, so we get at least a glimpse of his mood.

In comparison with the paintings with similar motifs from the 1980s and 1990s, the colors of *St. Joseph Dreaming* are clearer, and there is a liveliness; gone are the monochrome earth colors and the black that radiated an almost tragic mood. Now the skies are dancing, and the contrast between red and blue indicates a joy not present in the paintings of Gethsemane, Adam, and Elijah, in which the predominant emotion appears to be anguish.

The man sleeping on the ground is a central motif for O'Brien's understanding of salvation history and his form of imaginative biblical exegesis. In these paintings, man is primarily passive and spiritually receptive, and God is the one acting—for example, through dreams. Human insufficiency is combined with interior divine workings. O'Brien could instead have chosen the classic motif of Eve created from Adam's rib while he slept, or Elijah as he was awakened by the angel. We do not know which of Joseph's four dreams is depicted, and we do not see the angel. The glow around Joseph's head leaves it to our imagination to decide what is taking place his soul.

Other works, such as *Angel of the Dawn* (2001) and *Creation of the Birds* (2002), are variants on the tension between the interiority of the sleeping man and the Christian symbolic meaning. In the first, an enormous red angel takes the new moon in his hands while the man, with a shepherd's staff lying beside him, sleeps on the dark ground. In the second painting, different kinds of birds surround a sleeping face seen close up. Various hands release the birds, which seem to be both within the man's dream world and outside of it; they are, at the same time, psychological, physical, and spiritual birds.

This tension between traditional Christian symbols and the expression of interiority is not present, for example, in another Elijah painting, *Elijah and Elisha* (2002). Elijah is going into the sky in the fiery chariot, and Elisha takes hold of his red mantle. They look at each other. Once again, light- and dark-blue swirling shapes light up the sky; the landmass beyond the turquoise water is merely indicated by saturated red undulating lines. The colors and the celestial phenomena exude a joyful mood, but the painting could instead have focused on Elisha's pain in seeing his master departing. The shapes of the sky, the sea, and the hills are not formed and distorted by passions but are animated by the supernatural reality underlying the picture. It is as if the skies dance according to their own form of jubilation, not moved by human feelings. The pictorial language of the icon is dominant, and the characteristics of expressionism are not present. In this way, one can see how O'Brien moves on a scale between symbolic meaning, pointing to spiritual realities, and expressionist meaning, making lines and colors change according to human subjectivity. At one pole, there is spiritual depth, and at the other, there is psychological depth. In the inner world of the dreaming soul, these two coincide, hidden from our gaze.

Another Western influence on O'Brien's art, as he began to move beyond the boundaries of the classical icon, was realism—the painterly language with which he began: first with drawings of nature and then with portraits. Before taking up sacred art, however, he had given up this form of expression. To him, it was connected to a secular understanding of reality that he tried to leave behind. Despite his reservations, his main inspiration for integrating realism into his project of sacred art was William Kurelek (1927–1977), who combined a kind of dreaming naïve realism with intense Christian motifs. He became O'Brien's mentor for a year before his early death, and one can clearly see Kurelek's influence in some of O'Brien's colorful landscapes that have three-dimensional depth and are sparsely populated by small human figures. For example, *Christmas at Rosebud Creek* (1989) and *Christmas Eve in Canada* (2014) are similar to the illustrations in Kurelek's book *A Northern Nativity* (1976), which locate the Nativity in different Canadian milieus, among them an Inuit igloo, featured on the cover. O'Brien's two paintings with the name and motif *A Place Where We All Could Live* (1986, 1987), which present an ideal village life in the mountains, are painted in the same style. In *Homecoming* (2004) and *Sanctuary of the Heart* (2010), however, the level of realism is lower and they incline toward symbolism, even if the theme is the same: finding one's true home.

If Kurelek's style of realism is similar to idealized memories, then photographic realism, like expressionism, lets us confront reality in its rawness. Instead of psychological phenomena, it is the surface of material reality, devoid of symbolic meaning, that we encounter. Photo-realism in the 1960s and 1970s focused mainly on the artificial world of human creations, with its machines and modernist architecture, instead of on nature. Hyperrealistic painting techniques, which take photo-realism one step further, can be used in sacred art. Like expressionism, however, photo-realism moves the focus from the spiritual to the psychological, making us attentive to the materiality of the depicted objects and persons, not to their spiritual meaning.

One obvious area in which photo-realism becomes relevant for sacred art is in portraits of saints who lived in the twentieth century and of whom we have photographs, such as St. Teresa Benedicta of the Cross (Edith Stein) and St. Maximilian Kolbe. Often O'Brien chose to paint them in the style of old photographs with a faint monochrome warm hue, similar to sepia photographs. But with St. Thérèse of Lisieux, of whom there are several black-and-white photographs, he integrated a full-color, more classical style with the facial features derived from photographs.

Using photographic realism, even if here it is black-and-white photographs, gives the saints a distinct personality that is otherwise absent from O'Brien's sacred art paintings, in which the faces are highly stylized and similar to each other. Moreover, in his saint portraits that follow photographs closely, there are no halos or religious symbols. Instead, the peaceful, loving expressions on the faces provide the spiritual meaning. It is markedly different from the figures with closed eyes, inside whom we can guess that powerful emotions move. The modern saints of the photographic era direct their benign attention toward the viewer; but, without the title, as with some of the expressionist paintings, we would be at loss to know we were viewing sacred art.

As we have seen, O'Brien uses many styles in his paintings, but it is misleading to divide his art into periods, as he uses these styles in parallel and at times simultaneously. To order his art in this way would be to imitate the narrative of Western art in the many grandiose neoclassical art museums, arguing that one style leads to another in a kind of evolutionary process. Still, there are some distinct periods in O'Brien's half century of creative life: that of the early realist drawings, followed by a seven-year phase of Byzantine iconography and then different attempts at fusion of East and West—but this is not the real story. I think it is much more interesting and worthwhile to highlight the principles of his attempts to formulate Christian sacred art for the third millennium. It is as if he explored the scale rather than a single formula. In this way, what O'Brien gives us is not a perfected style, but attempts to work with these principles. In other words, how are symbol, interior passion, and representations of the physical world to be balanced in a way that speaks truthfully about the mysteries of the Christian faith in our times, characterized by de-Christianization?

Before I highlight the interconnection of these three dimensions in his sacred art, I need to present a guiding principle that underlies O'Brien's entire work. It is his scrupulous dedication to authenticity. He would rather burn his paintings than be unfaithful to his inspiration and beliefs. Therefore, he does not attempt to increase artificially the efficiency of his style, his aptitude for skillful persuasion, or to develop a brilliant technique meant to dazzle the viewer. He wants to be absolutely true to the interior promptings of the Holy Spirit and his imagination and also to the spiritual realities of the Catholic faith. This approach is for him a deep realism, in distinction to realisms limited to the phenomenal world by rationalism. Personal authenticity means that he himself has to live what he paints. The artist is not merely a skillful manufacturer of devotional objects according to specified rules. I believe that this is the master principle in O'Brien's attempt at renewing Christian art: the way of the artist is that of the Cross, the central mystery of the Christian religion.

Of course, this exalted value given to authenticity, in order to overcome spiritually inadequate forms of art, inclines O'Brien toward expressionism, which reveals that the artist himself is sharing in the Passion of Christ. But then the religious symbolism is caught in a tension between, on the one hand, pictures and scenes in the imagination of the artist that present themselves with an immediacy and authority that cannot be doubted and, on the other hand, the conventional signs and symbols of the Christian tradition.

On the sliding scale between interior authenticity, tending toward the mysterious and idiosyncratic, and exterior theological truths, written with the help of images, realism intersects the material world, that is, the lived, human, moral world. In a sense, these three principles correspond to three "parts" of the human person: the spirit, the soul (psyche), and the body, which, in their turn, are active in contemplation, the will, and the senses—and in another threesome: truth, goodness, and beauty.

The major question in O'Brien's attempt at formulating sacred art is how to find a balance between these fundamental aspects of reality that pertains to the human person and society—and to the triune God. The symbol points to spiritual truth, expression to moral goodness, and realism to the beauty of the created world. If the balance is upset, symbolic art becomes didactic, expressionism suffers from sentimentalism or chaotic emotional uproar, and realism indulges in either sensationalism and exhibitionism or cold materialism.

Sometimes O'Brien gives more weight to expression, sometimes to symbols, and sometimes to realist renderings of faces and landscapes. Where is his balance? Did he really find it? Perhaps it is beyond a single artist to overcome the disjunction between truth monopolized by science, goodness claimed by ideologies, and beauty taken over by the entertainment industry. To do this, I am afraid, it is necessary to overcome the whole of the modern project. A mighty task indeed!

For O'Brien, as I have stated, the underlying principle is personal authenticity: the artist must live what he paints or writes. And as he is Christian and believes in the existence of the soul and of a loving, omnipotent God, and in the helping power of angels, the source for living this reality is foremost spiritual and interior. It is in deep prayer and in a simple life in accordance with one's spirit, which inevitably is that of the Cross, of slowly dying to oneself, that we, according to O'Brien, should search for this balance. In a sense, this makes failure the solution—not in a tragic way, the death of a hero against overwhelming odds, but as a recognition of the inadequacy of human power and the necessity of divine intervention. We cannot find spiritual, moral, and aesthetic balance on our own.

On a similar note, I would like to close this introduction not with more analysis but with a synthesis, with a red thread that runs—or, rather, flies—through O'Brien's images.

If you look carefully, you will see that there is a bird, usually a swallow, in many of O'Brien's paintings. Sometimes it plays a central role, as in *The Rescuer*, in which a man with closed eyes, his head turned horizontally in an anatomically impossible pose (he thus appears to be sleeping even if he stretches out both his arms), releases a swallow, which flies upward toward a horizon of light. Meanwhile in the lower left corner, there is a fire from which many small swallows escape. It seems that the swallows signify individual souls, emphasizing their spiritual speed and agility; and, once more, the closed eyes of the man indicate that the significant part of the action takes place outside our vision. Similarly, in *Transcendence*, a man is standing on a hill in the lower left corner, releasing a swallow, while higher up, closer to the viewer, three swallows dash through the air. From the man, lines flow up into the sky. Perhaps it is the artist letting his thoughts and creations swirl up into the sky, passing in front of our eyes for a moment and then quickly darting away with a cry of joy toward heaven.

It is no coincidence that O'Brien chose as the cover picture for this volume the painting *Freedom*, in which a man with a solemn face looks intently at a white bird lying in his outstretched right hand, as if trying to tell the bird that it is now free. The man is more a composition of body parts than an anatomically correct human figure, which gives the image an intense expression. It is as if the artist waits for his own spirit, his inspiration, to rise and spread its wings and fly toward eternal freedom.

We can go on and on. In *The Healer* (2015) the spirit descends toward one of the hands of the healer. In the background of *Mother and Child Reading the Word* (early 1990s), a swallow races in flight along the curvature of the mother's hair. In *The Swallow* (2016), a figure in a boat rocked by heavy waves carries a swallow in her hand, exhorting it to fly high in the sky, as the other swallows do.

That the interior title page and the last page of this book both carry a small, light-orange silhouette of a swallow in flight against a black background is a way of saying that here is the solution: the unwavering attention to the spirit, the experience of interior freedom, the lightning-quick movements of the spirit's ethereal wings. It is not a style, a trademark, that O'Brien provides; instead, he puts before us the principles that we need to harmonize and the means to do so. The results will depend on our circumstances, both as persons and as communities.

The next time you visit an art museum, think of this: through the difficult combination of interior passions and exterior symbolic meaning, of jubilant colors and monochrome, there flies a swallow with astonishing speed through art history. You catch only a glimpse of him, but it is he who opens up the perspective, the depth of the painting. And much of what he inspires is not displayed there. There are lines of tradition living on outside those thick walls; he whispers even into the ears of those who have retreated deep into the wilderness.

Dr. Clemens Cavallin
Director of Religious Studies
University of Gothenburg, Sweden

PREFACE

Painting, unlike theater, sculpture, or architecture, must exercise its particular virtue in two dimensions only, while appealing to a single human sense—the visual. Even so, it has at its disposal the medium of light, which means that its potential for expressing seen and unseen realities is practically infinite.

Its scope is limited only by the artist's level of skill and the quality of the materials and instruments that come to his hand. And by his eye, of course. On the purely human level, every artist paints what attracts him, moves him, sometimes emotionally and sometimes spiritually, or a combination thereof. These aspects of the creative life vary from artist to artist, but the universal principle is always at work: "Man is a maker", says Aristotle. And as St. Thomas Aquinas writes, a millennium and a half later, man is drawn through the beauty of created things to the One who is the source of beauty, who is Beauty itself. *Id quod visum placet*, "that which pleases when seen", is the first level of encounter, yet it beckons beyond itself. A thing is truly beautiful, says Aquinas, if it has integrity (fidelity to its nature), proportion or harmony (order and unity), and *claritas*, by which he means not only a certain clarity but, above all, a radiance of being.

It is important to keep in mind that when an artist makes beautiful things, he himself is a medium, though not in the sense of a tool or a mechanism or an indifferent conduit. He is concerned not so much with the portrayal of external reality for the purpose of merely replicating it (a camera, after all, can perform this task more efficiently and precisely); rather, he is about a more difficult process: that of making manifest the mysteries and barely perceptible inner beauties of his subject. He is a vehicle of perception, an interpreter, and when he lives his calling to the utmost, he is a contemplative.

Every artist emerges at a specific time and place in history, immersed in a culture that is contemporary to him, formed to a great degree by what he perceives around him even as he looks backward at what has gone before and, simultaneously, blindly, forward into the future. This is as true for the man making his bison and mammoth murals on the walls of the cave at Lascaux as it is for the ingenious painters of the mummy portraits at El Faiyûm, Egypt, for the Byzantine iconographer and the medieval manuscript illuminator, for the Impressionist landscapist and the postmodernist anarchist. Each in his way strives to be master of a multidimensional assortment of elements in the creative process—his eye's perception, optics, the color spectrum, the form of his subject, shadow and light, details and textures, the illusion of three dimensions, the mind-brain-muscle control of his hand, the unstable behavior of pigments and, not least, his feelings, his intuitions, and the elusive imagery that appears spontaneously in his imagination; moreover, let us not fail to mention a dash of reason as he takes a step back and ponders what is materializing on his canvas, his paper, his wall.

This is a roundabout way of saying that an artist is a co-creator. Made in the image and likeness of God, he exercises in a subsidiary manner a power bequeathed to him by the Creator, who gave him his nature and his life. He may be entirely ignorant of this truth. He may even adamantly deny it, but the gift is there nonetheless. For the Christian artist, the meaning of his labor vastly expands, and with it—it is to be hoped—his creative vision. The artist must be tireless in perfecting his practical skills and knowledge of the art, for without the discipline of craftsmanship, the vision will be indistinct and may even fail altogether. Grace builds upon nature, says Aquinas, and thus the artist of faith must be as dedicated to prayer as he is to his tools. He must be ceaselessly concerned with the authenticity of the work and the good of those who will one day gaze upon it. In this way, with a sensitive awareness of the demands of *ora et labora*, he will grow personally, and the fruit of his labors will develop into living words—words that give life to others—first calling them through the medium of beauty to silent attention before a mystery; then evoking profound questions within their hearts and souls; and then drawing them to a state of wonder, and from there into reverence for being itself.

This no small task. It is no small vocation. Indeed, no artist ever realizes it perfectly. Mozart and Raphael notwithstanding, few, if any, artists are geniuses from birth, though flashes of genius may appear early on in a life. For most of us, the path is one of long, hard labors combined with a spirit of exploration and, above all, a spirit of love, which is the means and motive of the growth. At the core of all genuine love is the willingness to sacrifice, to die to oneself so that others may live. Jacques Maritain, in his *Art and Scholasticism*, says that "it is the actuality of love, contemplation in charity, which is here required. A Christian work would have the artist, as man, a saint. It would have him possessed by love. Then he may go and do as he likes."[1]

Maritain is not naïve about the stresses and obstacles involved. He writes:

> But it may be objected, is this Christian art not a myth? Can it so much as be conceived? Is not art pagan by birth and tied to sin—even as man is born a sinner? But grace heals the wounds of nature. Do not say that Christian art is impossible. Say rather that it is difficult, doubly difficult—difficulty squared, because it is difficult to be an artist and very difficult to be a Christian, and because the whole difficulty is not merely the sum but the product of these two difficulties multiplied by one another, for it is a question of reconciling two absolutes. Say that the difficulty becomes excruciating when the whole life of the age is far removed from Christ, for the artist is greatly dependent on the spirit of the time. But has courage ever been lacking on the earth?[2]

The whole life of our age, at least in its dominant perceptual consciousness or psychological cosmos, is far removed from life in Christ. All too easily, gifted young people who have been denied their real identity, their own true story, turn away from the vocation of art—and especially sacred art—believing it to be not only impractical but impossible. If they value their creative gifts sufficiently, they will not, perhaps, abandon

[1] Jacques Maritain, *Art and Scholasticism*, trans. J. F. Scanlan (New York: Charles Scribner's Sons, 1930), 55.

[2] Ibid., 53–54.

the making of images altogether but instead may fall into various traps. These can take a myriad of forms, such as a habit of making superficial decorations, or prettiness, or sensuality, or the posturings of revolutionary "transvaluation of values". This latter is the most tragic, for the artist who sees himself as a hero or a prophet, or a priest of the sociopolitical forces to which he is loyal and which he believes are the historical necessities of his times, too easily becomes a puppet. He has no external measure with which to assess reality. Whether he submits to the forces entirely or in part, he becomes a parody of himself, and then, without knowing it, he surrenders his gifts to the demons of his era. Having lost his place in the continuity of time, he becomes dependent on social affirmation and the drug of exalted feelings common to all revolutionaries. He destroys even as he thinks he creates.

But we must not lose hope for him, for his desire for exultation is really a damaged longing for the transcendent. And, in time, he may come to understand that the real challenge for the artist is to distinguish between his tendencies to genuine creative intuition and the impulses of the self-centered ego. By seeking to understand himself without falling into the trap of self-obsession, by suffering, and most of all by learning to love, he will find the true story of man and his own identity. Is this still possible in our age, which is so saturated in the false story? I know that it is possible, because, for a time, I was that man, a lost man, an agnostic, a practical atheist, carrying within myself a void that I presumed was the reservoir of superior vision.

My conversion to Christ at the age of twenty-one was a pure gift from God. It was sudden, totally unexpected, instantaneous, like St. Paul's on the road to Damascus. It was a radical shock, a shattering of the illusions that had enslaved me and a revelation that everything the Church and Scripture had taught about God was, in fact, *reality*. I swiftly ran to him, and my life began.

One of the extraordinary gifts with which I was blessed shortly after my conversion was the gift of art. Until then, I had never been seriously interested in it; indeed, I had failed miserably at it in elementary school and high school. There were, in my case, no early "flashes of genius". To put it simply, I was the least likely to succeed. Even so, one spring day, while wandering in a wood, I absentmindedly took a pen and paper and drew a small budding sapling growing up out of a pile of rocks. It had moved me somehow, and I made a sketch of it in order not to forget it. Only later did I understand it as a metaphor of my newfound faith bringing me to life out of the absolutely barren soil of modernity. I was startled by the strength of the drawing, and I began to draw other things in the forest around me. Like a spring of water, this trickle of creativity flowed more and more until I was soon drawing continually as a pile of sketches grew in quantity and quality, a tumbled archive that I had no idea what to do with. What it all meant I could not then foresee, though the joy I felt when drawing was unprecedented for me, and I did not want to lose it.

To condense a complex story that involves much grace and providence, a year later I had my first solo exhibit at a commercial art gallery. And that led to a growing sense that I might possibly find my way in this world as an artist. And a few years after that, in 1976, I made the decision to paint overtly Christian works from then on, trusting that God would continue to do the impossible. It has now been nearly half a century since I began to draw, more than forty years since I made the commitment to serve

Christ and his Church as an artist. Through it all, there have been constant trials and tribulations, but more importantly, an abiding joy.

In this collection of my visual art, the reader will find only a fraction of the paintings I have made, presented rather loosely according to themes and styles. I have not arranged them in chronological order because I have been a very poor record keeper and a haphazard photographer. I have no memory of the precise years many of the images reproduced in this volume were created, though I am fairly certain about the decades. In addition, some of the best paintings are lost, though I should say they are not really lost, as they are out in the world somewhere, doing their work. Then and now, many of my works are unsigned and undated. They have lives of their own. It is my hope, therefore, that the images will speak for themselves.

Michael D. O'Brien

Early Drawings

This chapter presents a miscellany of sketches in pencil, charcoal, and ink, with subjects from nature, life portraits, mini renditions of family photographs from the nineteenth century, and whimsical flights of fancy, from 1970 to 1973.

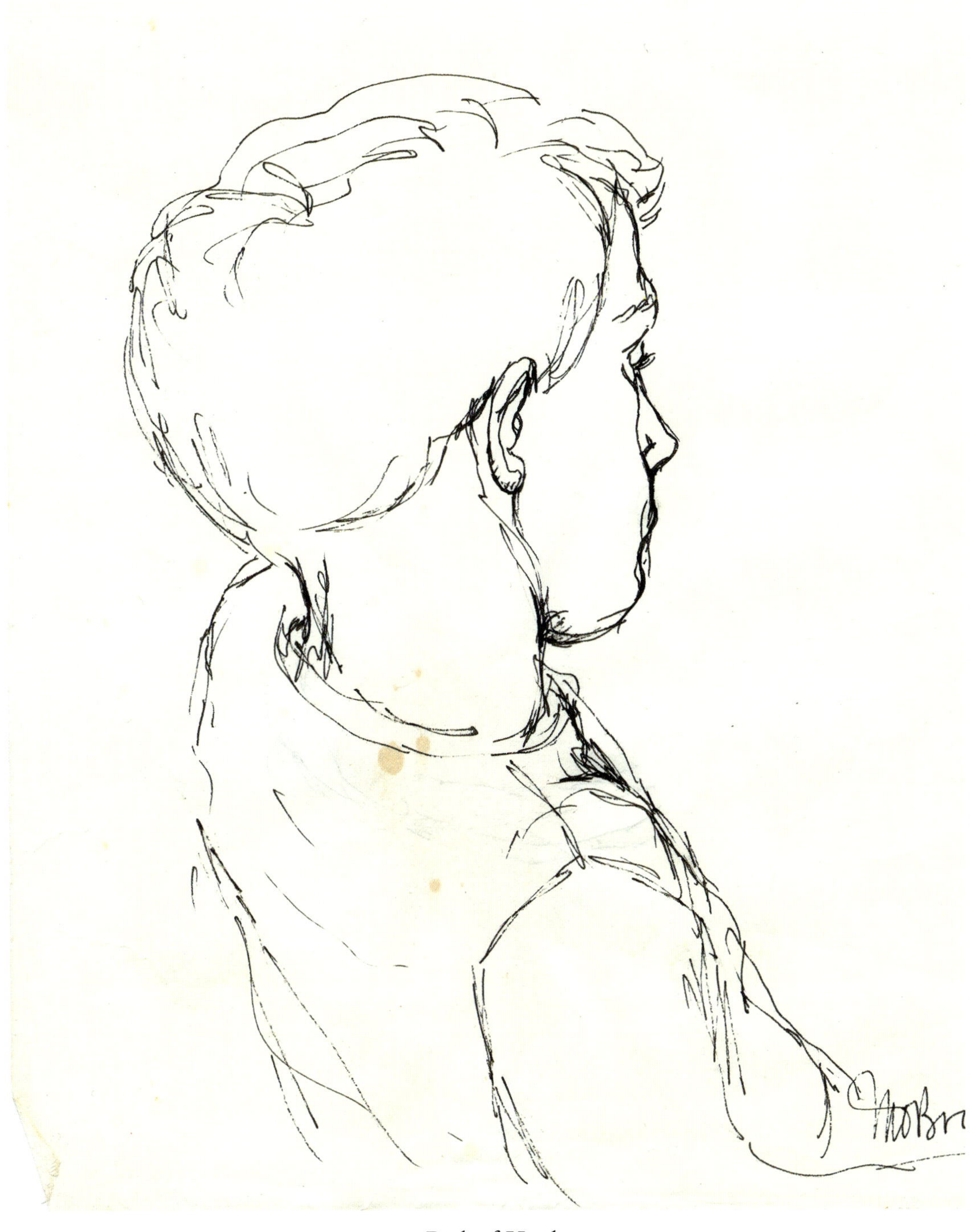

Back of Head

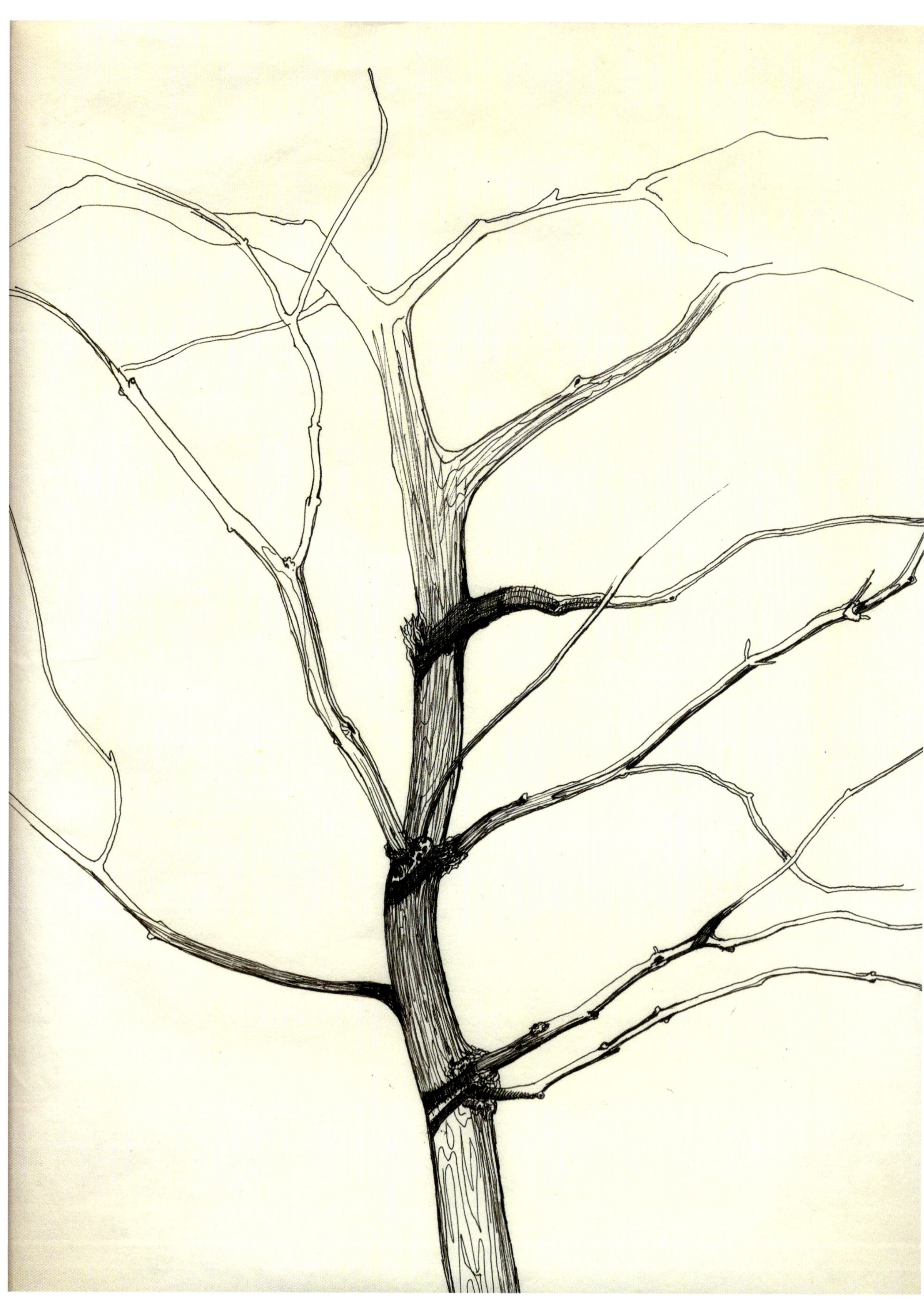

Barren Tree

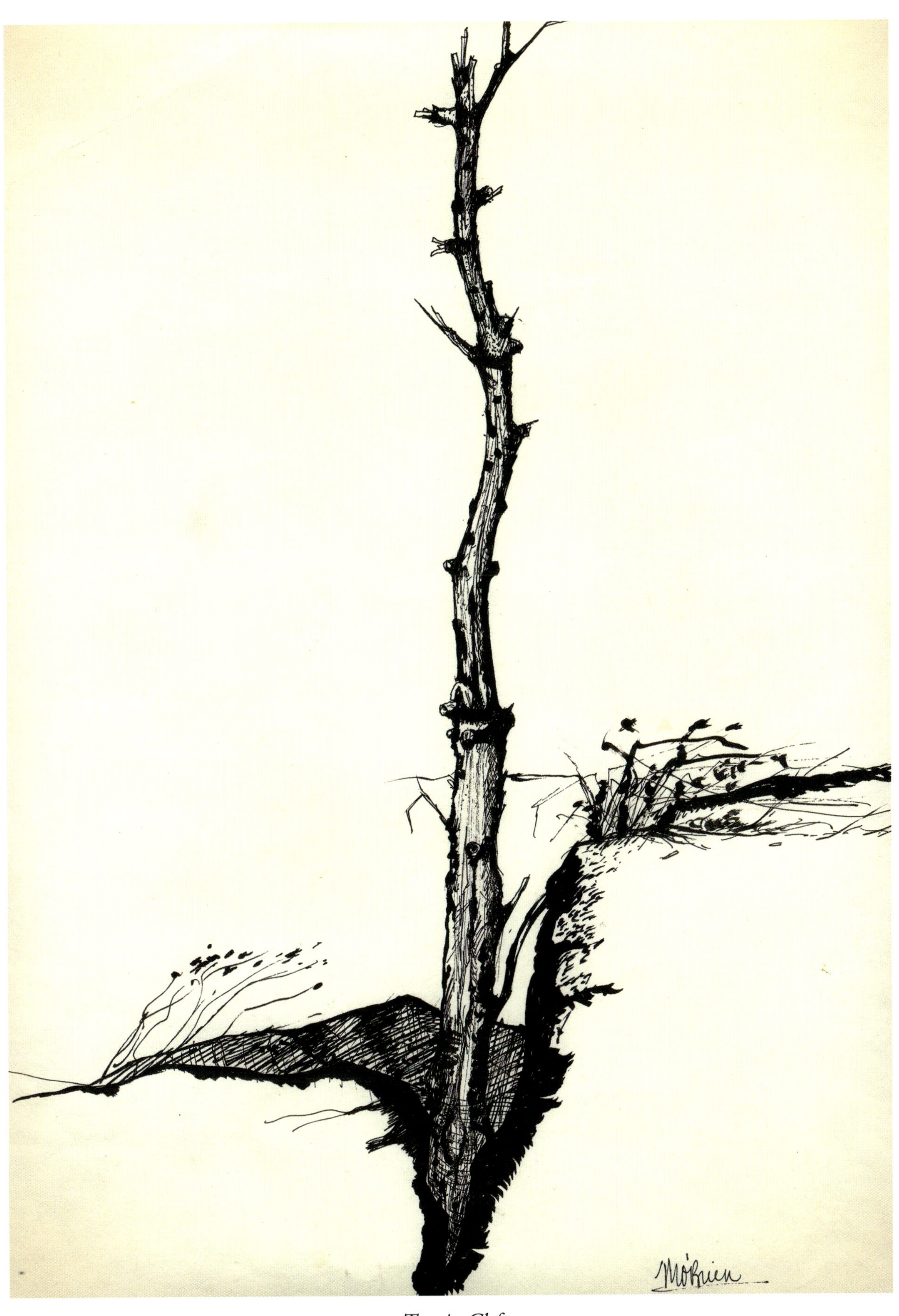

Tree in Cleft

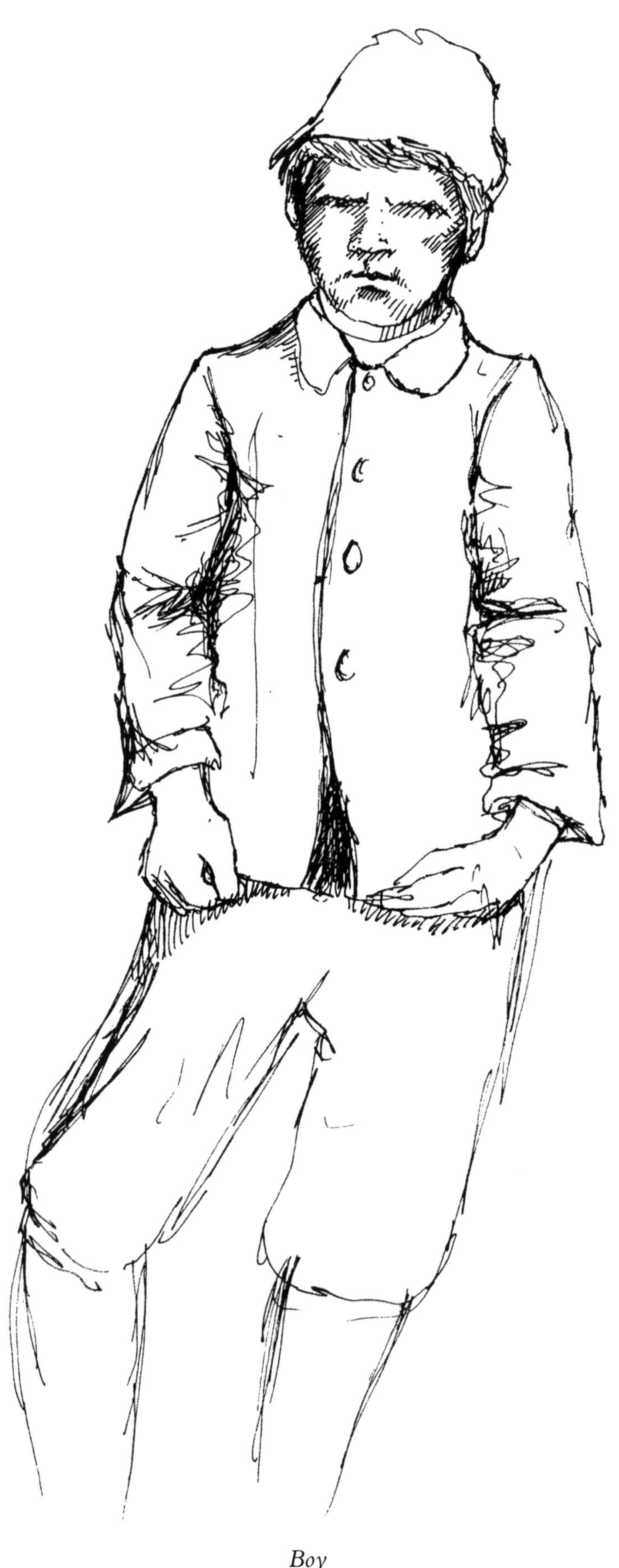

Boy

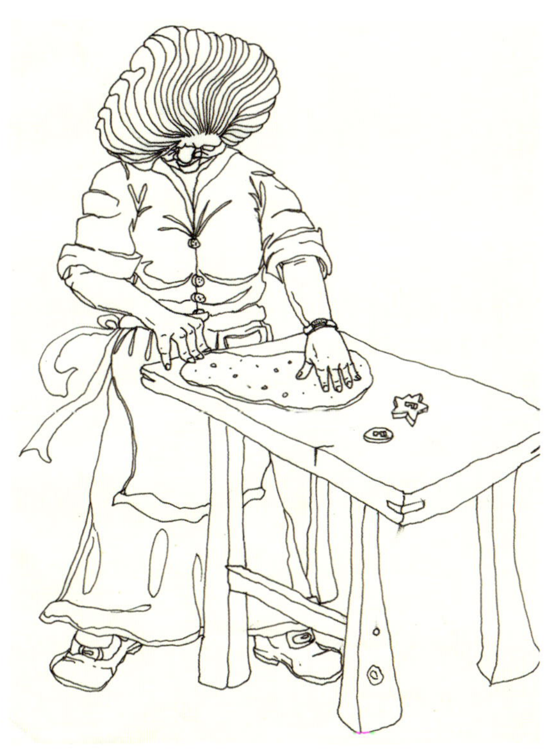

Woman Kneading Dough

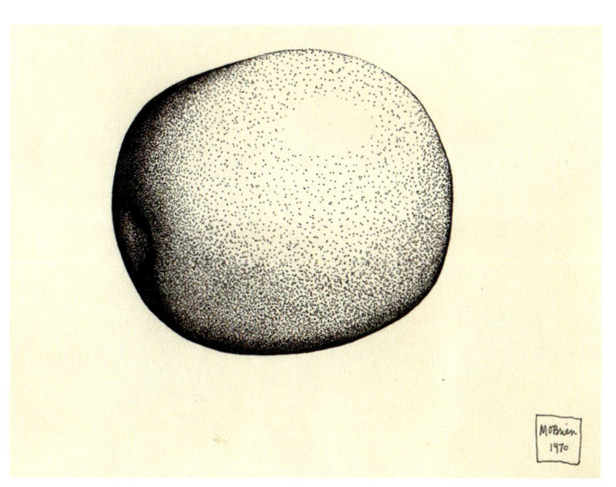

Fruit

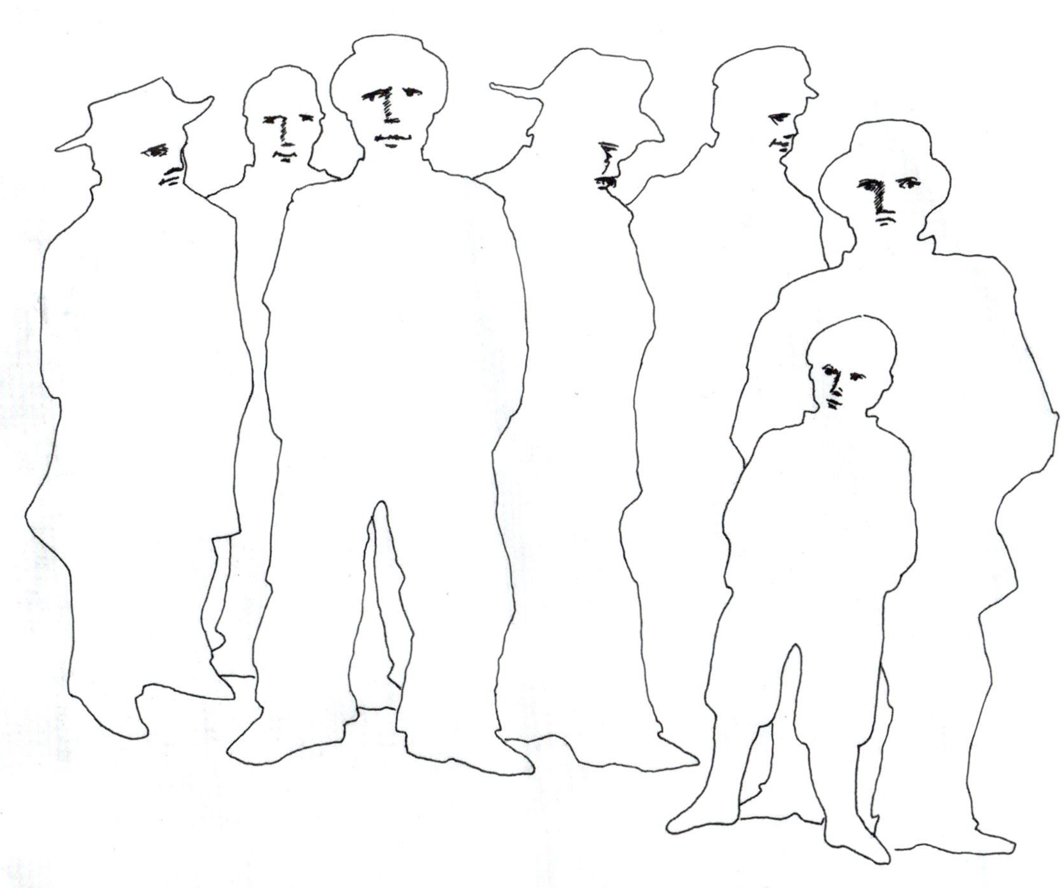

Group with Boy

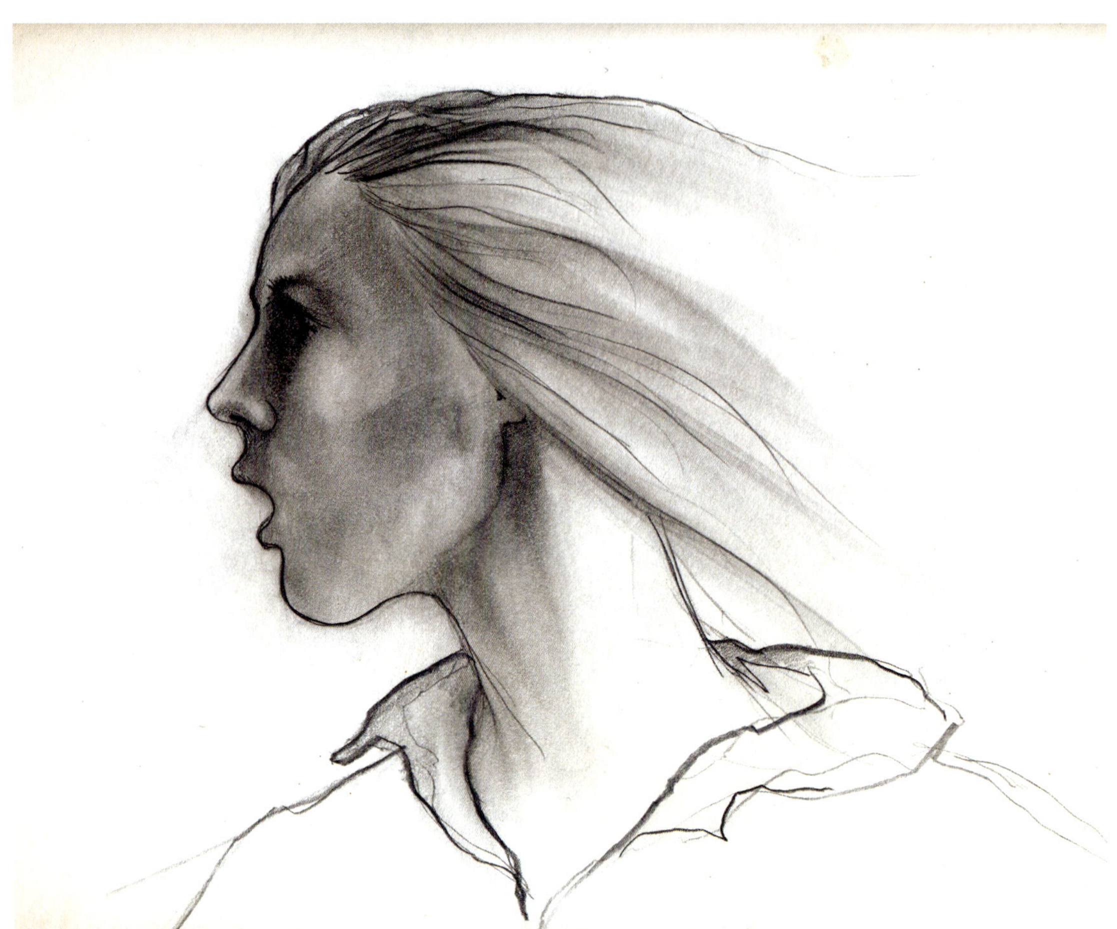

Woman with Wind in Hair

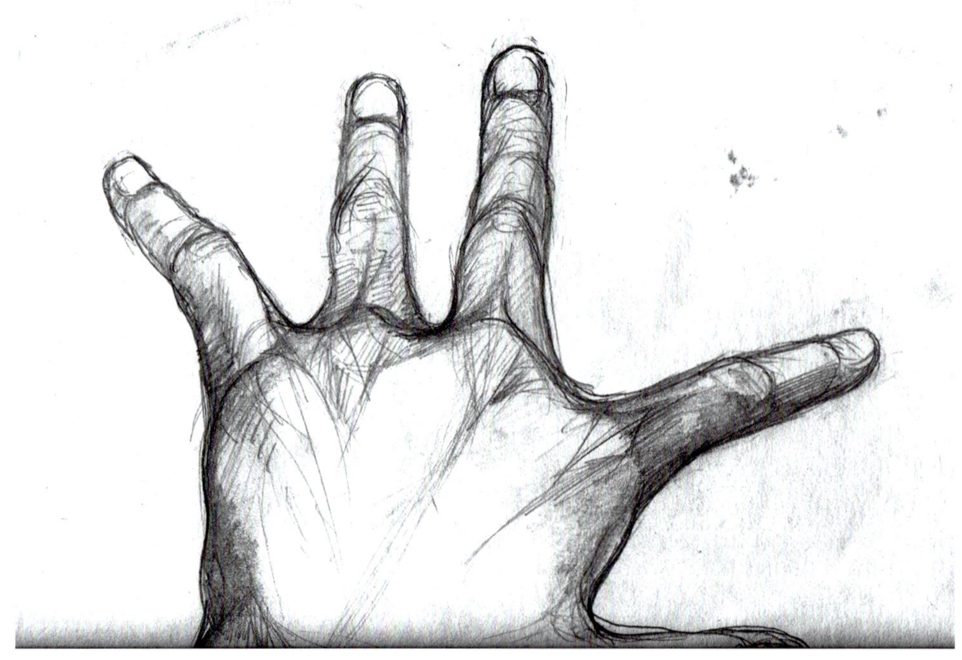

Hand

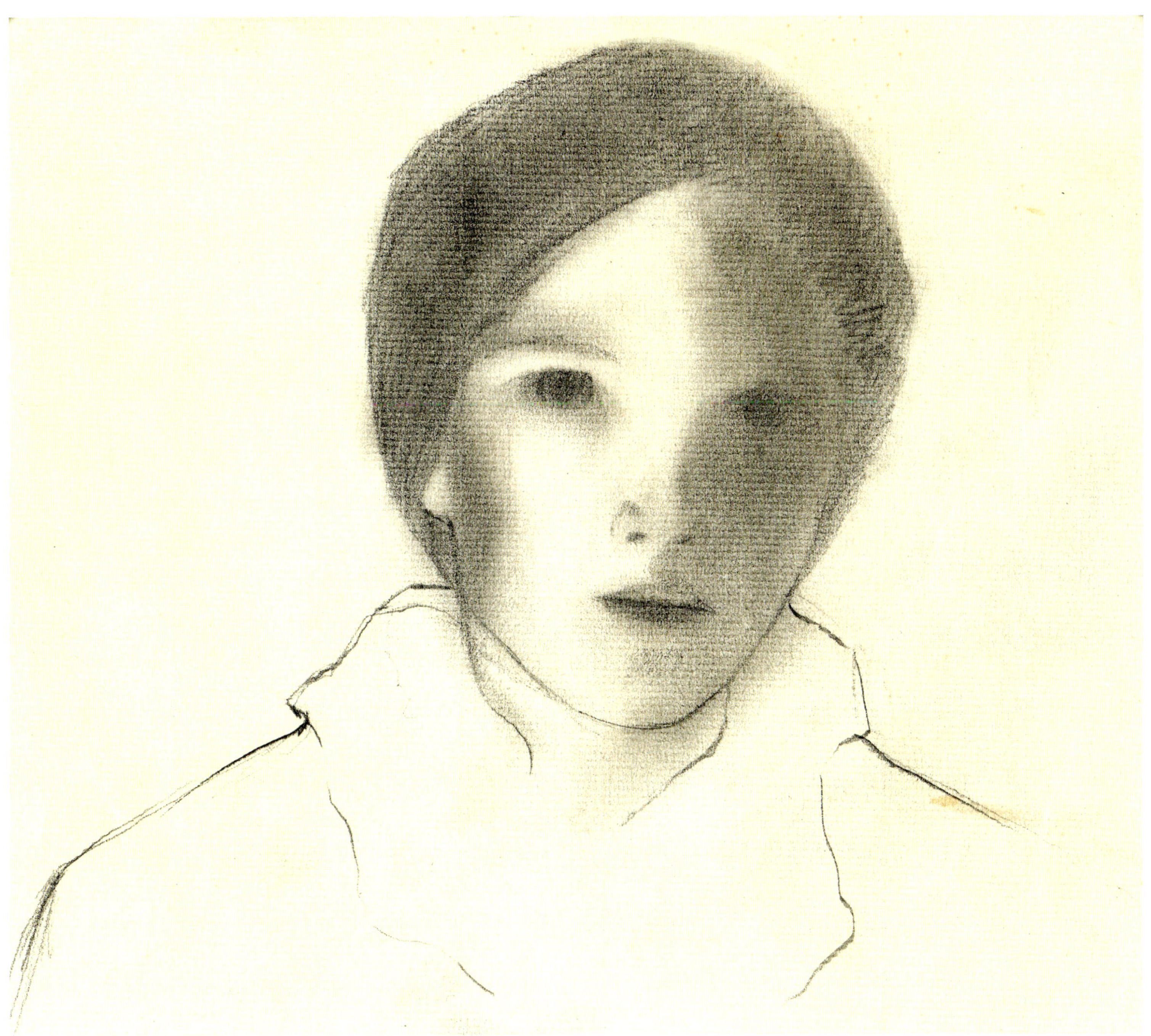

Girl

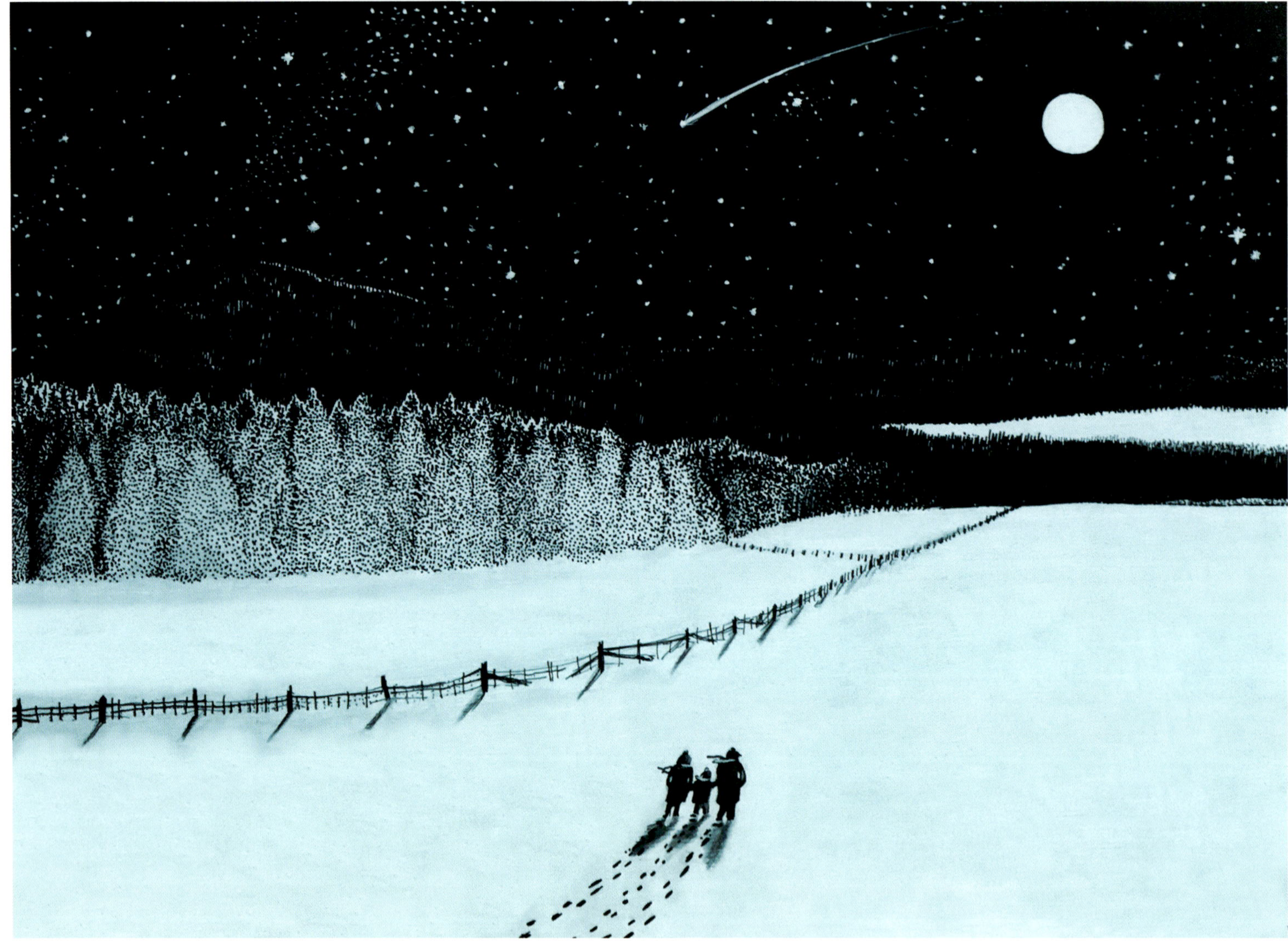

Winter Moon-Walk, ink drawing

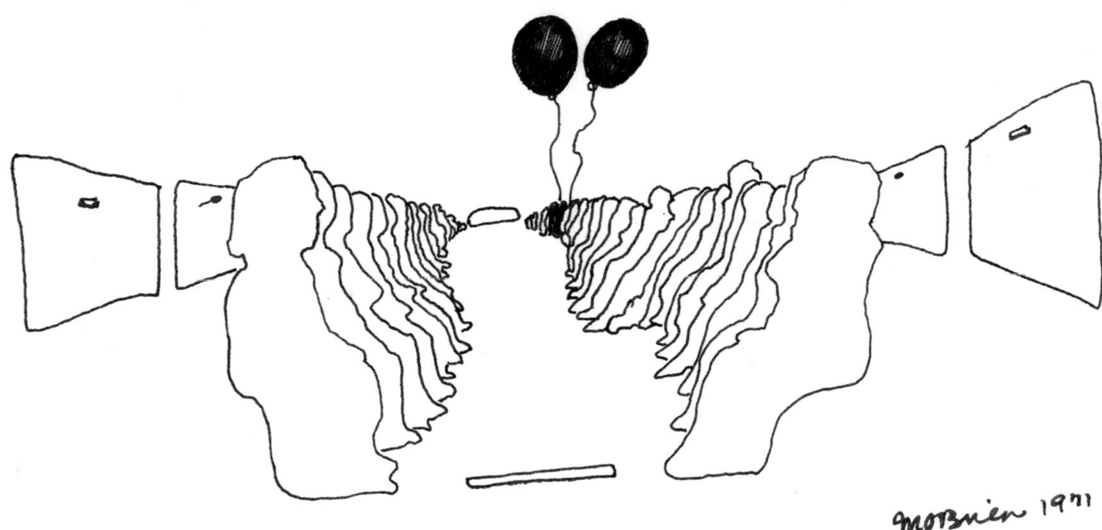

Balloons on Bus

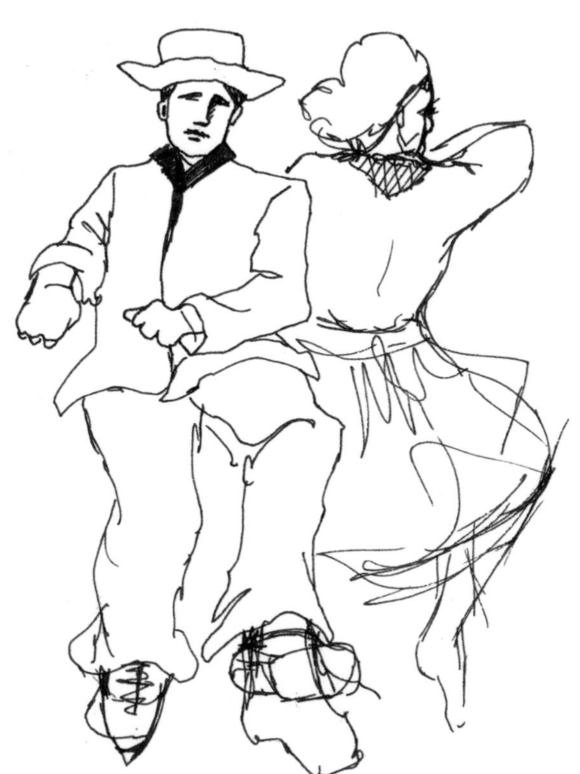

Dancing Couple

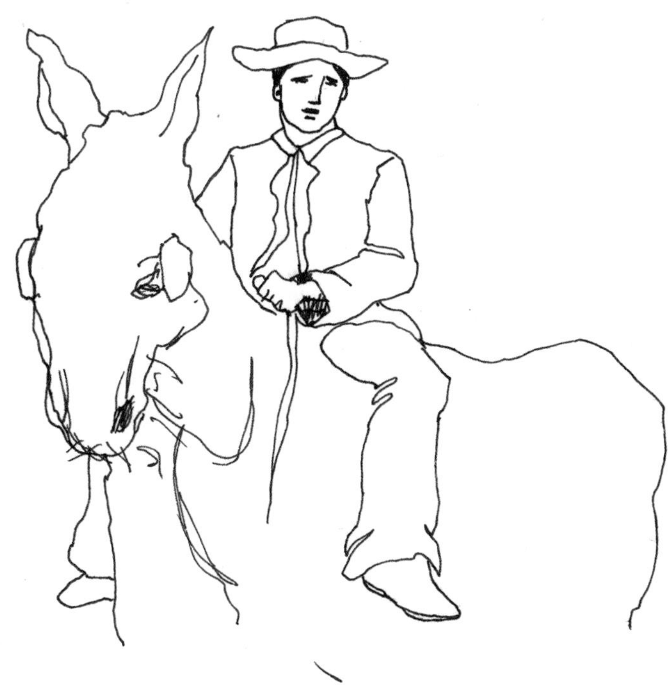

Man on Mule

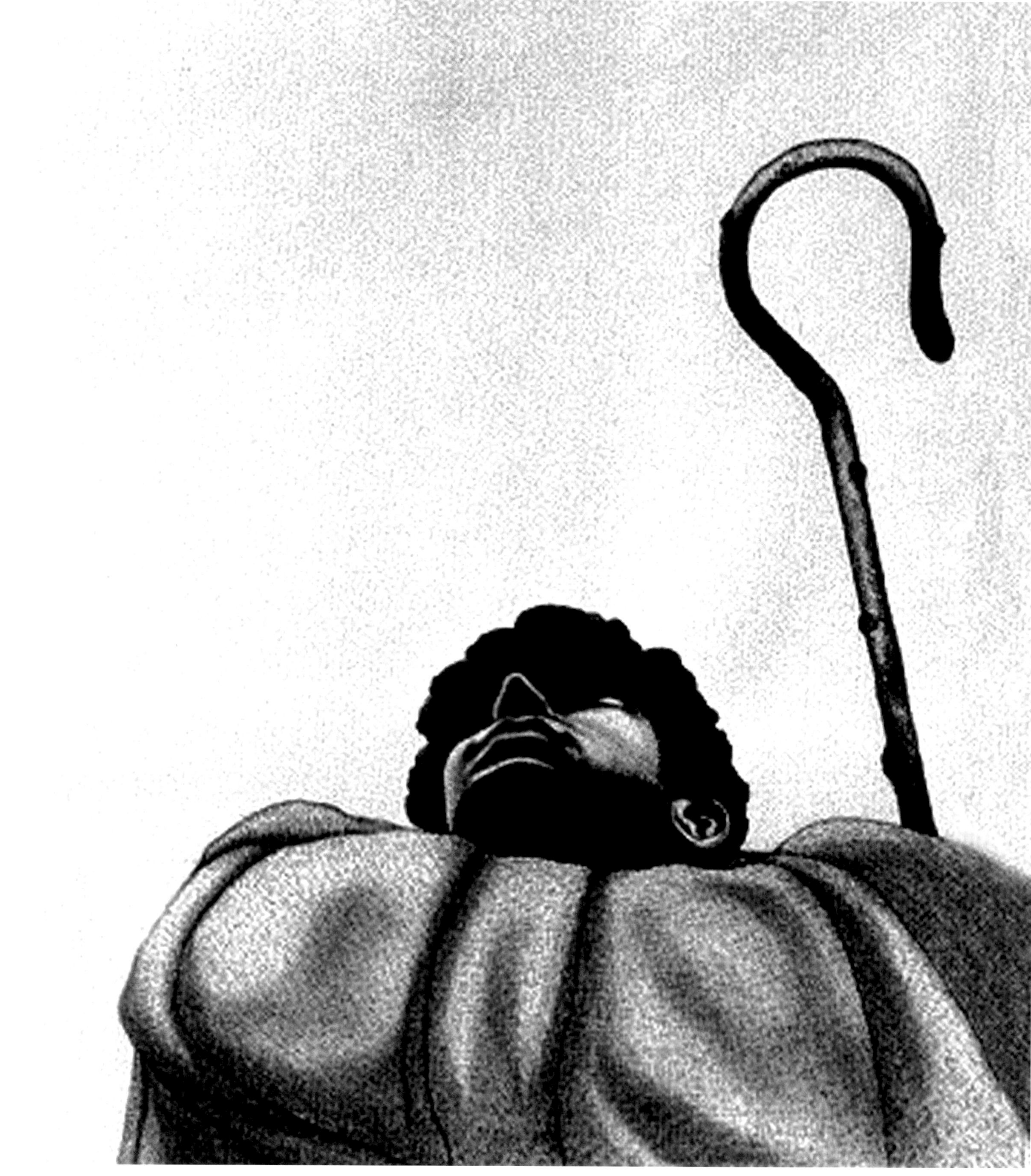

The Shepherd, ink drawing, early 1970s

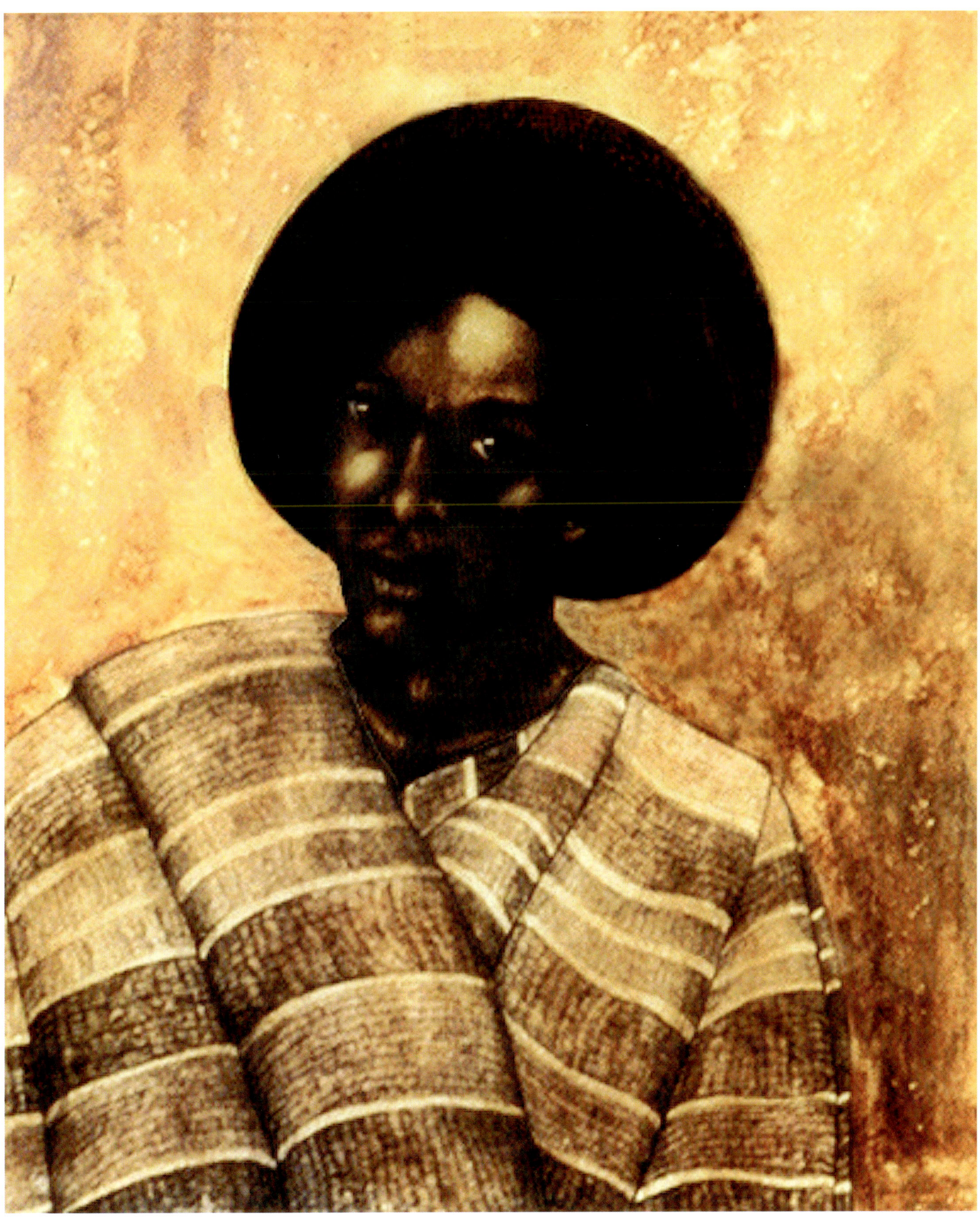

The Voice of Man, colored inks, early 1970s

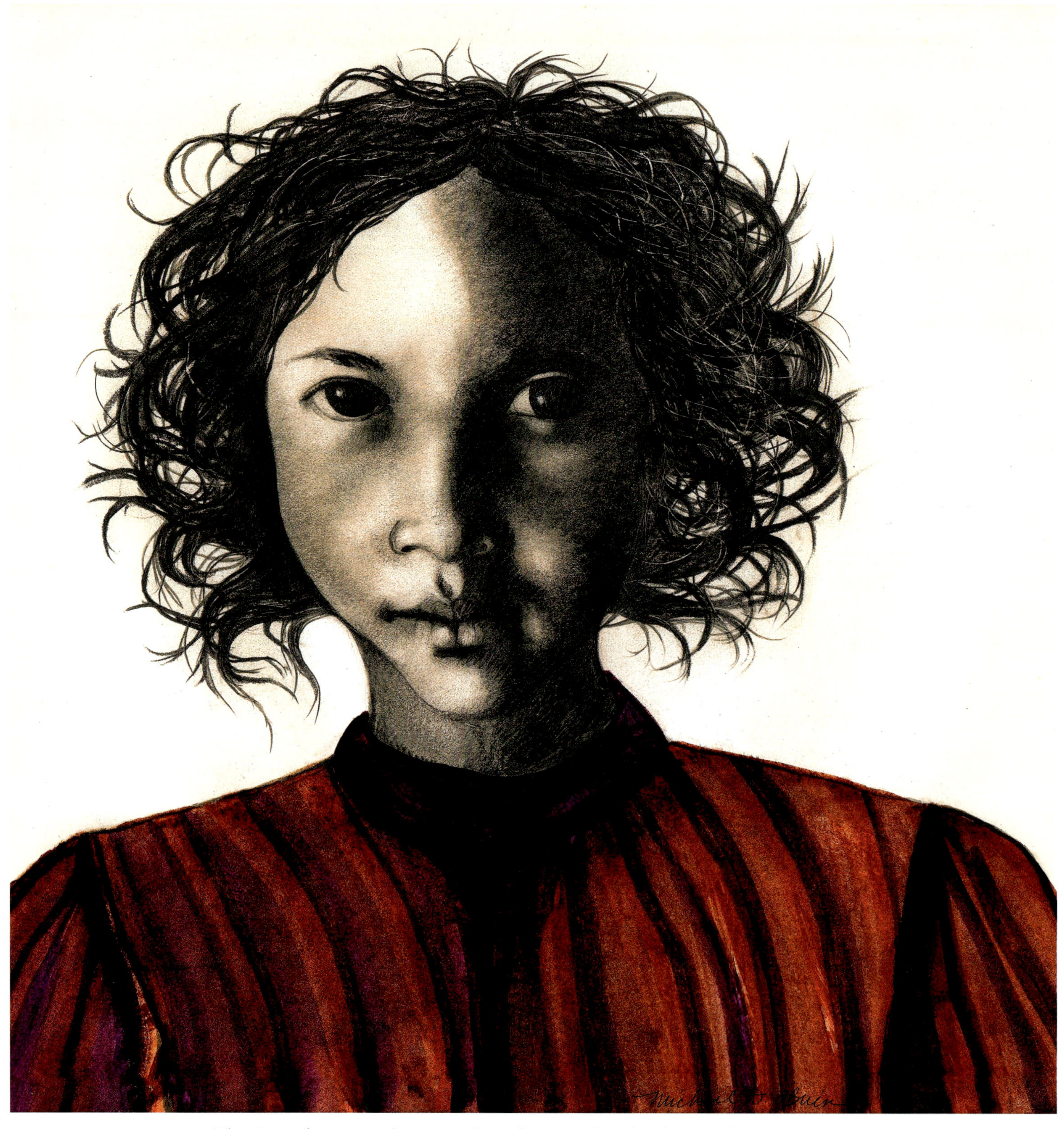

The Coat of Many Colors, mixed media, pencil and colored inks, early 1970s

Byzantine Iconography

Between 1976 and 1983, the majority of my work was in the discipleship of Byzantine and neo-Byzantine iconography. In this tradition, the anonymity of the icon painter is an essential part of the vocation. *Non nobis Domine, non nobis, sed nomini Tuo da gloriam!*—"Not to us, O Lord, not to us, but to your name give glory!" (Ps 115:1). In those early years, I kept a photographic record of only a few examples of my icons; the following are representative of a much larger number.

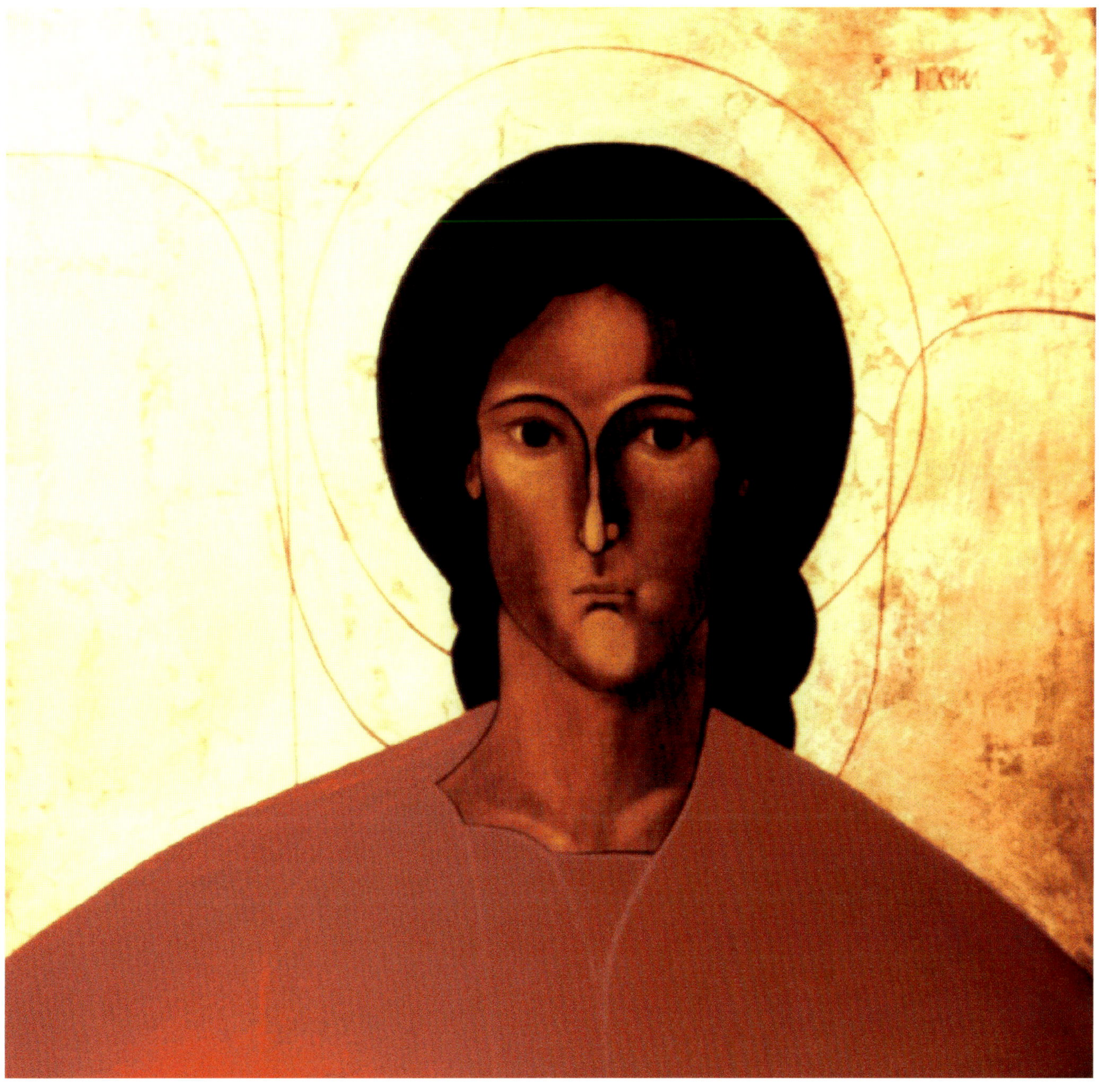

St. Michael the Archangel, circa 1977

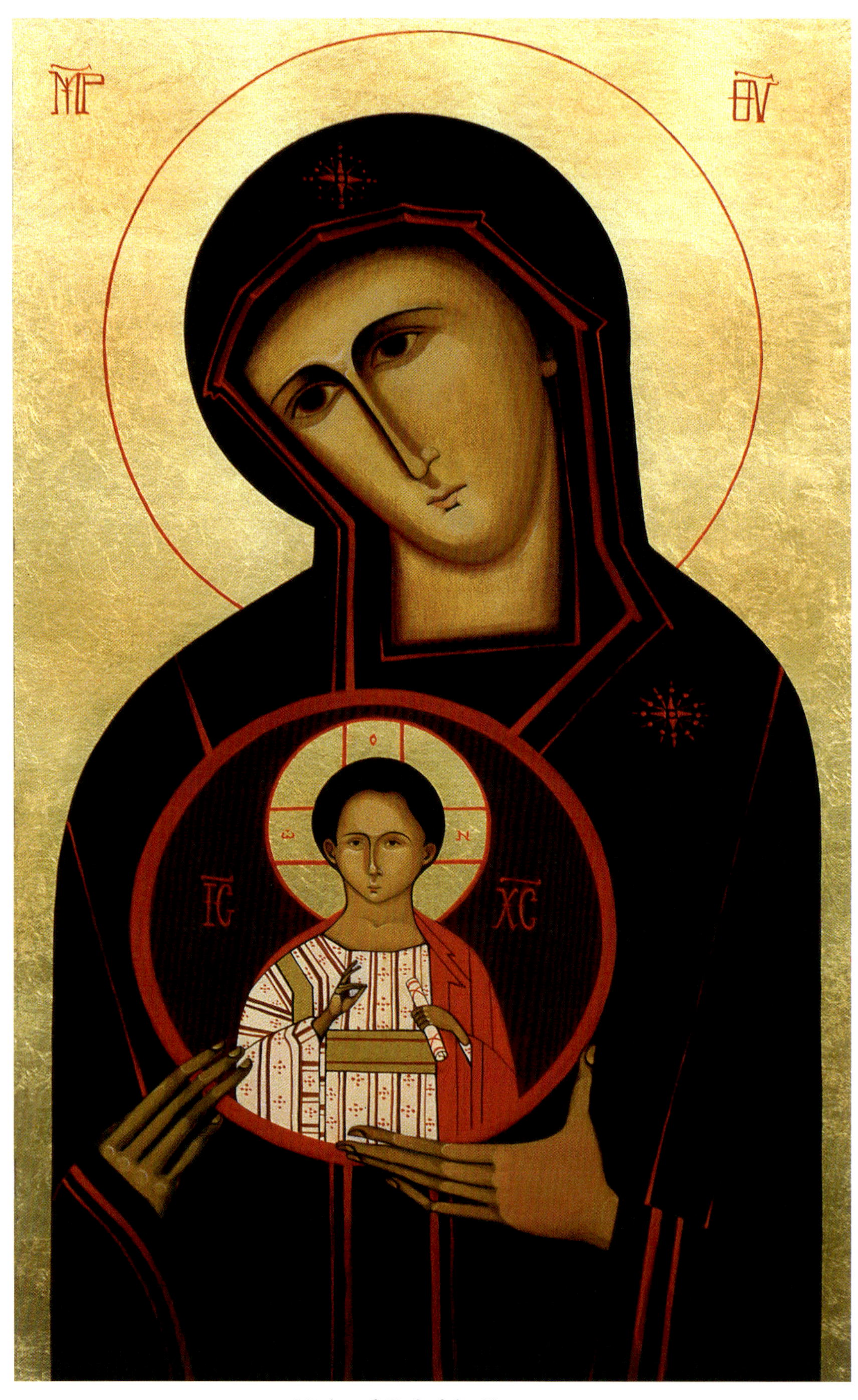

Mother of God of the Sign, 1983

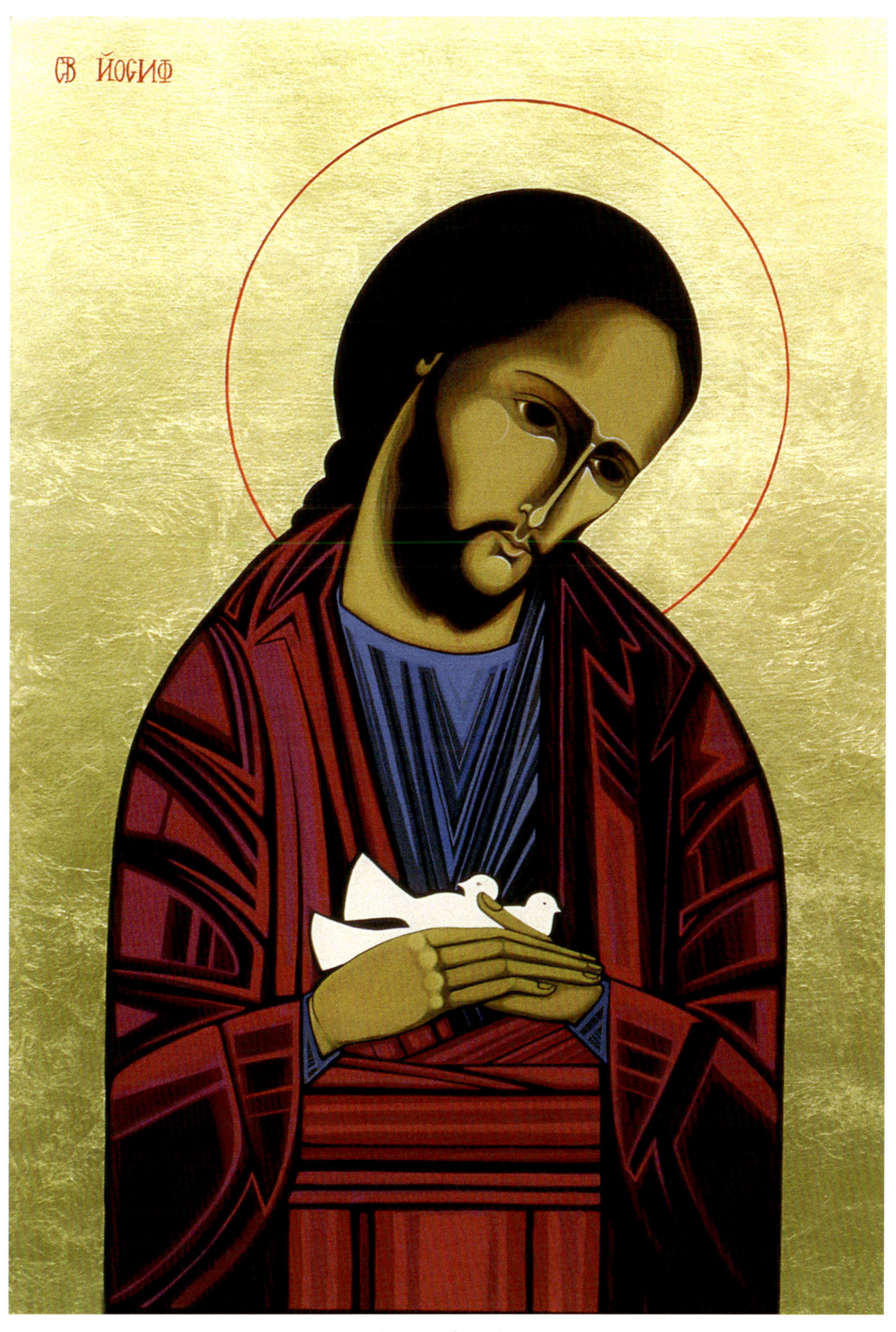

St. Joseph, 1983

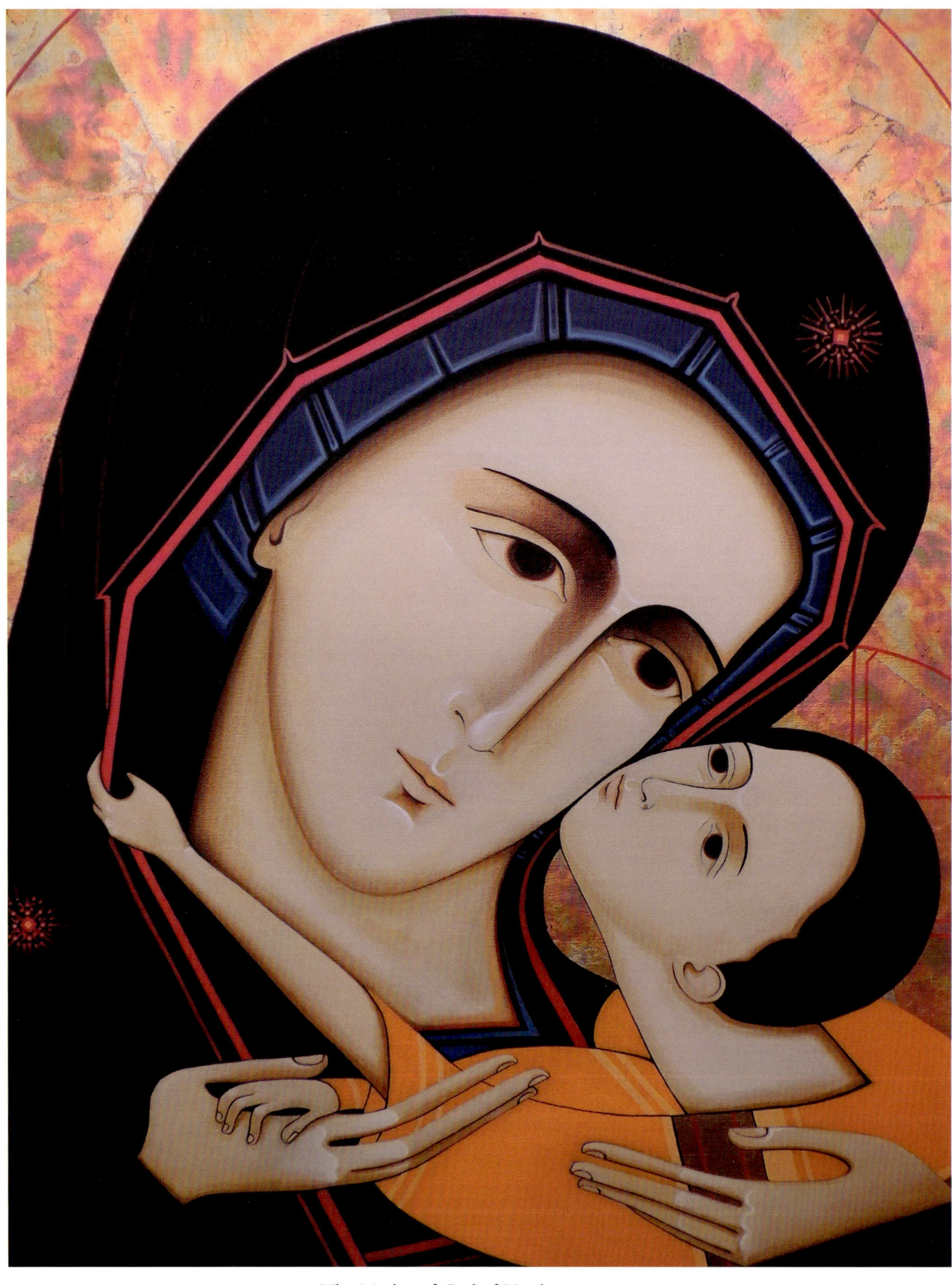

The Mother of God of Tenderness, 1985

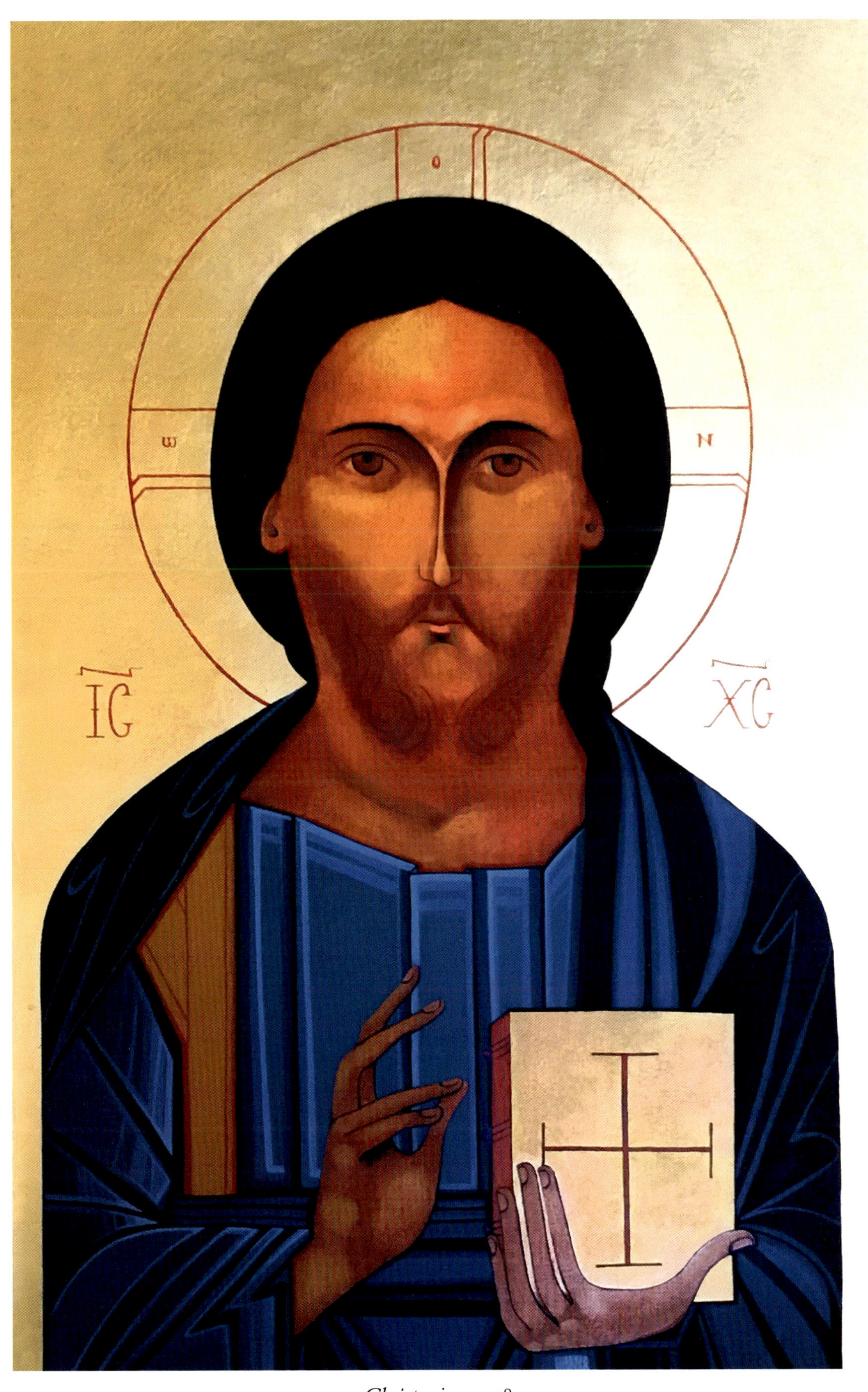

Christ, circa 1984

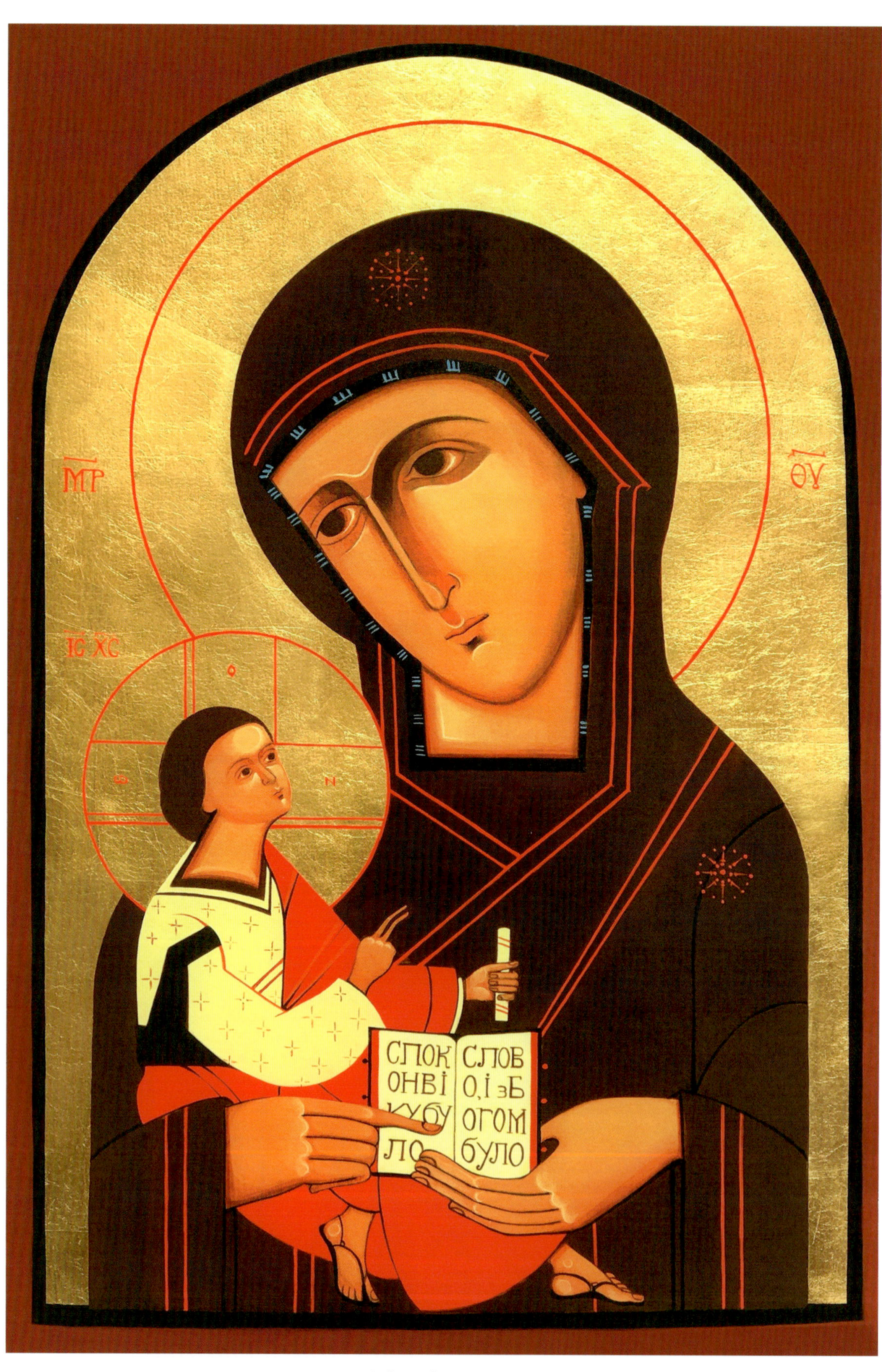

Theotokos, 1986

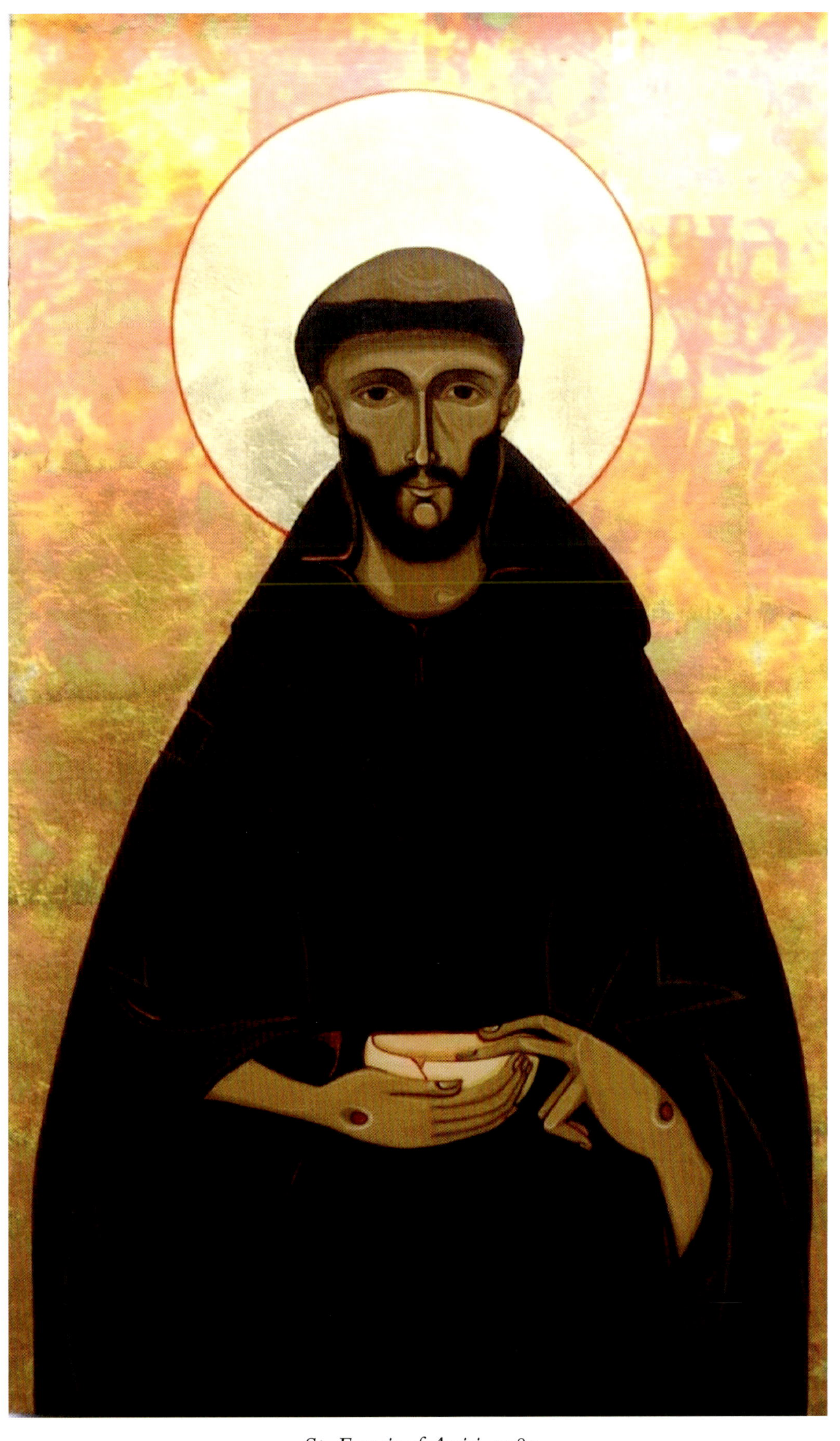

St. Francis of Assisi, 1983

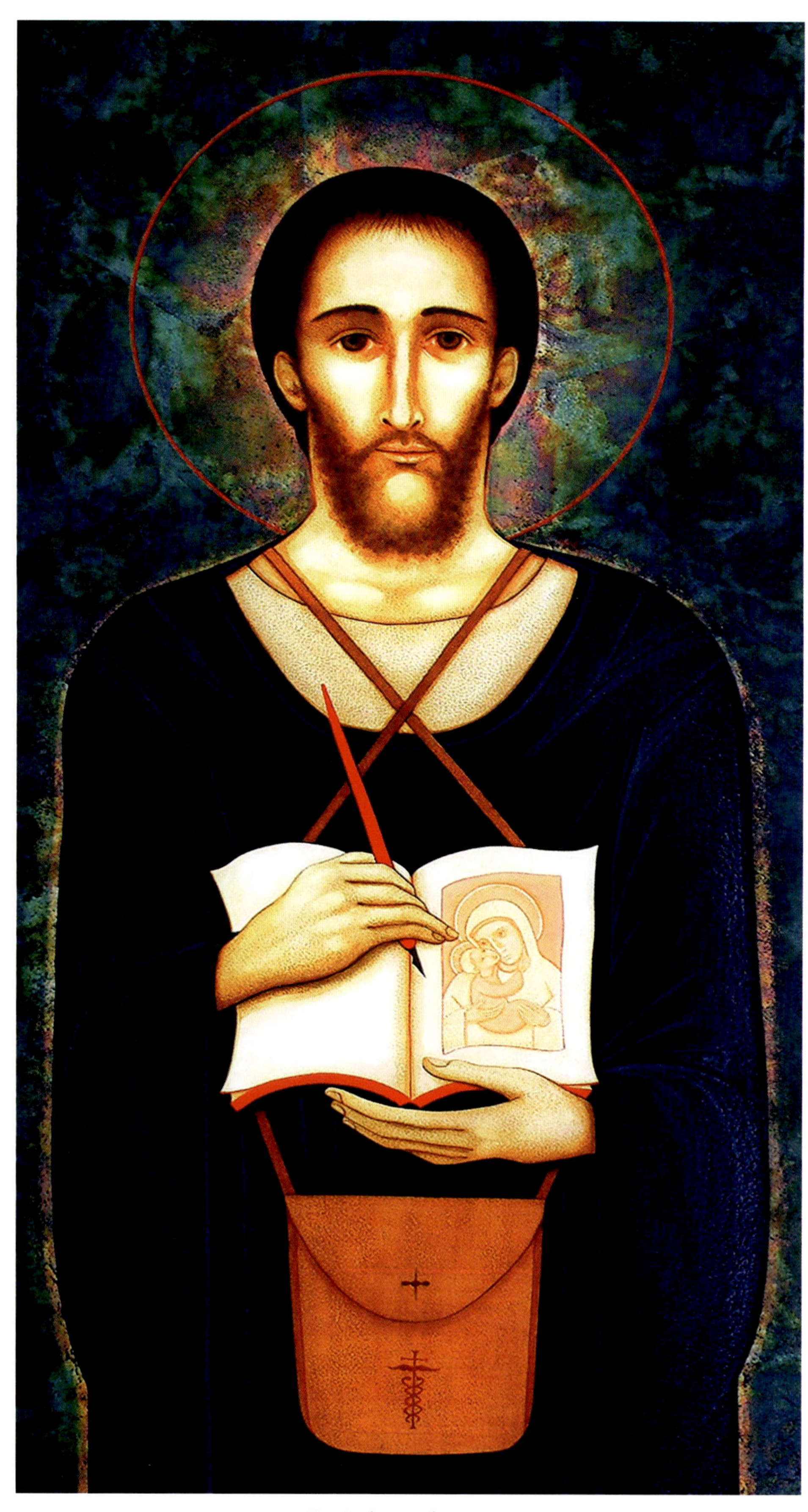

St. Luke, early 1990s

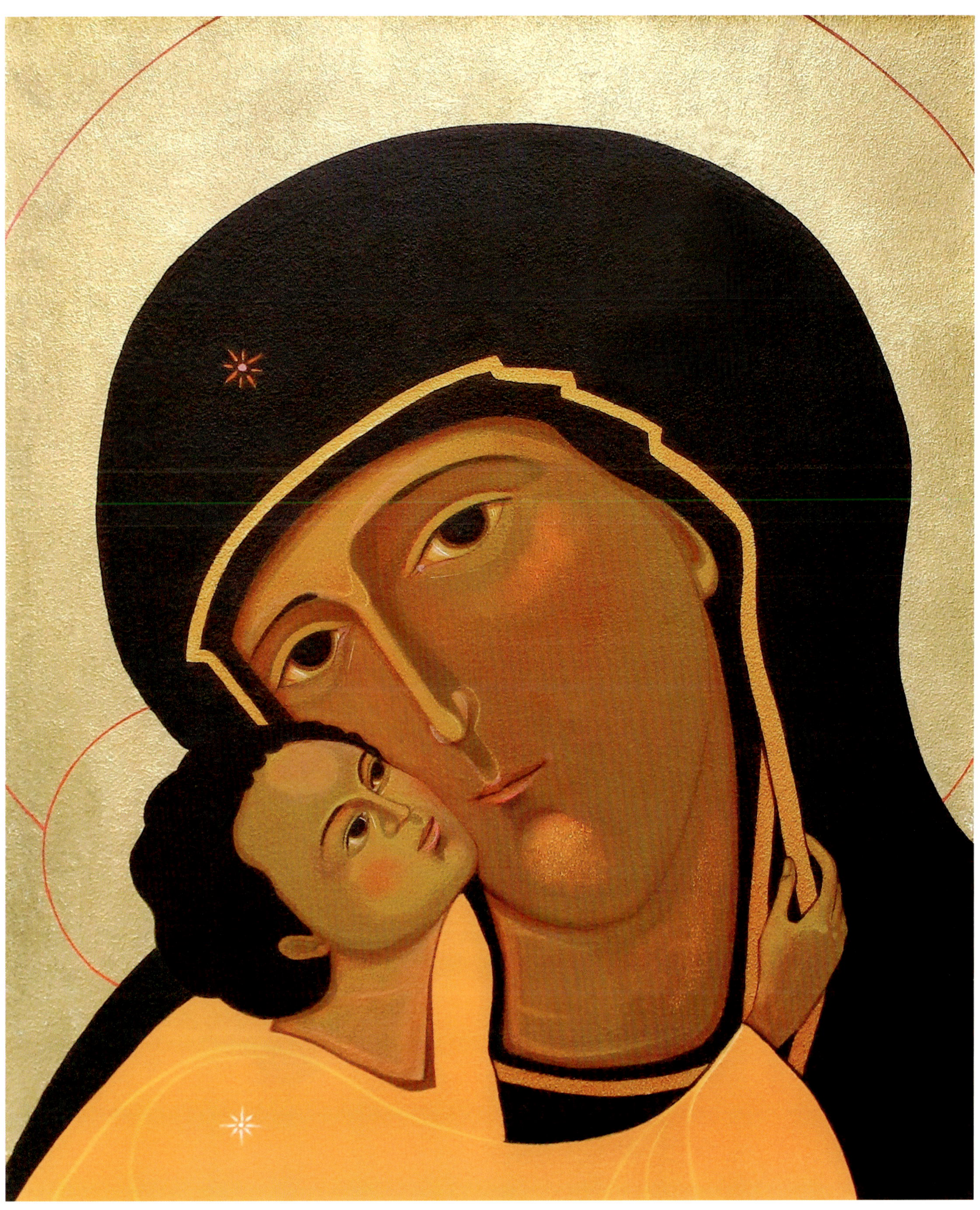

The Mother of God of Vladimir, 1979

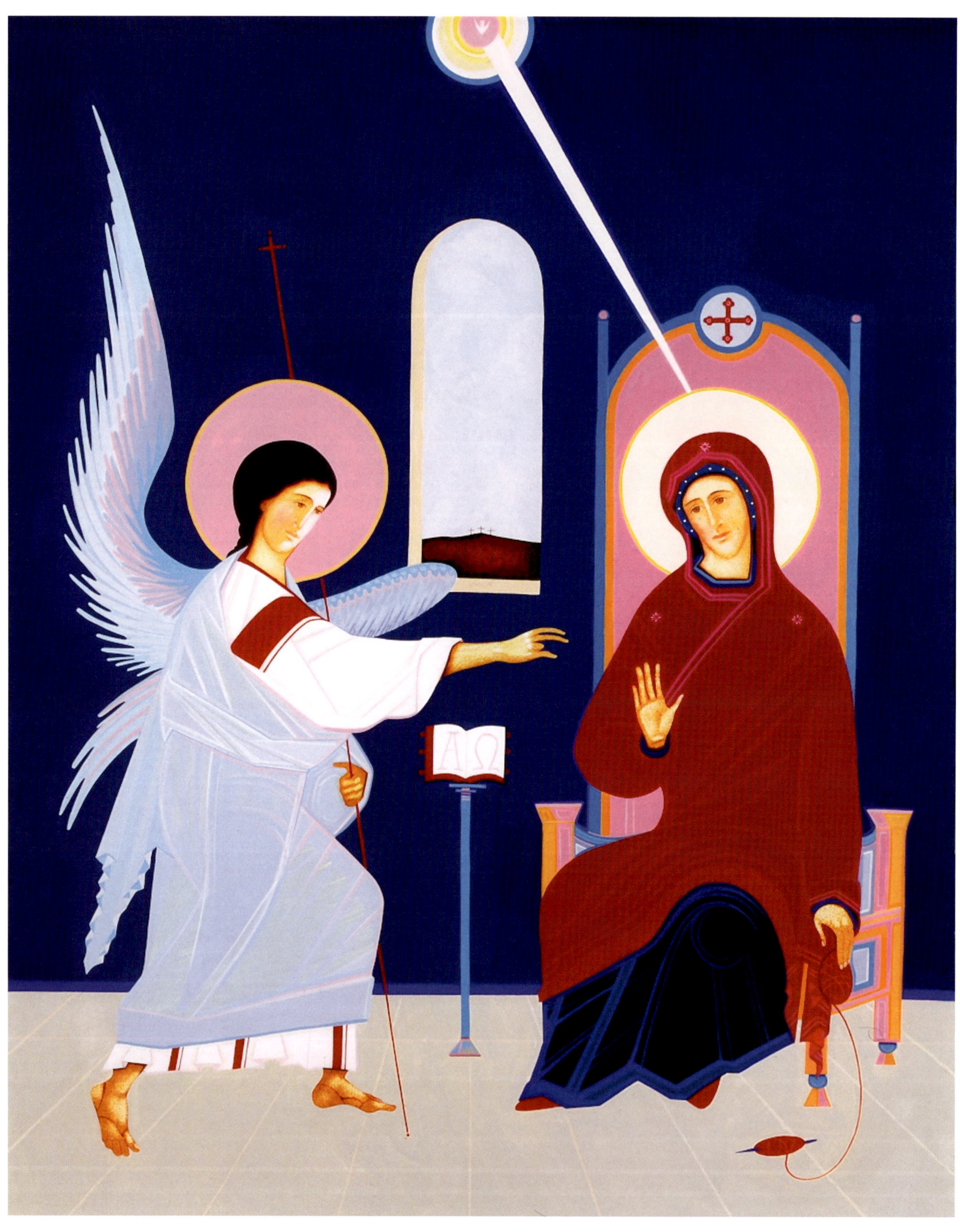

The Annunciation, 1990–1991

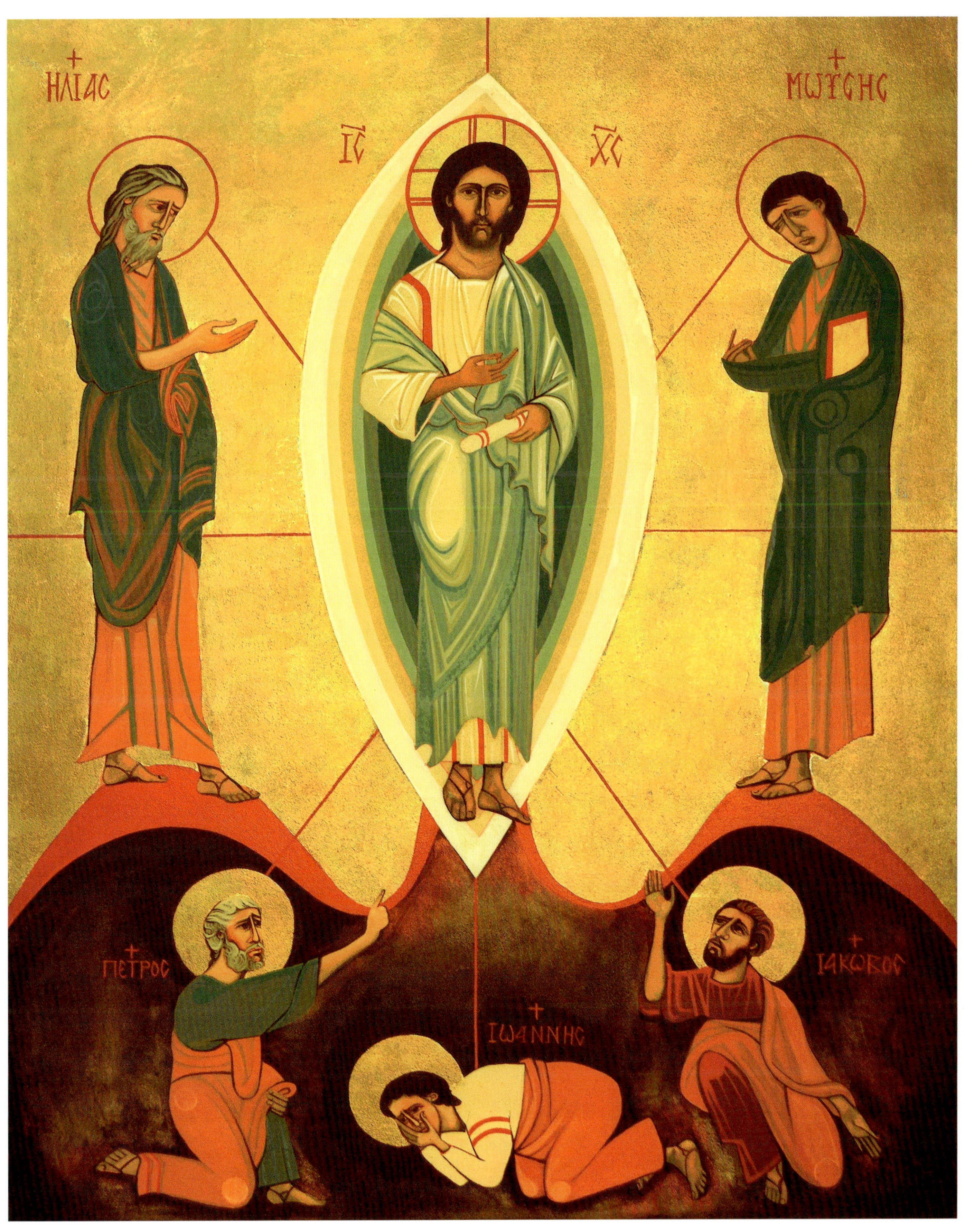

The Transfiguration, 1983

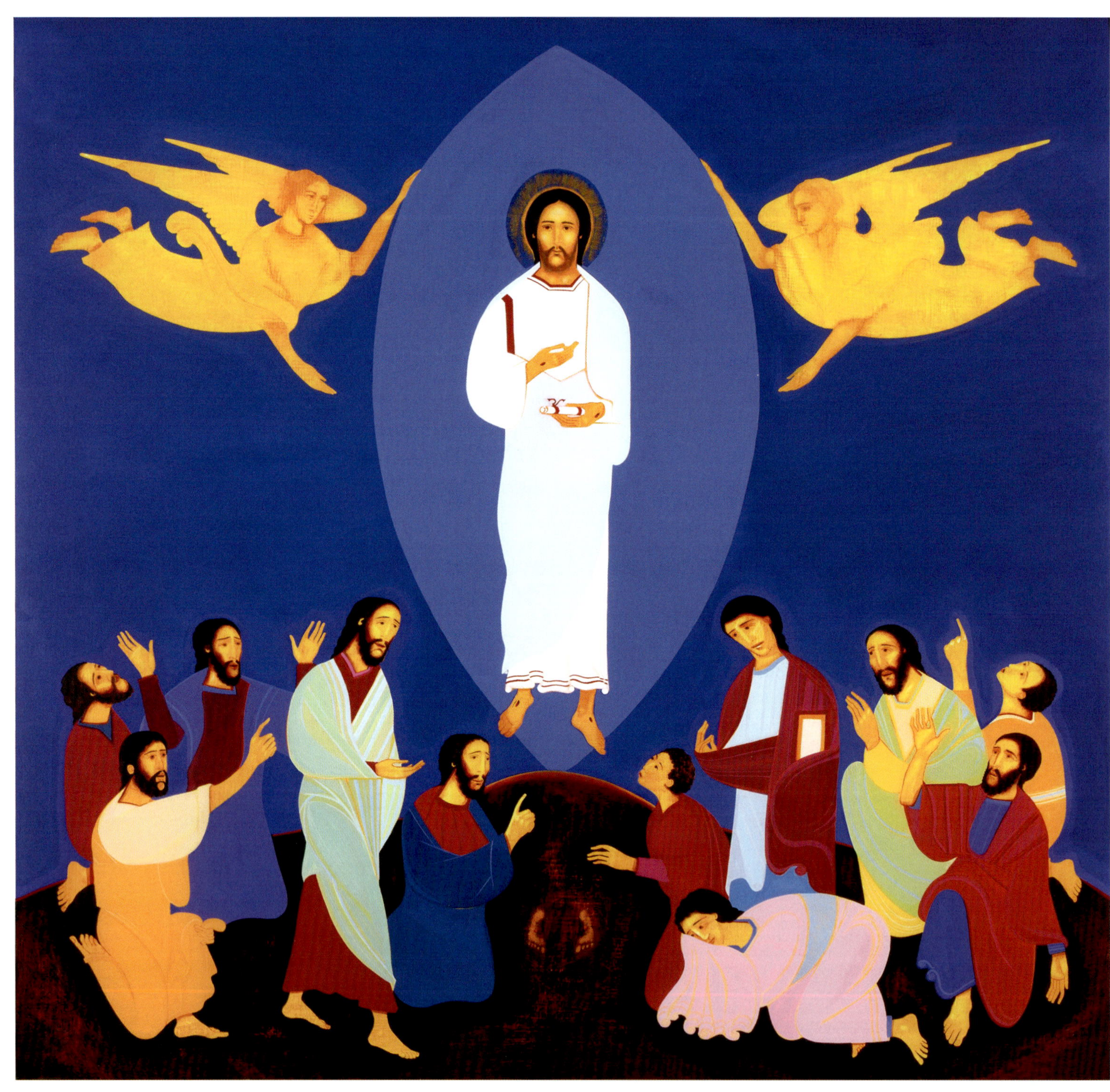

The Ascension, 1990–1991

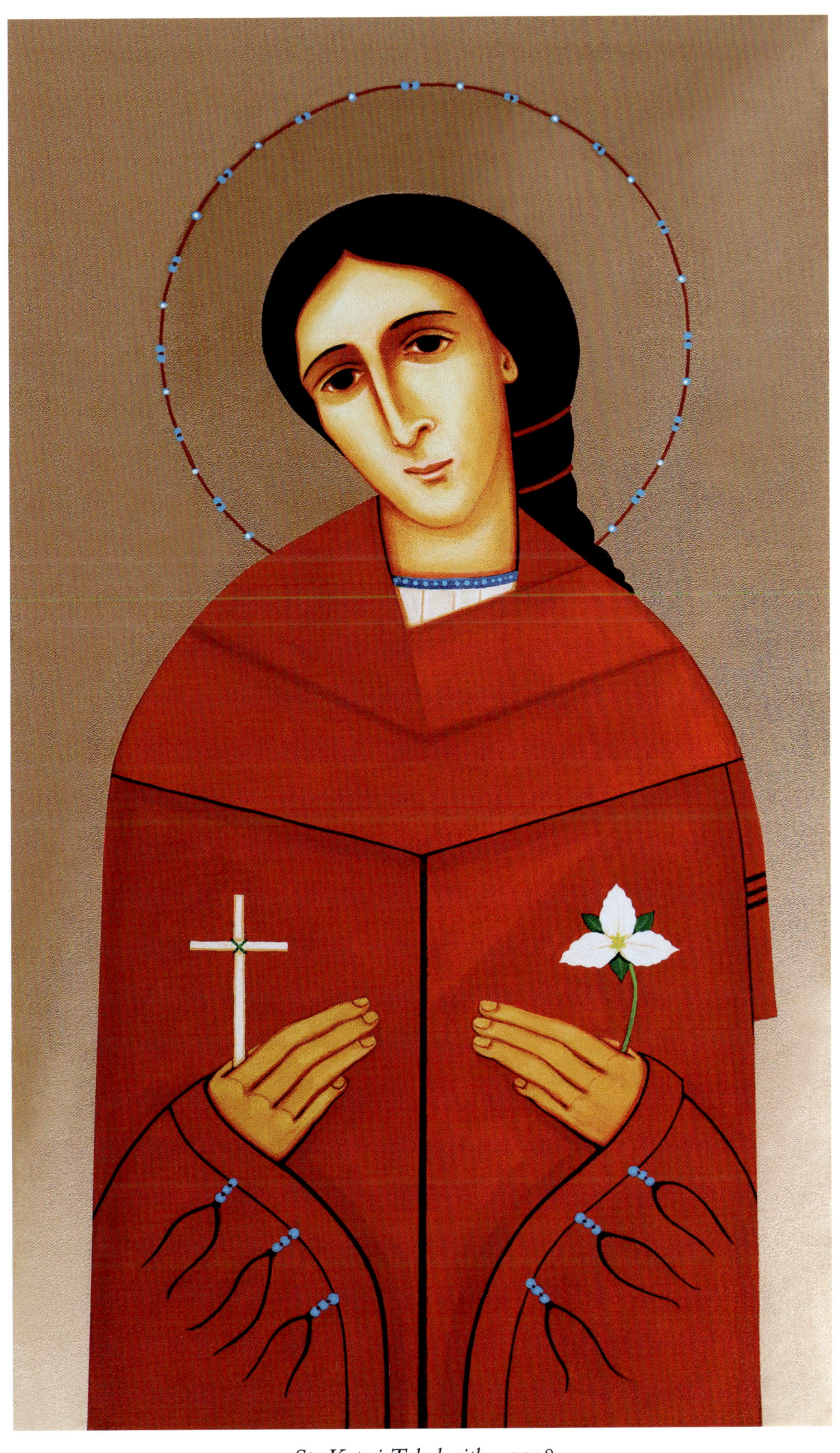

St. Kateri Tekakwitha, 2018

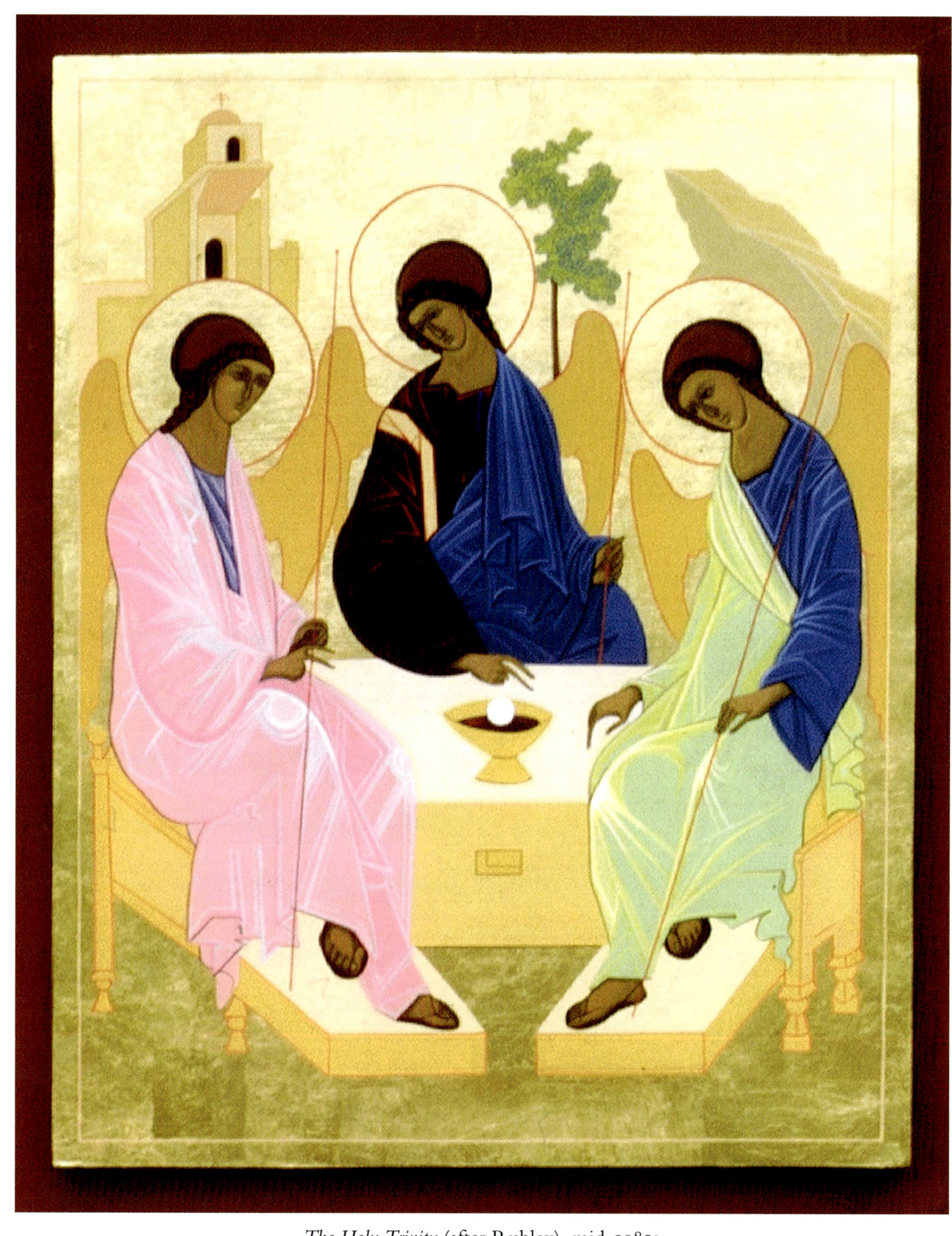

The Holy Trinity (after Rublev), mid-1980s

The Cross

The mystery of the Cross is *the* sign of contradiction, a blow to human consciousness, for we recoil instinctively from suffering and death. And yet it is the royal road, the golden gate unto the Resurrection. Christ has gone before us on this path and beckons us to follow him with trust. His Passion and death, and our sorrows united to his, have been a continual theme in my work—from the beginning until the present day.

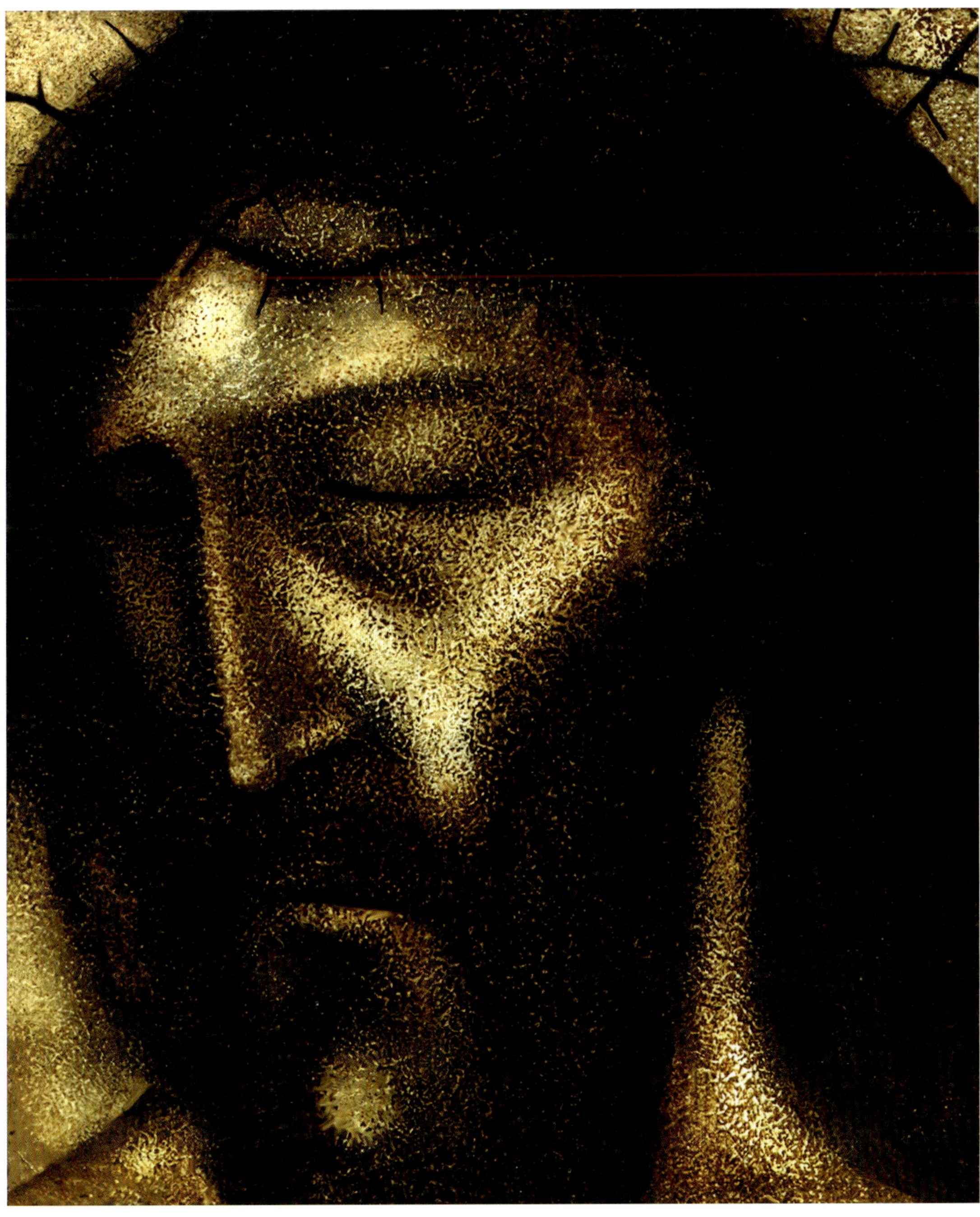

Ecce Homo, 1977

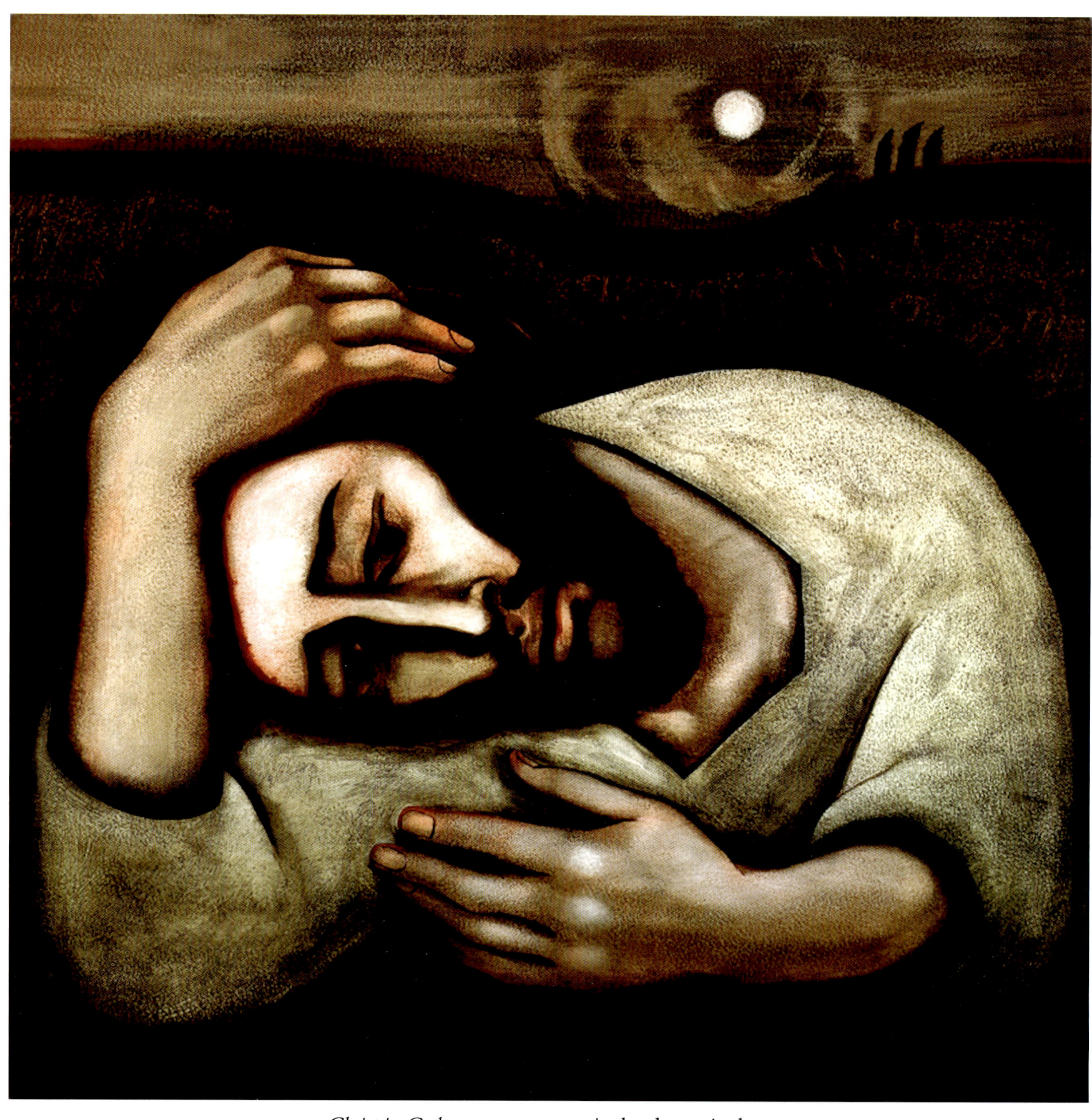

Christ in Gethsemane, 1991, 24 inches by 24 inches

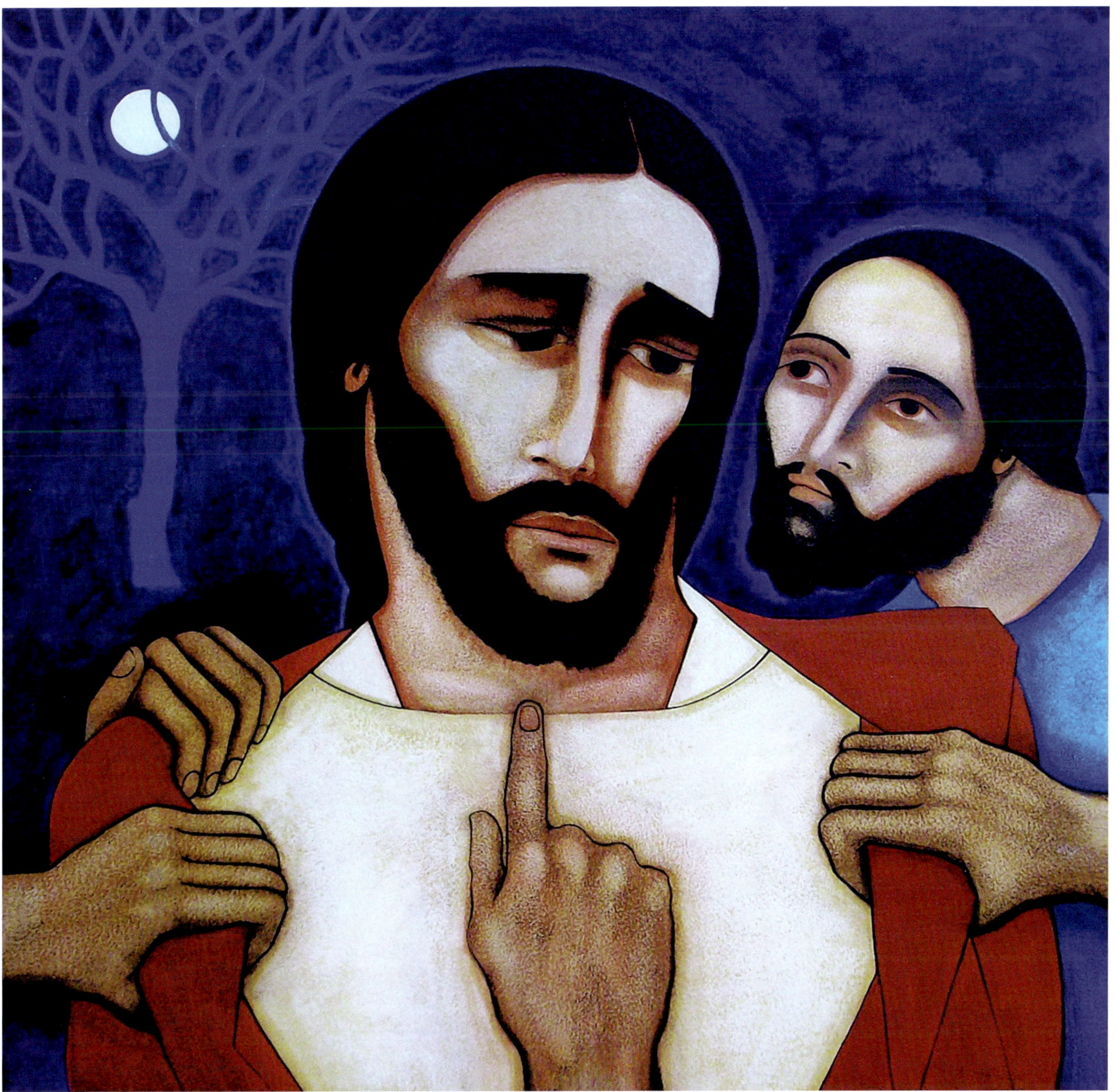

Betrayed by a Kiss, 2008, 24 inches by 24 inches

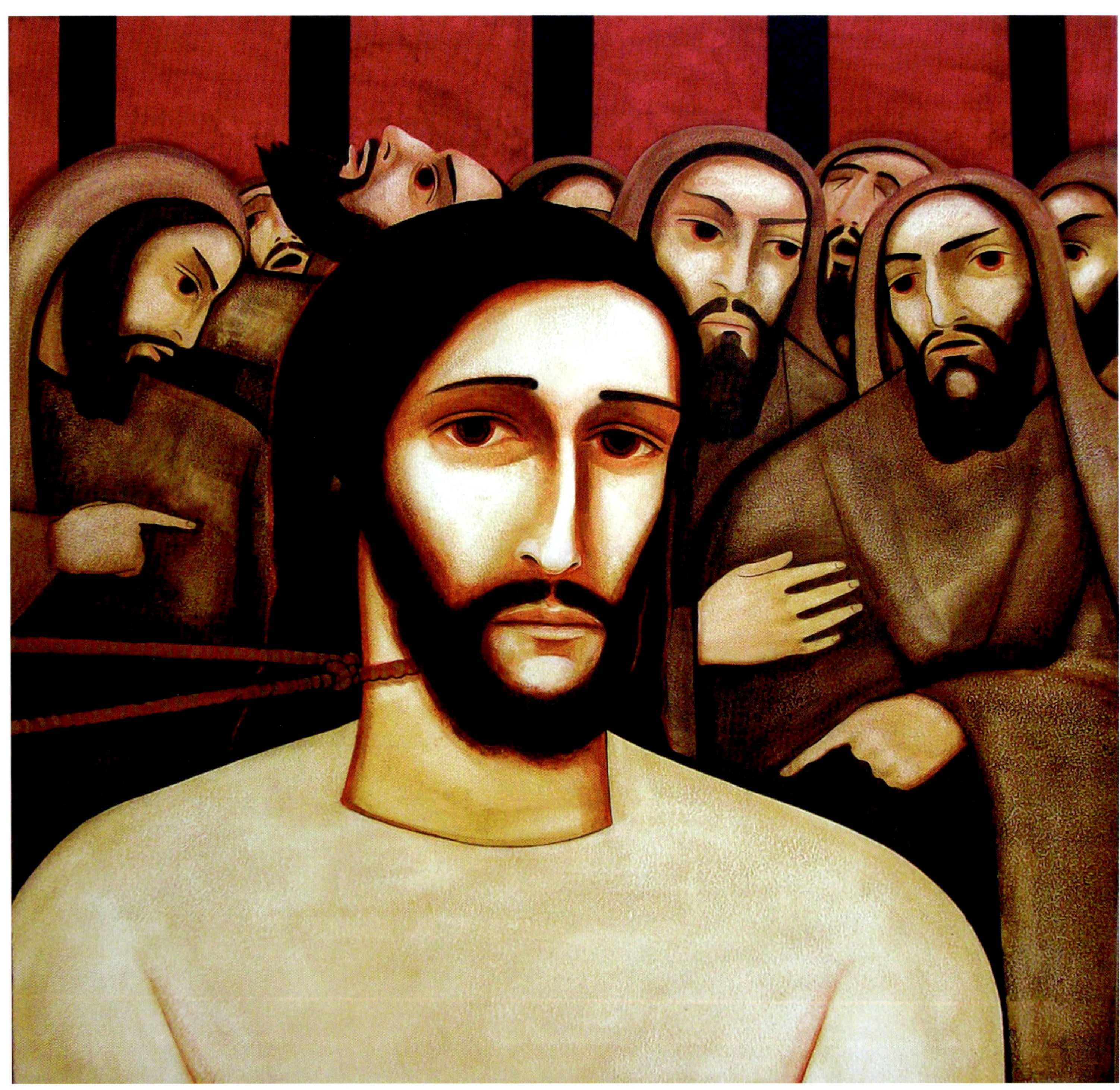

Jesus Condemned by the Sanhedrin, 2008, 24 inches by 24 inches

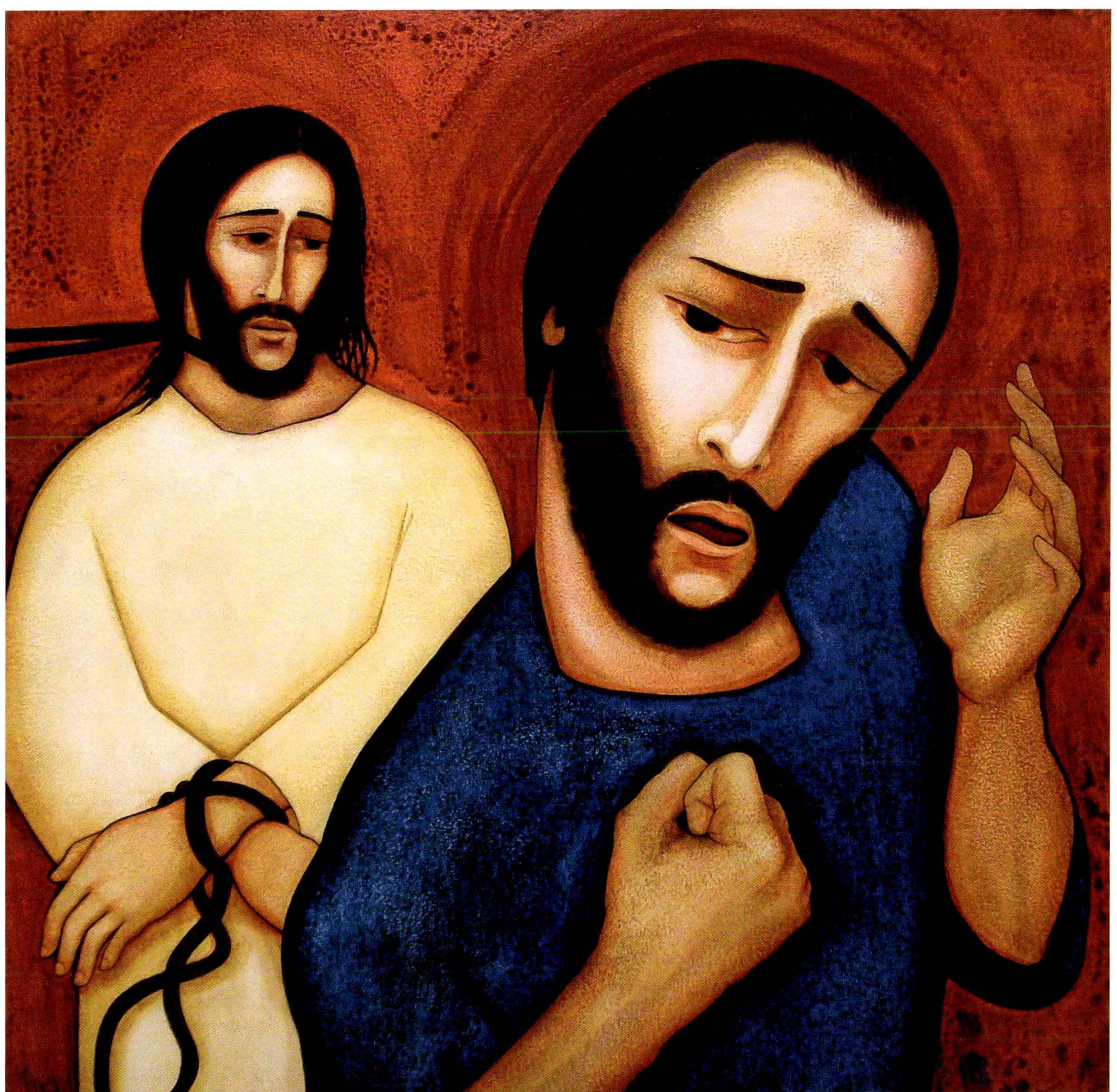

Peter Denies Knowing Jesus, 2008, 24 inches by 24 inches

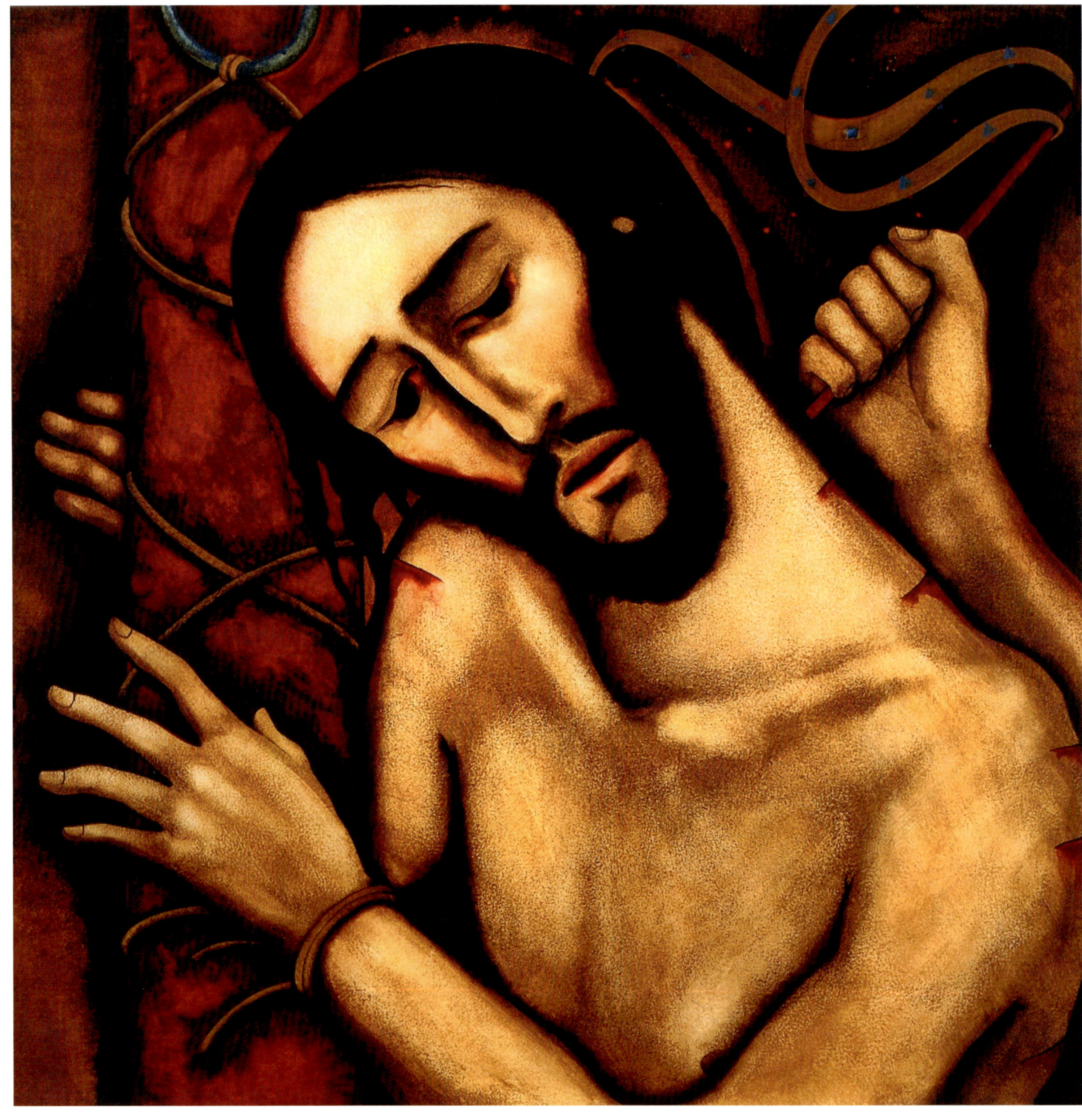

Jesus Scourged, 1991, 24 inches by 24 inches

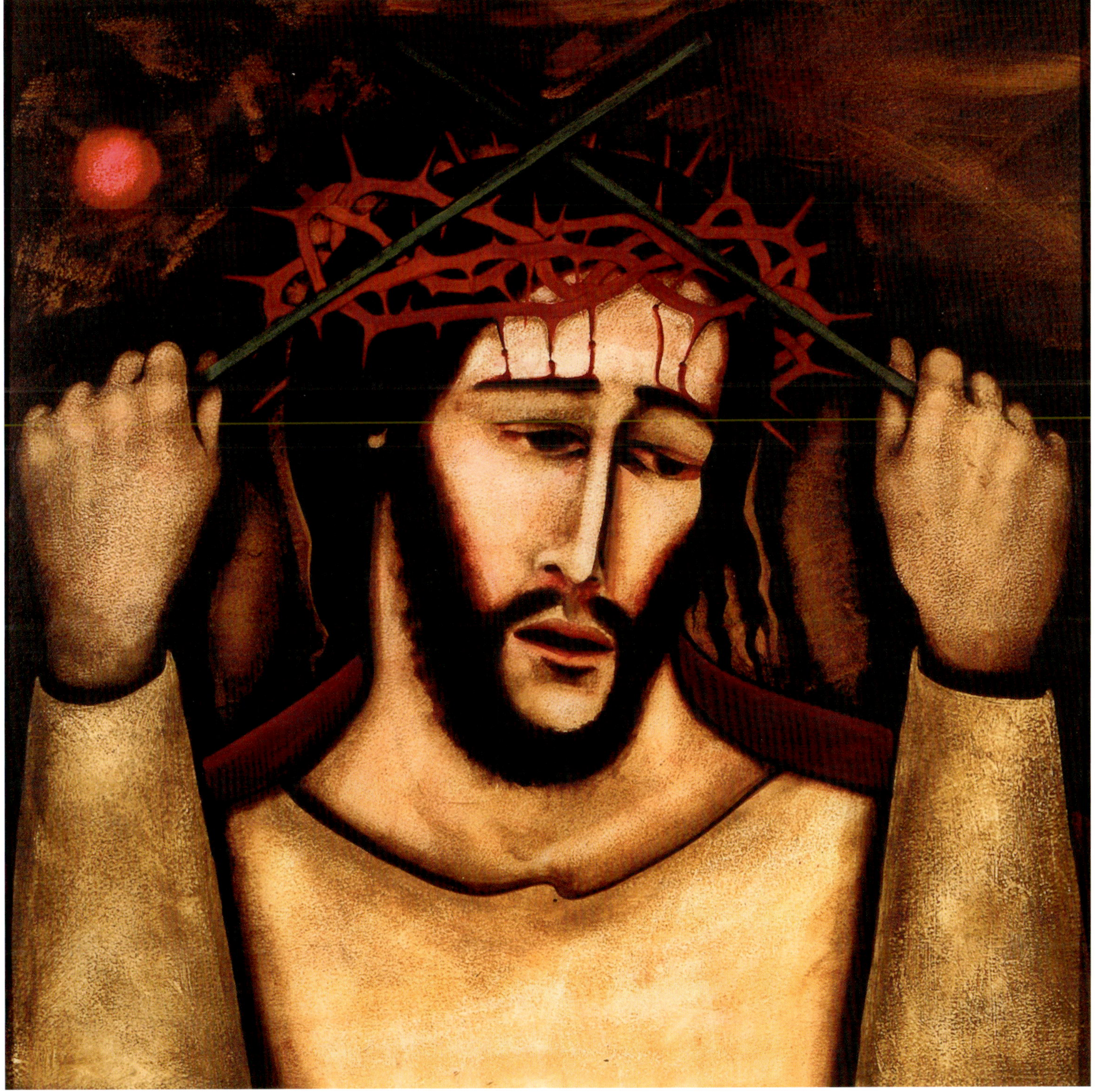

Jesus Crowned with Thorns, early 1990s, 24 inches by 24 inches

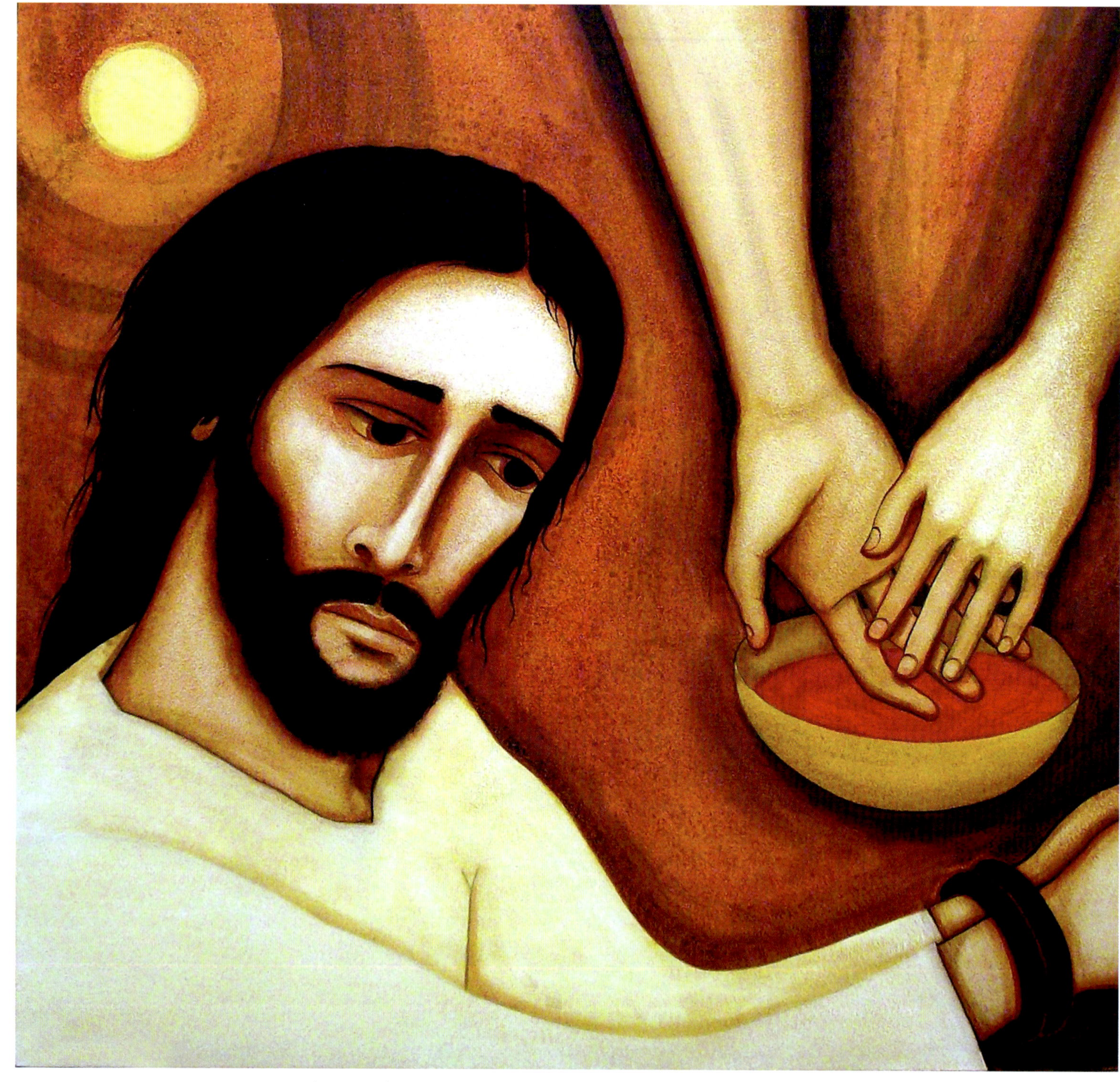

Pilate Washes His Hands of Jesus, 2008, 24 inches by 24 inches

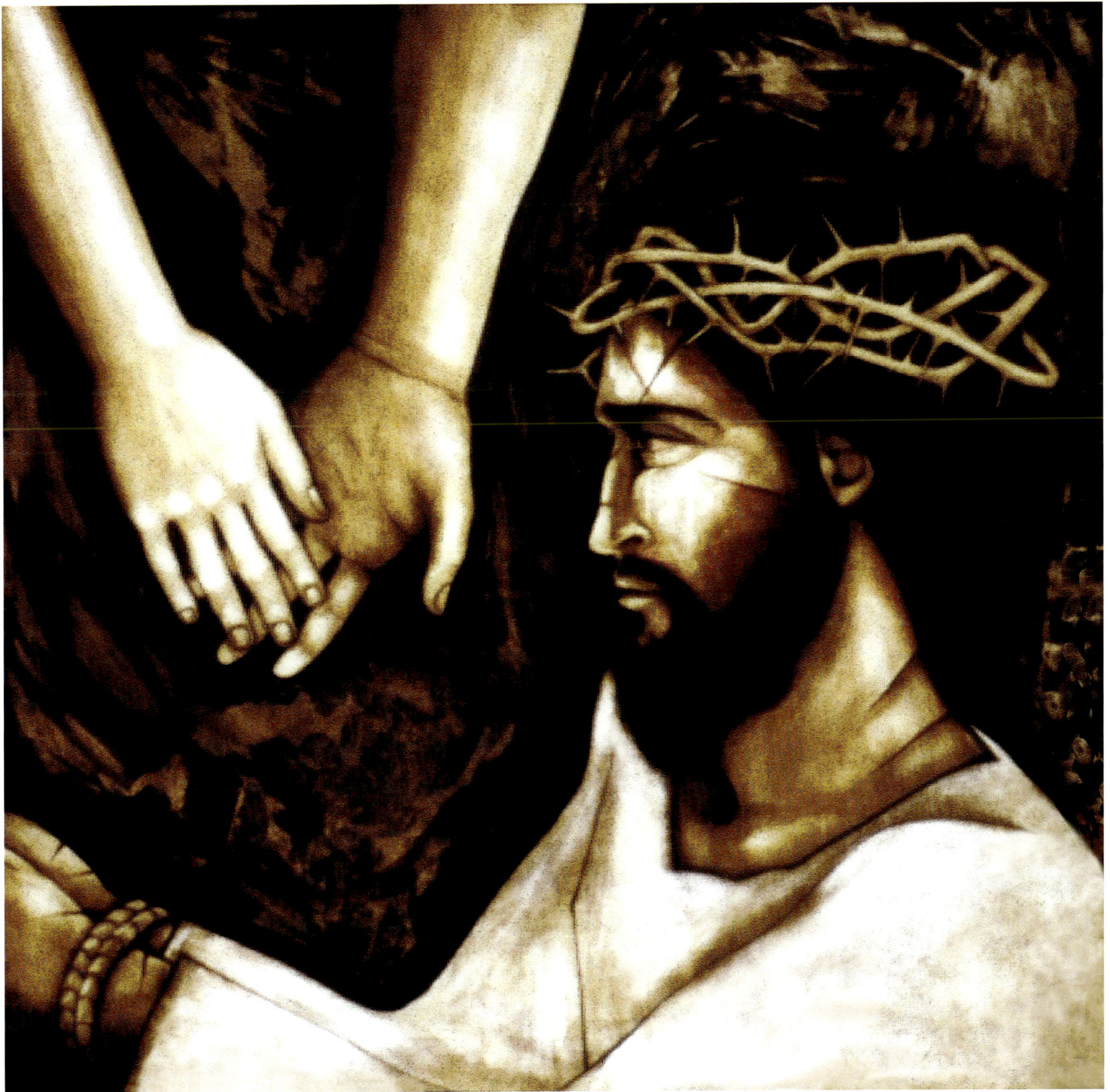

Jesus Condemned to Death, mid-1990s, 24 by 24 inches

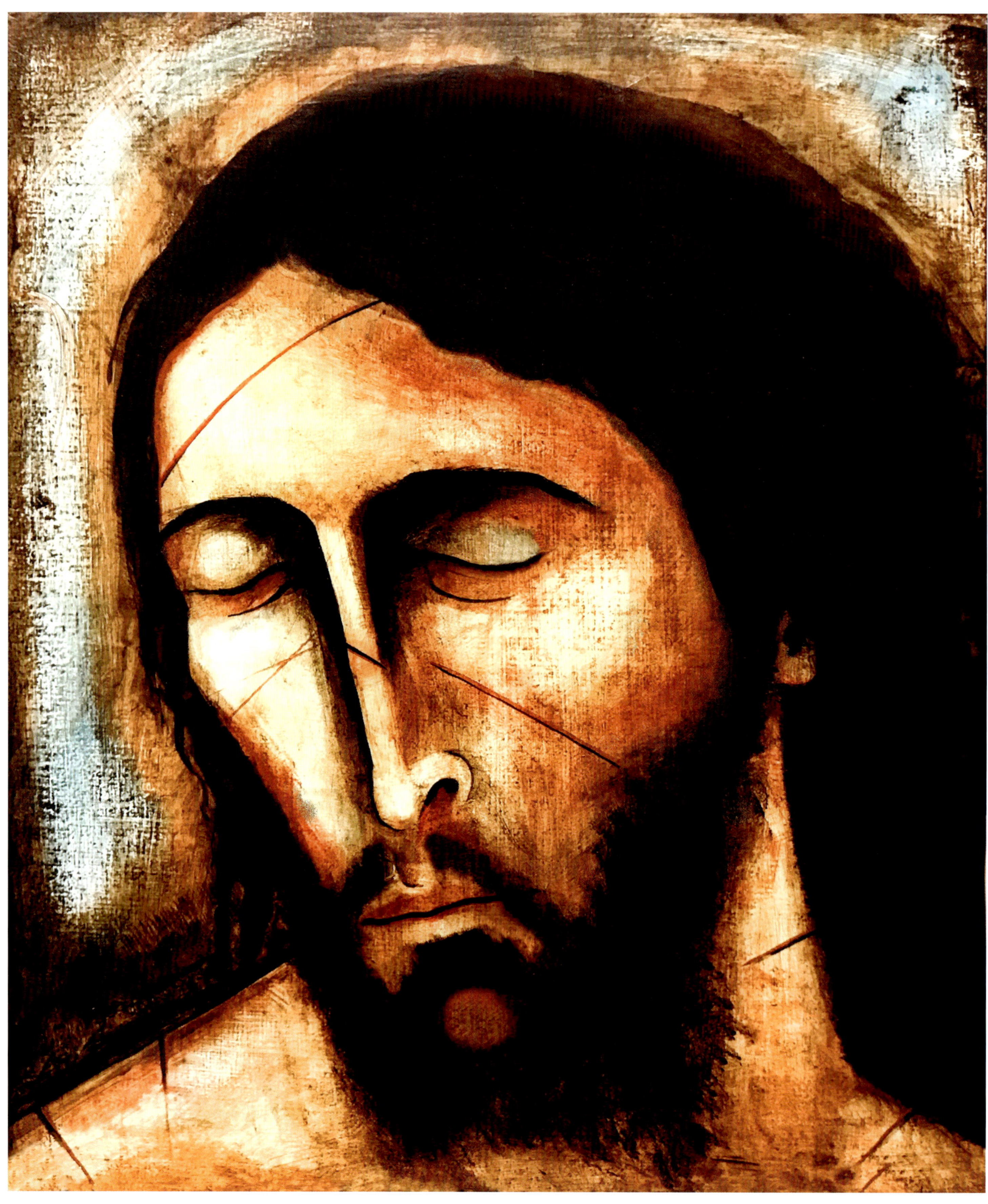

Christ Mocked, 1986

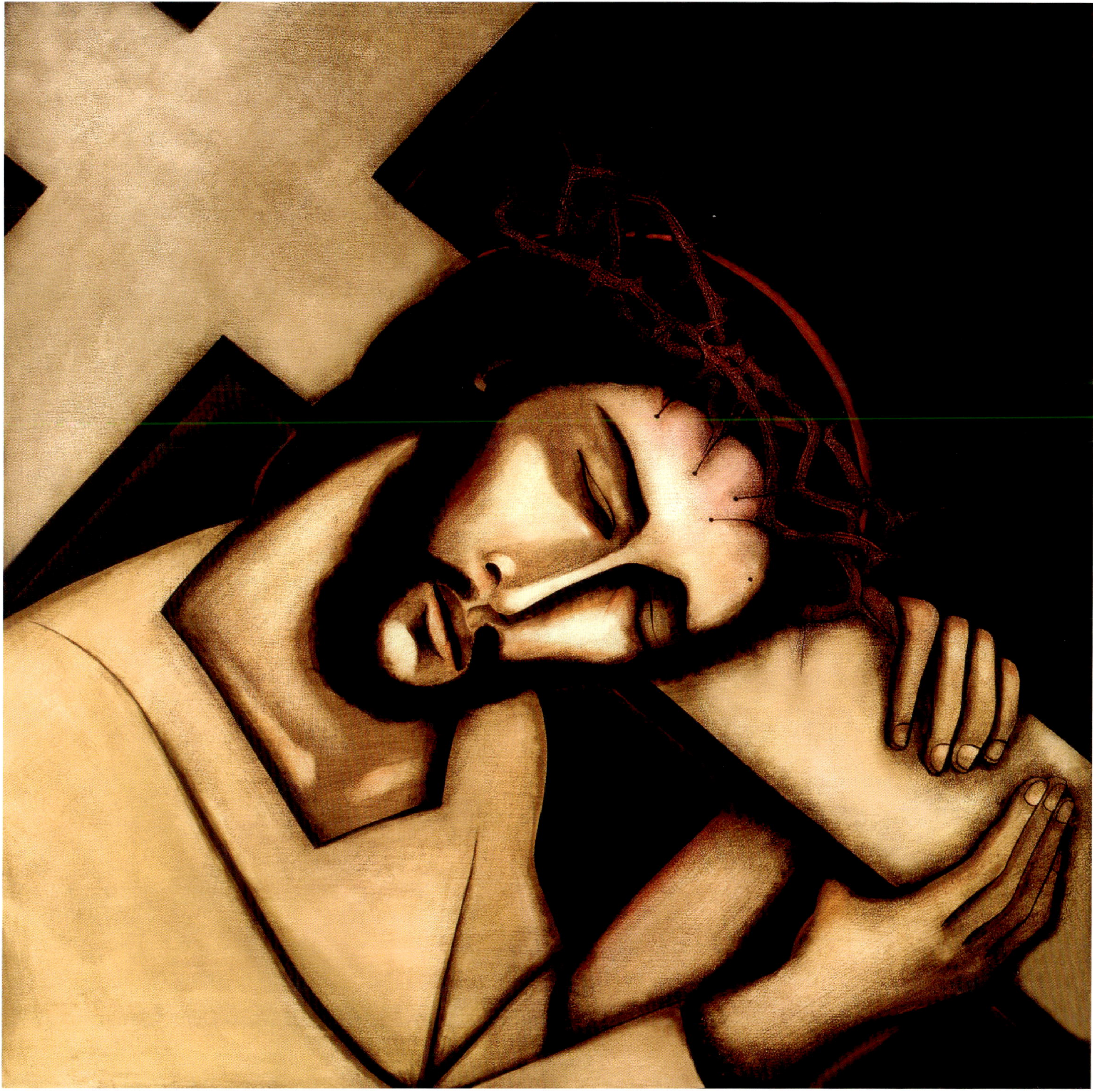

Jesus Carries the Cross, mid-1990s, 24 inches by 24 inches

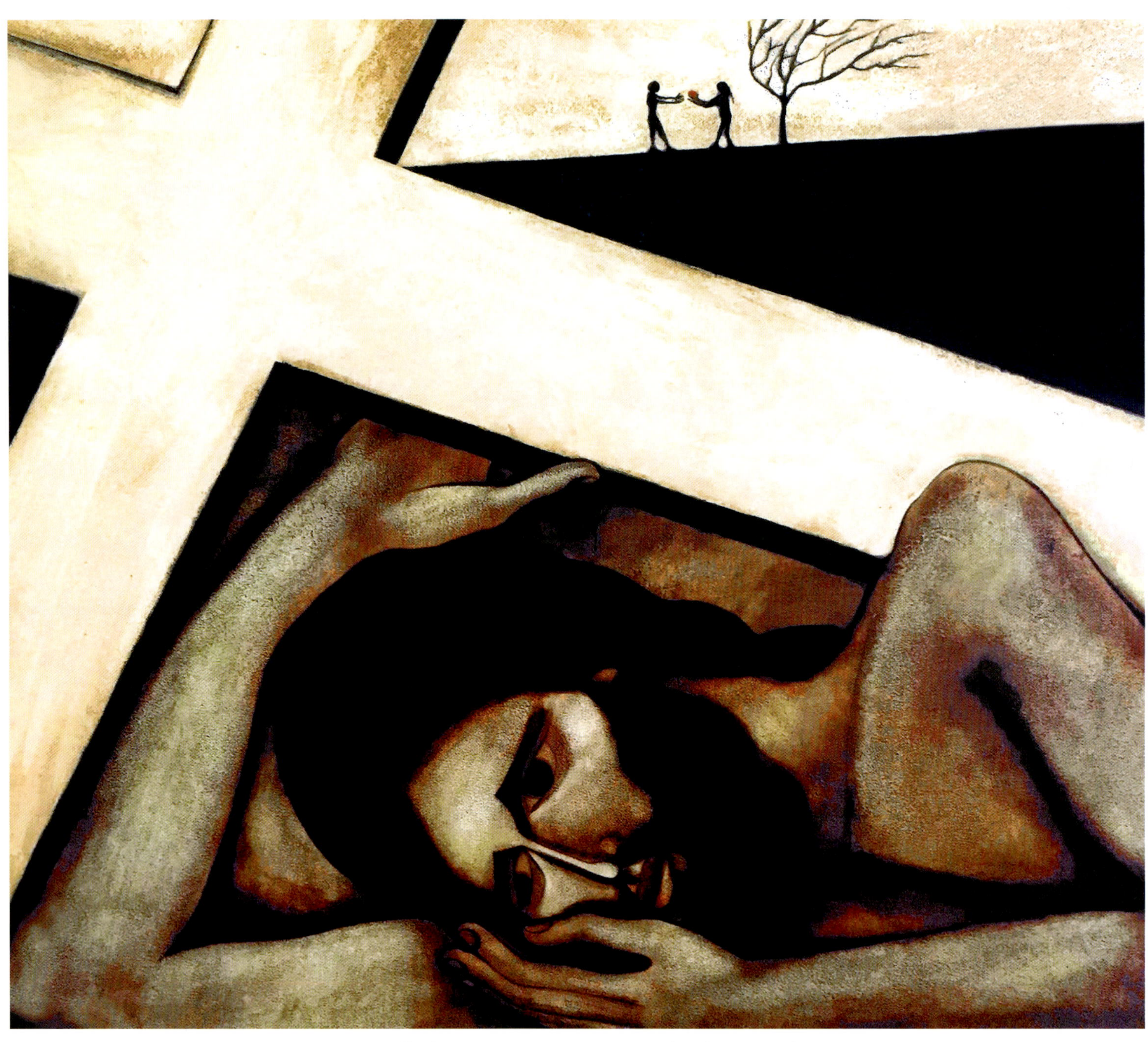

Jesus Falls the First Time, 1983, 24 inches by 24 inches

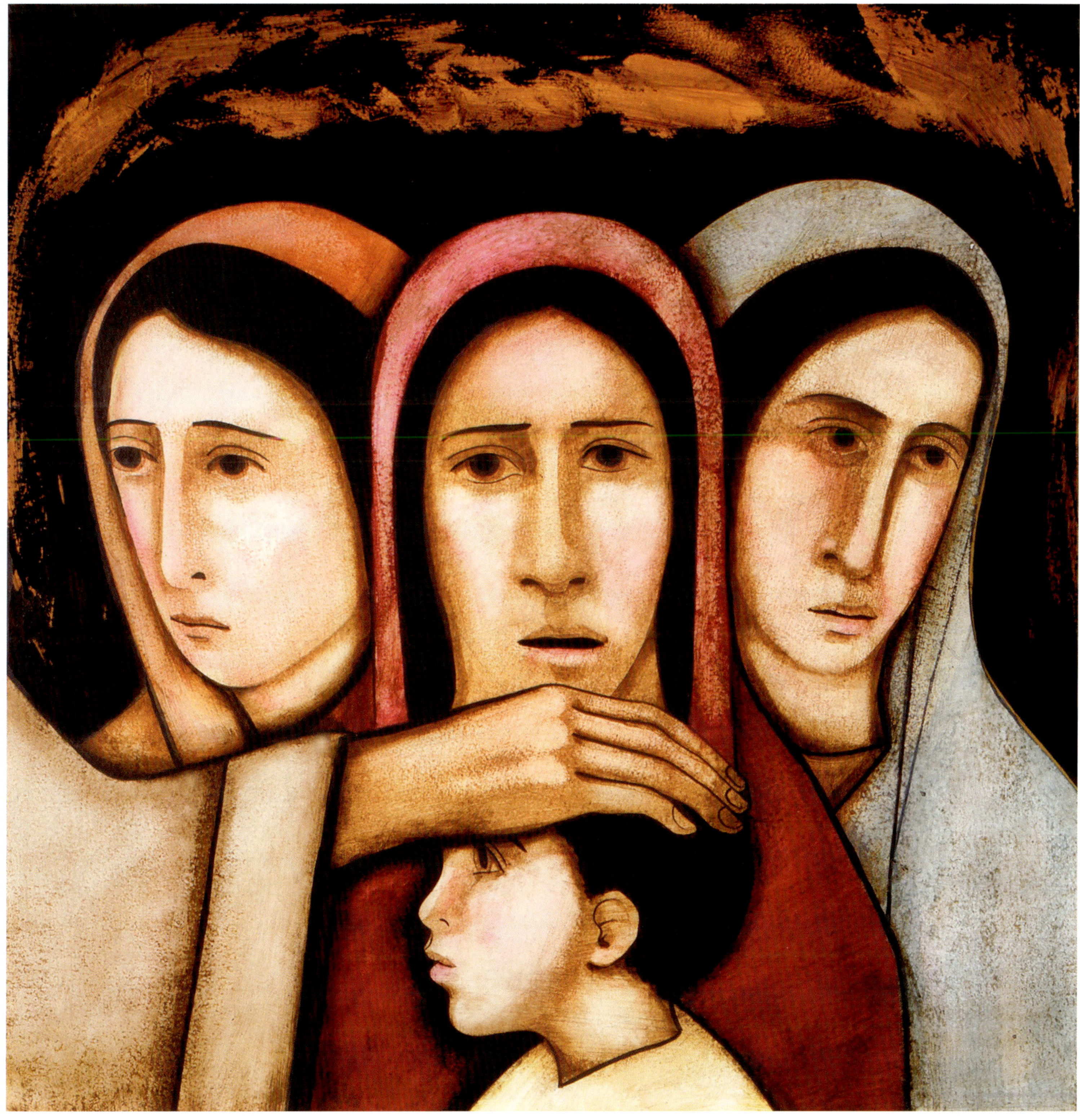

Jesus Meets the Women of Jerusalem, early 1990s, 24 inches by 24 inches

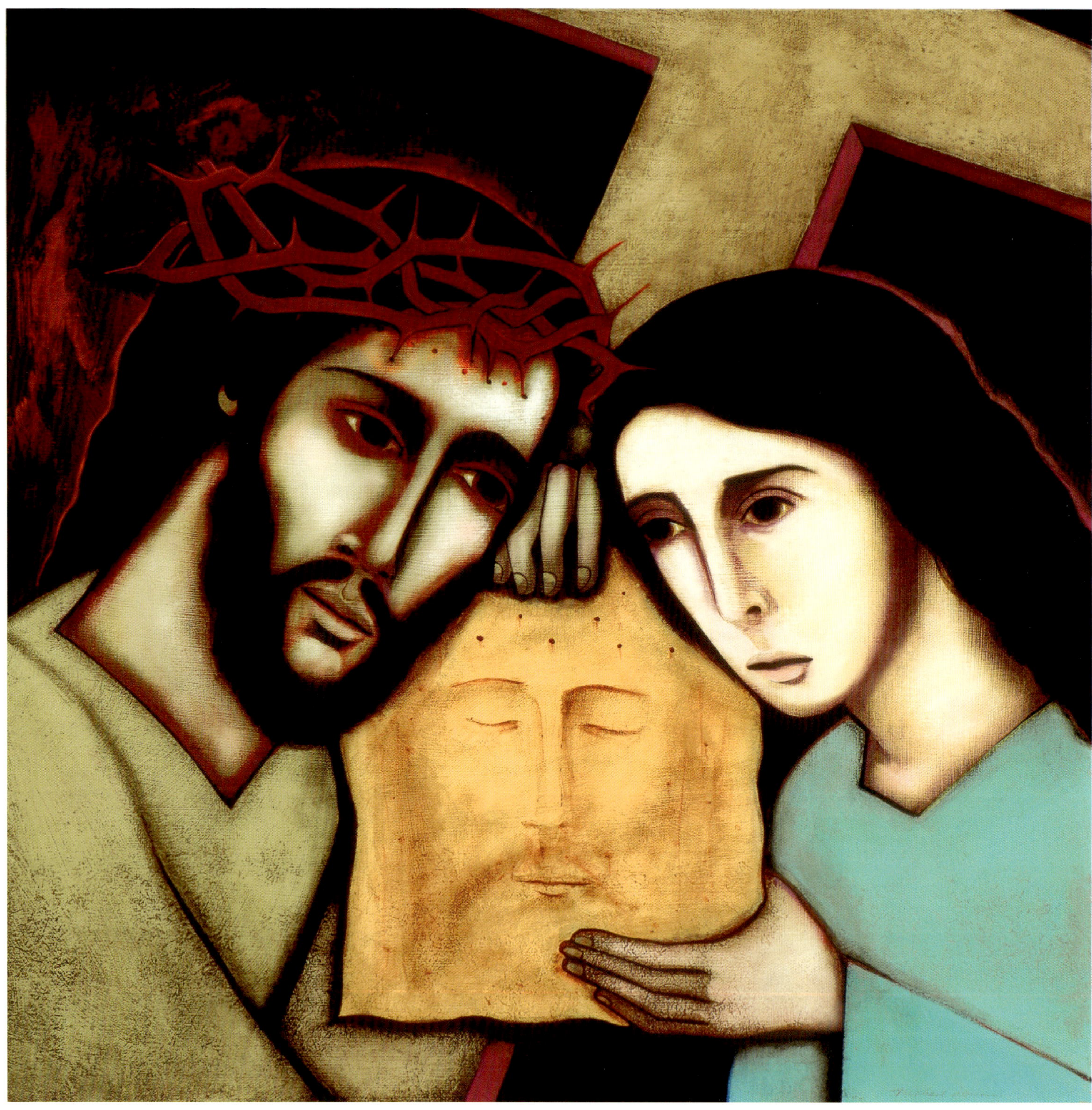

Veronica Wipes the Face of Jesus, 1989, 22 inches by 22 inches

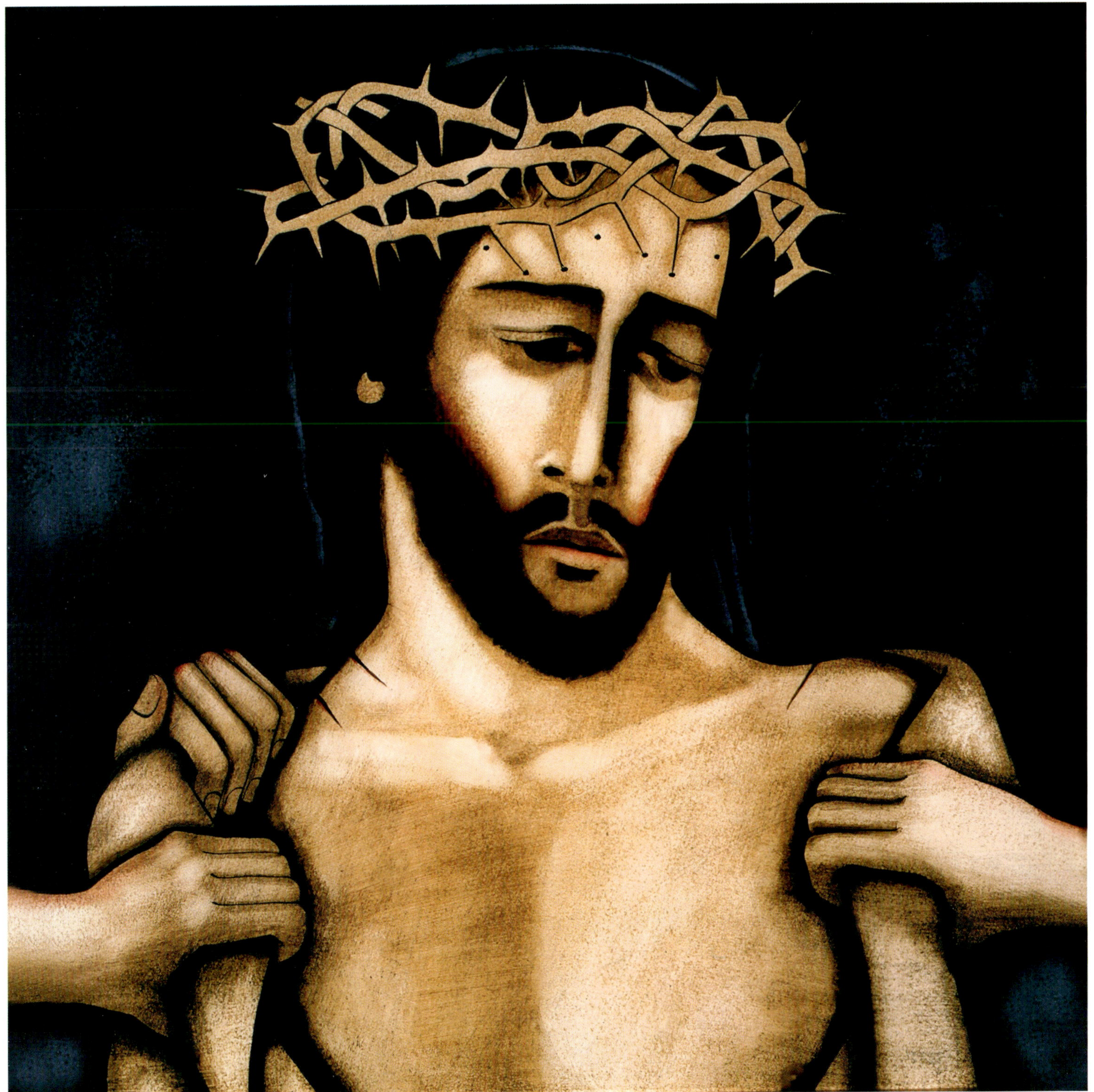

Jesus Is Stripped of His Garments, early 1990s, 24 inches by 24 inches

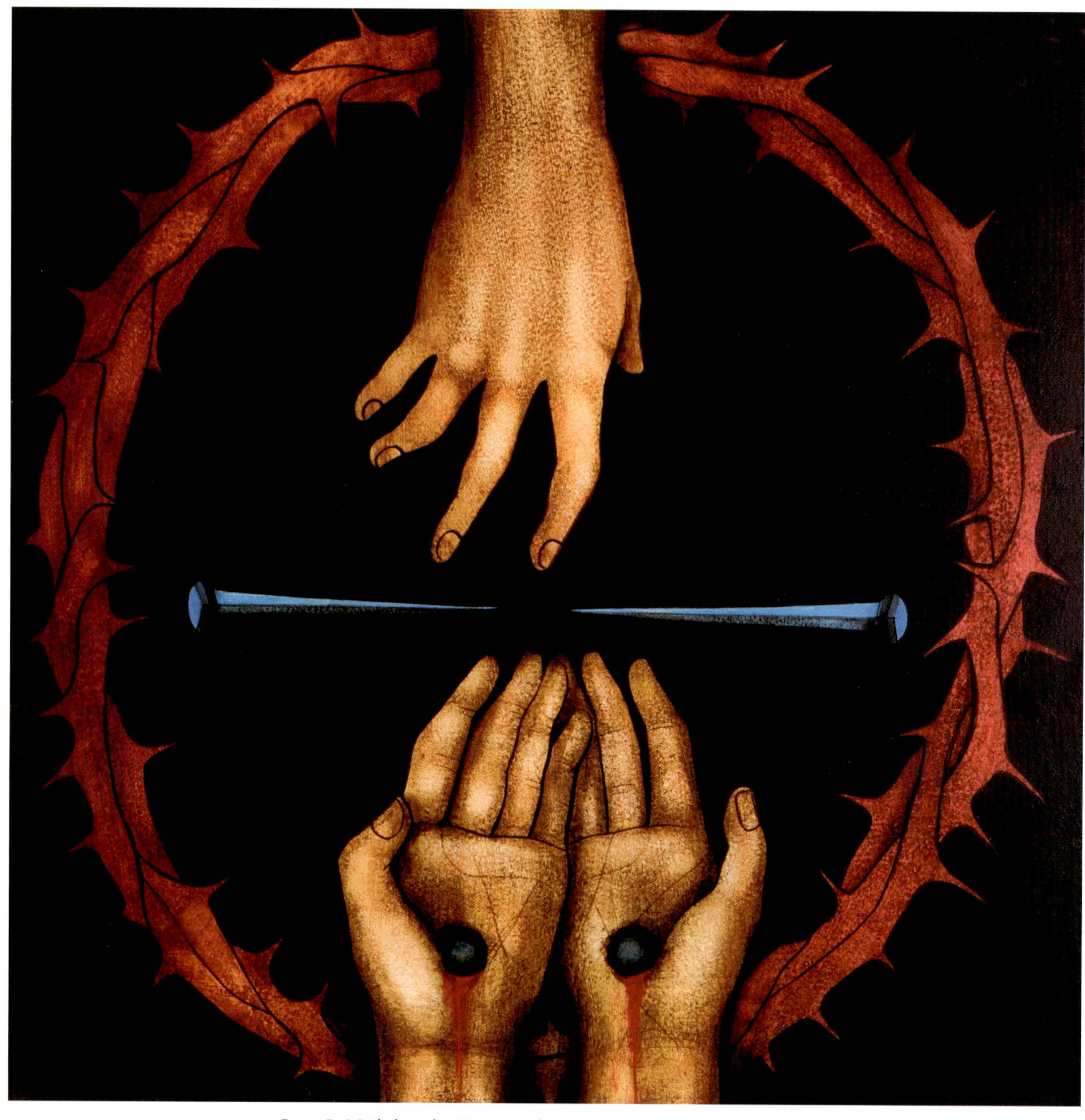

Jesus Is Nailed to the Cross, mid-1990s, 24 inches by 24 inches

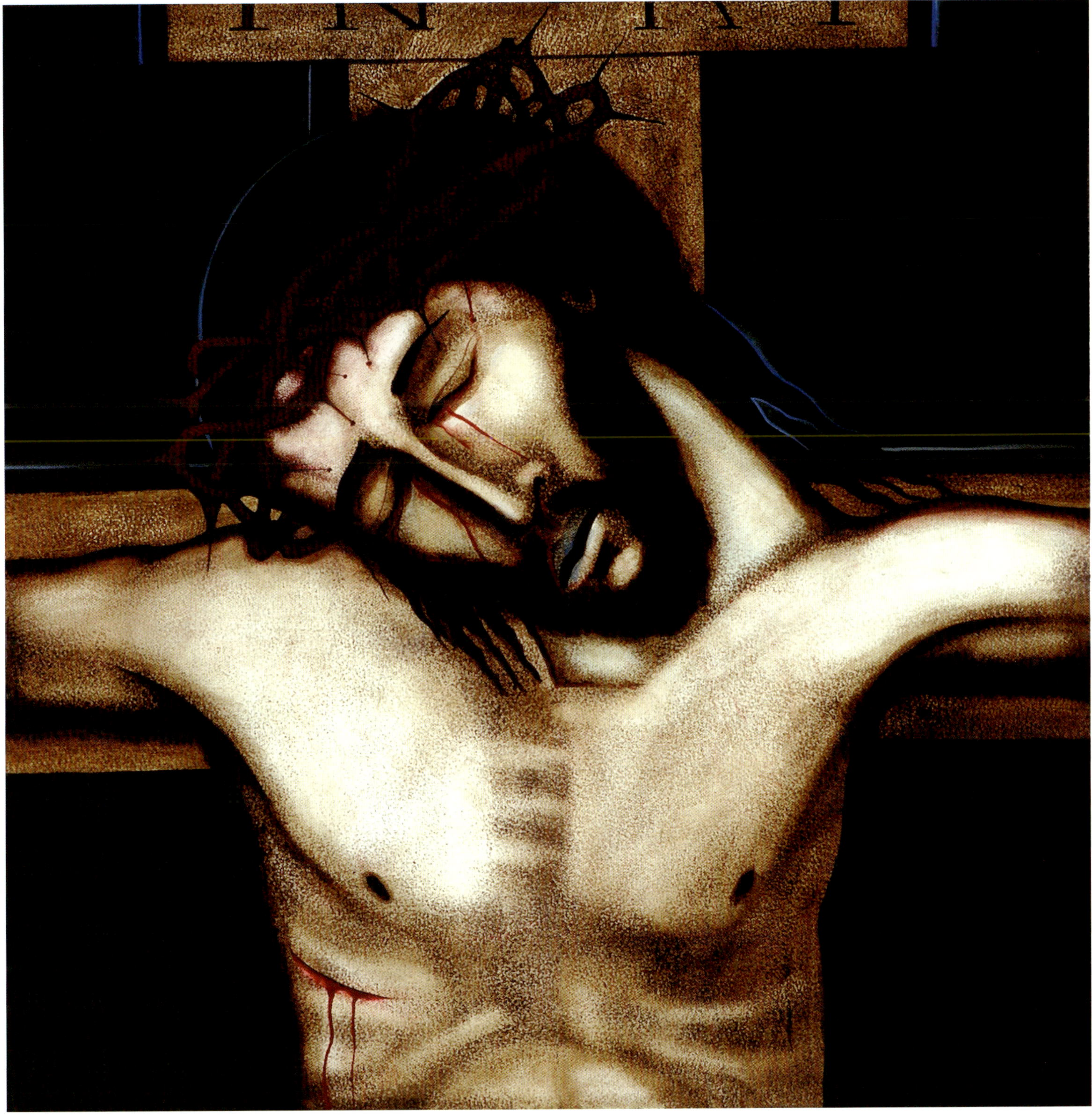

Jesus Dies on the Cross, 1991, 24 inches by 24 inches

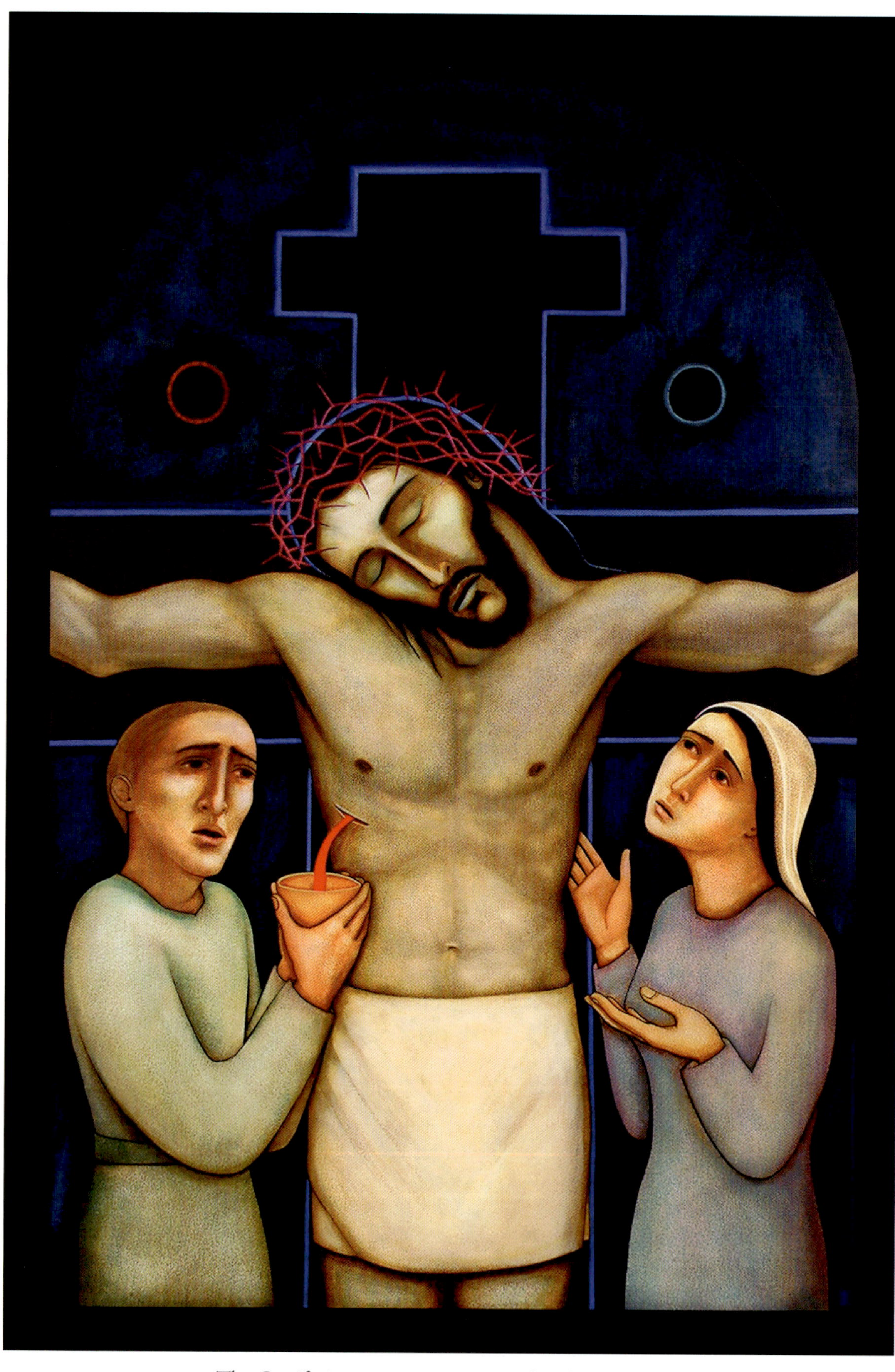

The Crucifixion, 2003–2004, 29 inches by 45 inches

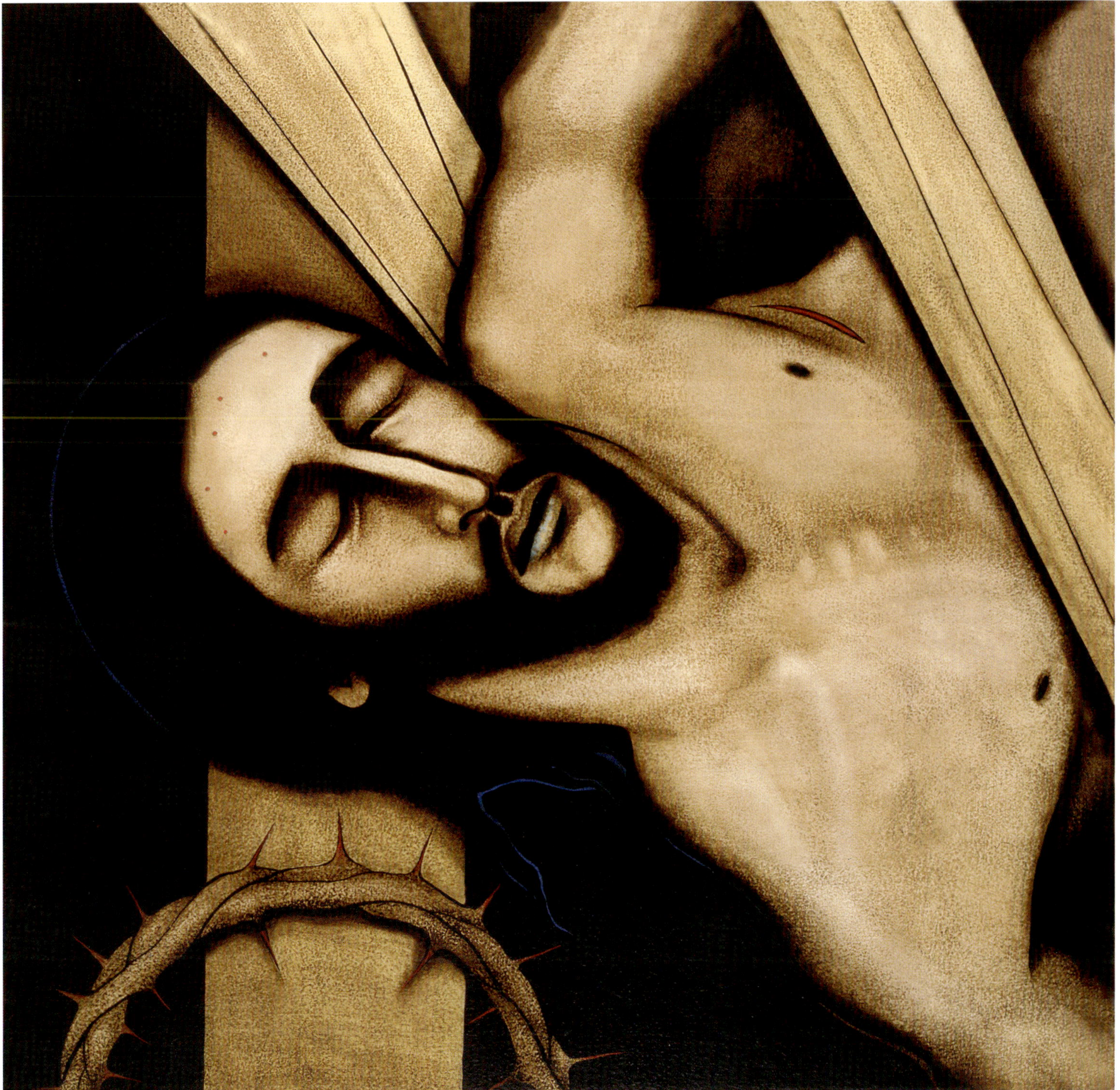

Jesus Is Taken Down from the Cross, 2010, 24 inches by 24 inches

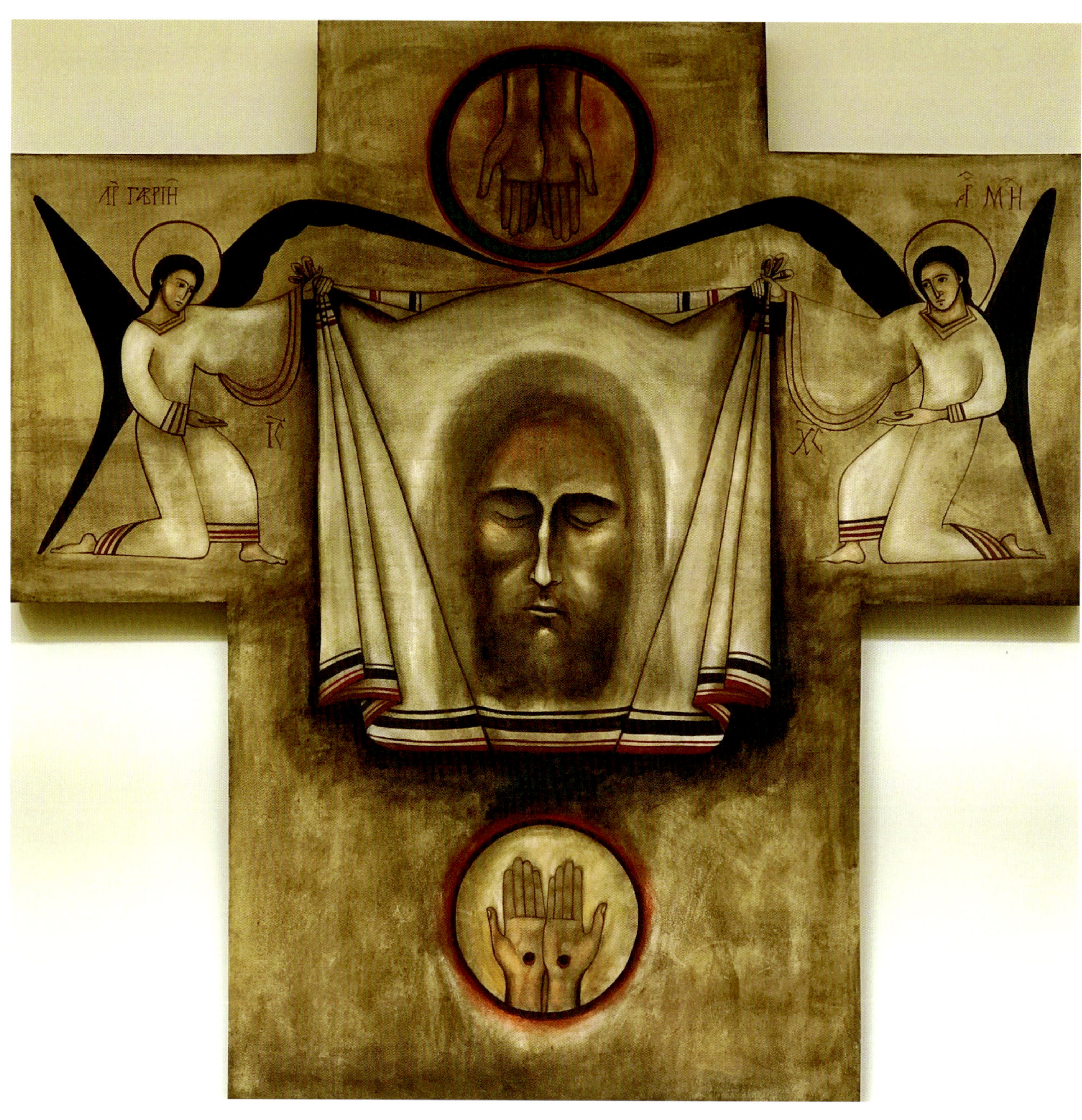

Cross of the Holy Face, wooden structure, 1983, 4 feet by 6 feet

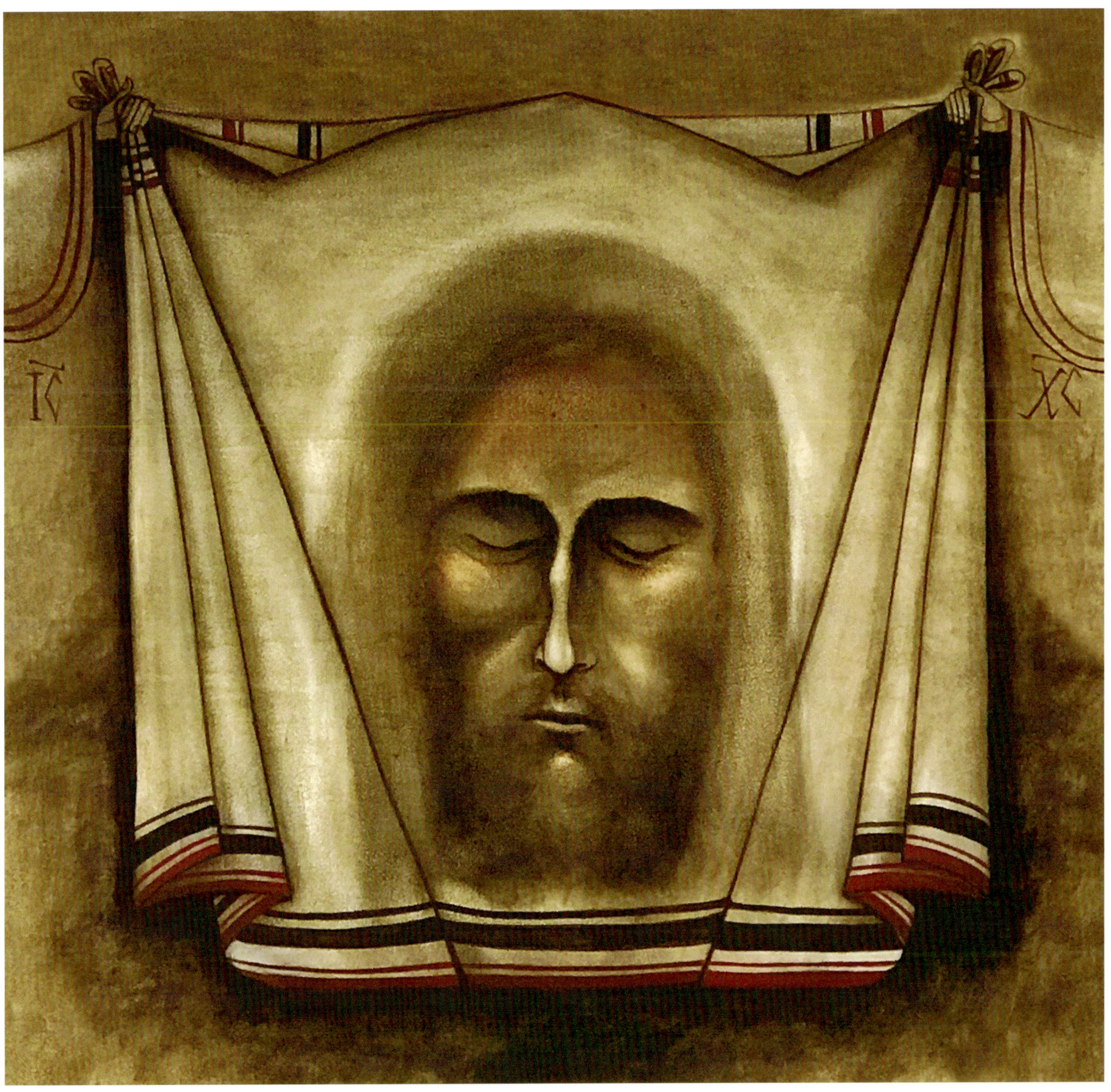

The Holy Face, 1983

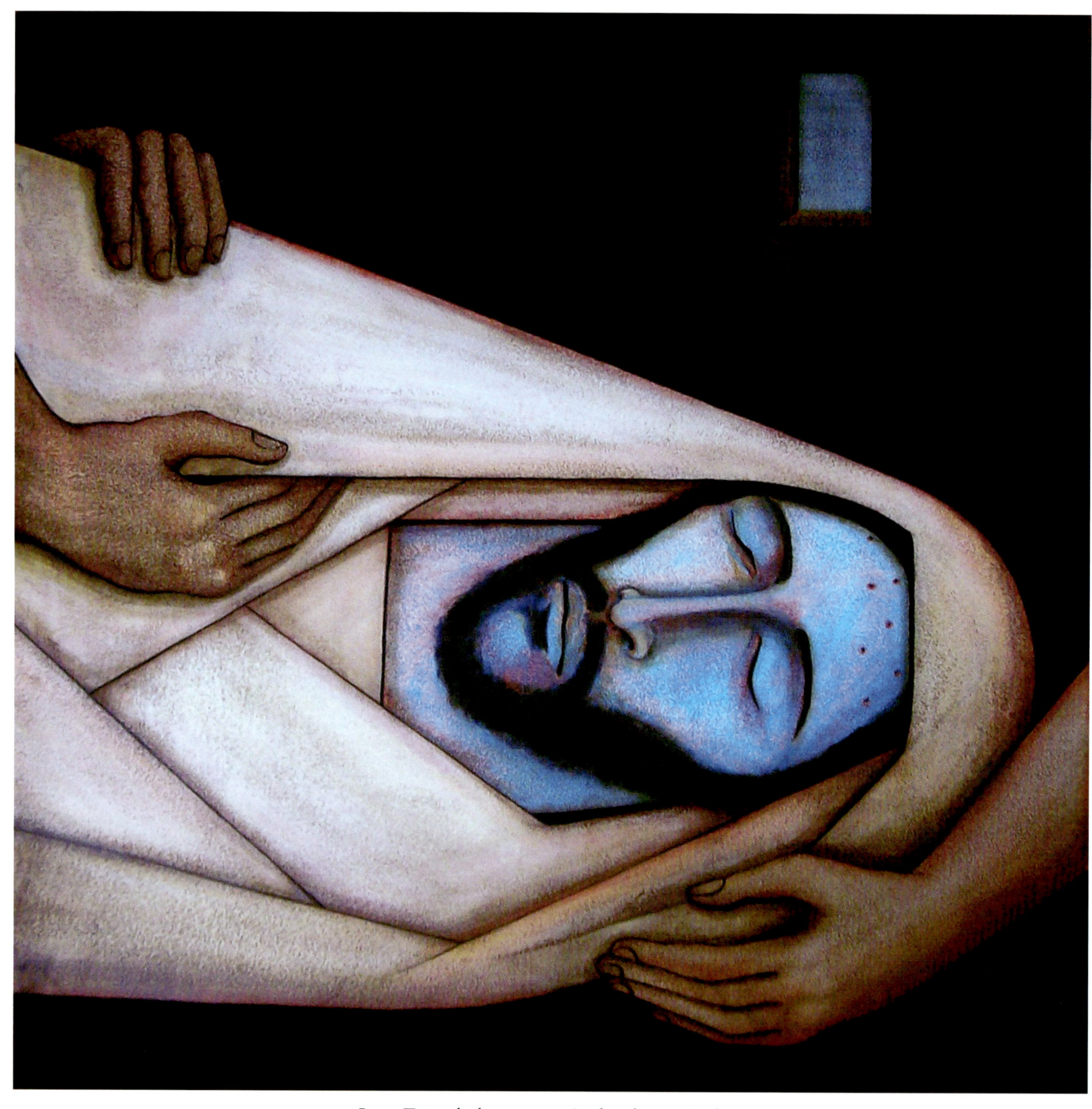

Jesus Entombed, 2013, 24 inches by 24 inches

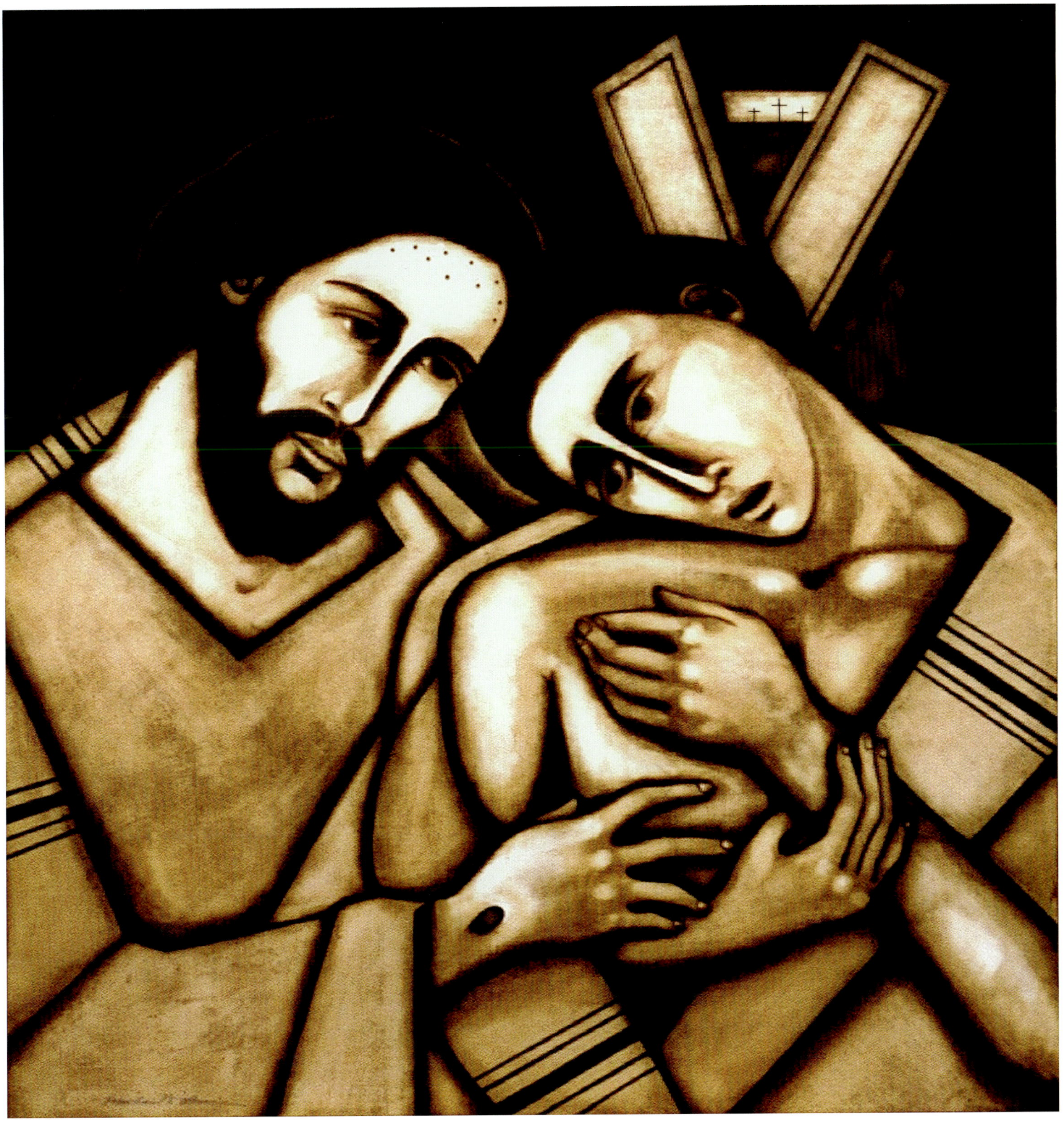

Christ and Adam, early 1990s, 24 inches by 24 inches

Scriptural Illuminations

The stories of the Old and New Testaments are inexhaustible, their dramas and mysteries ever revealing new layers of meaning. The arts, like Sacred Scripture, can offer multiple dimensions of exegesis.

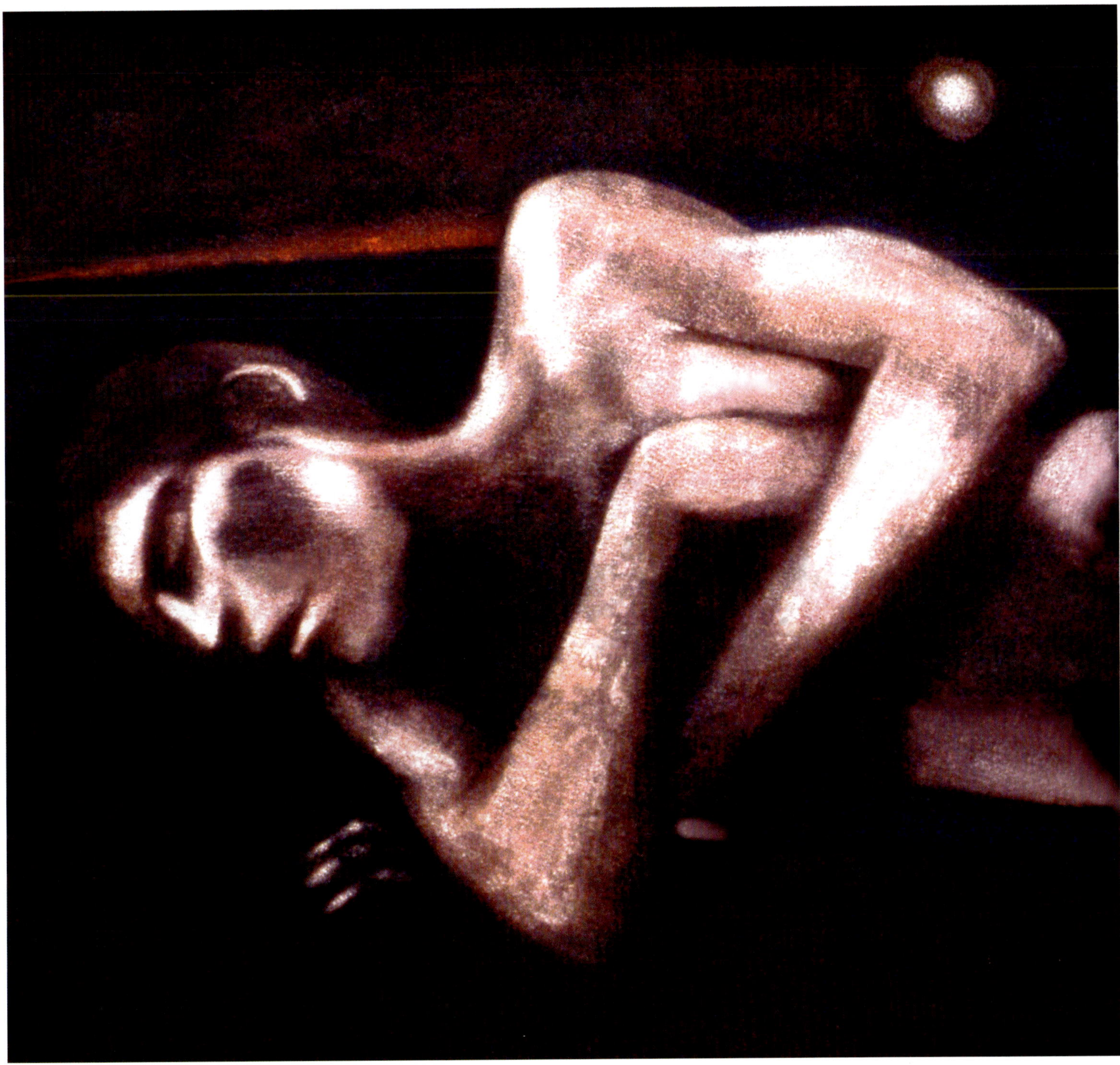

Adam Sleeping, 1986

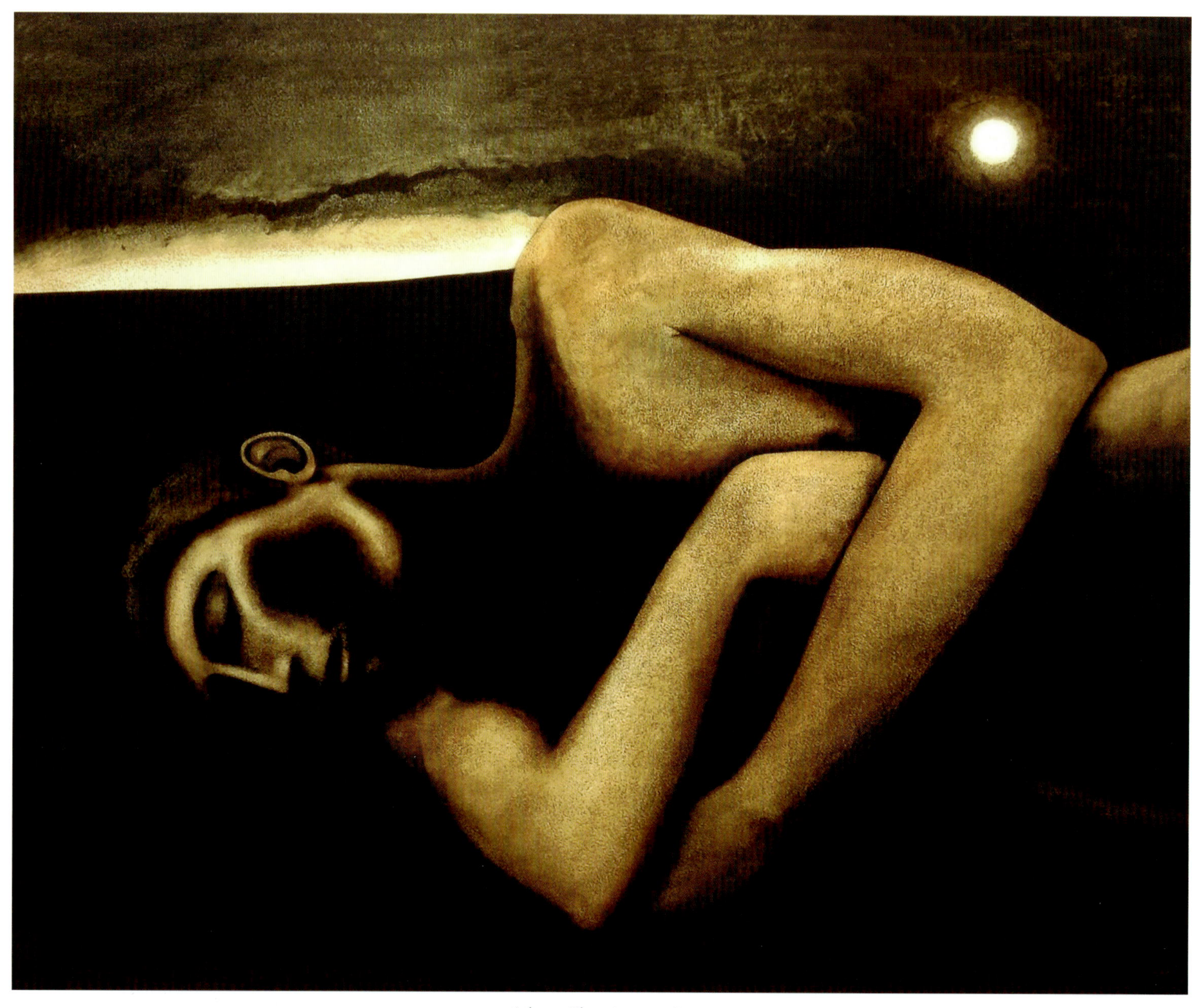

Adam Sleeping, 1985

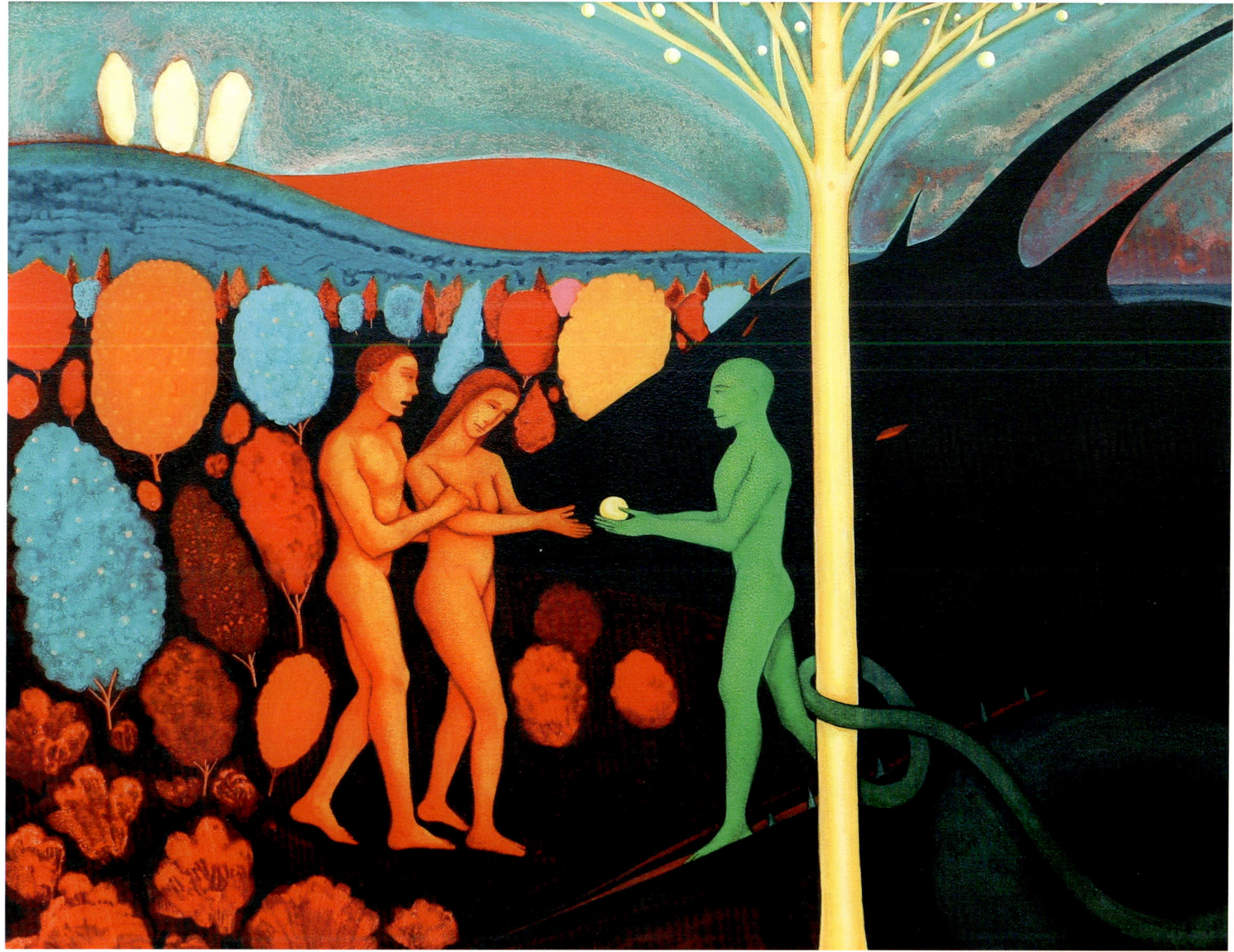

The Temptation in Eden, 2005

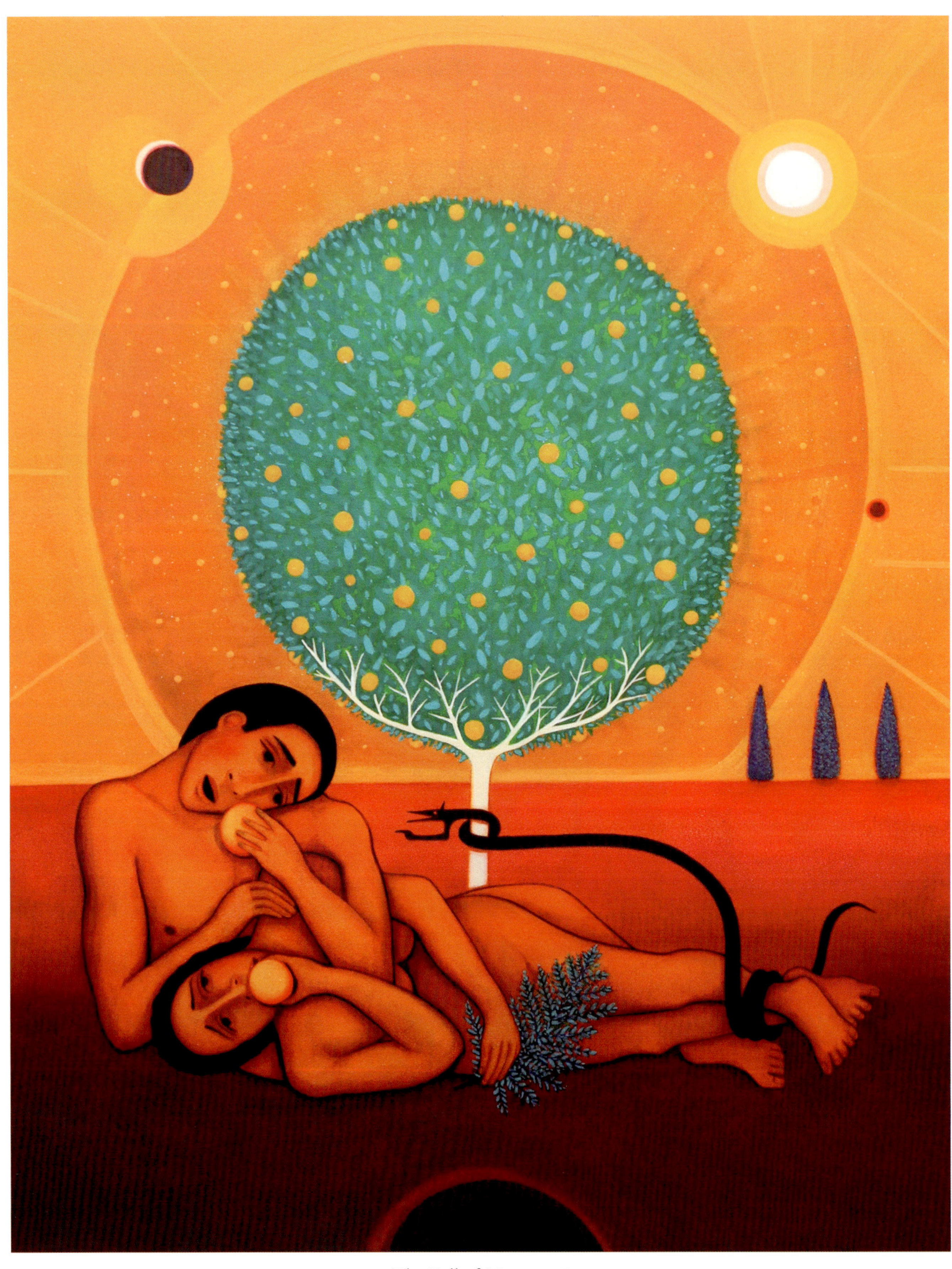

The Fall of Man, 2018

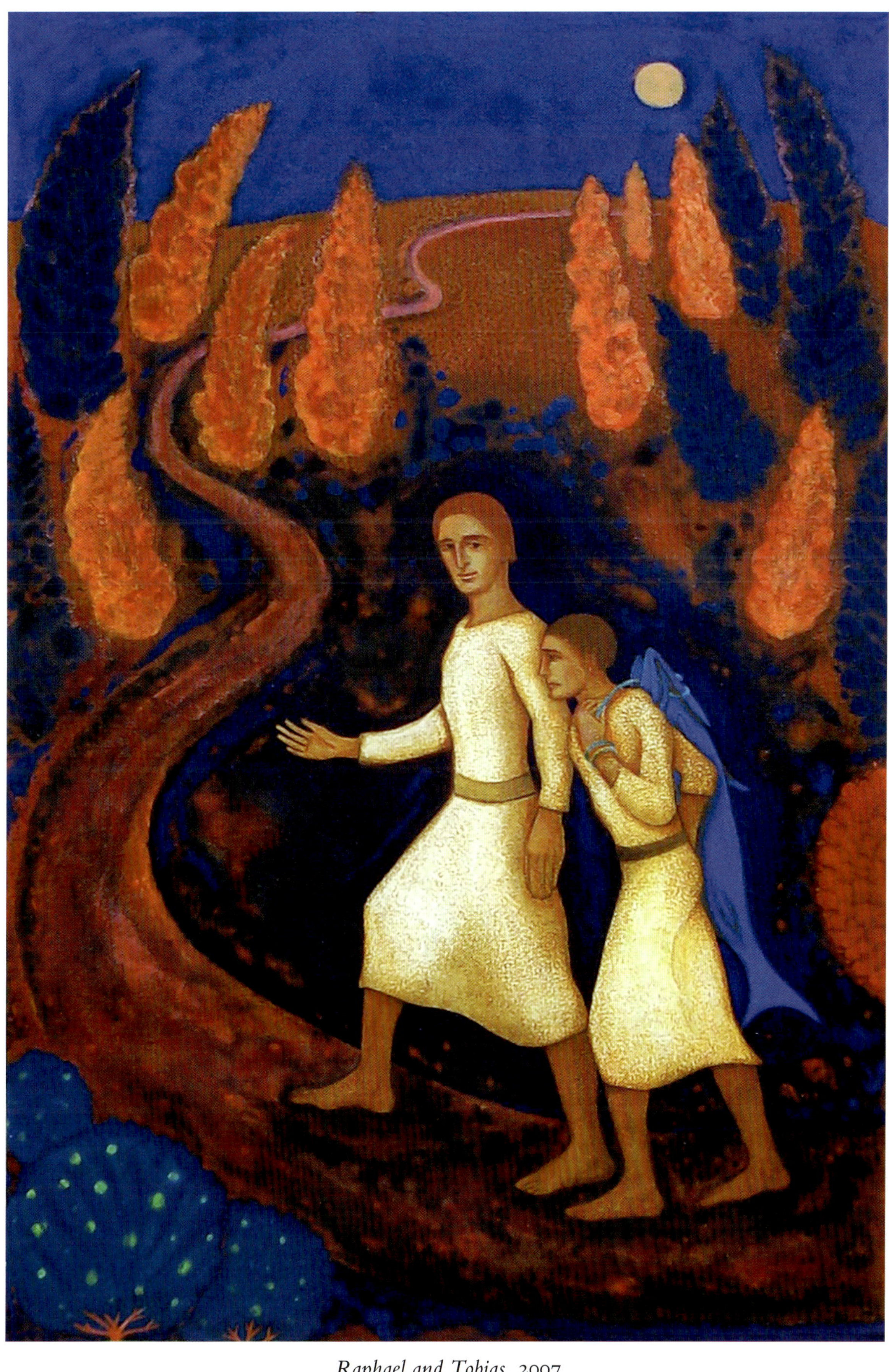

Raphael and Tobias, 2007

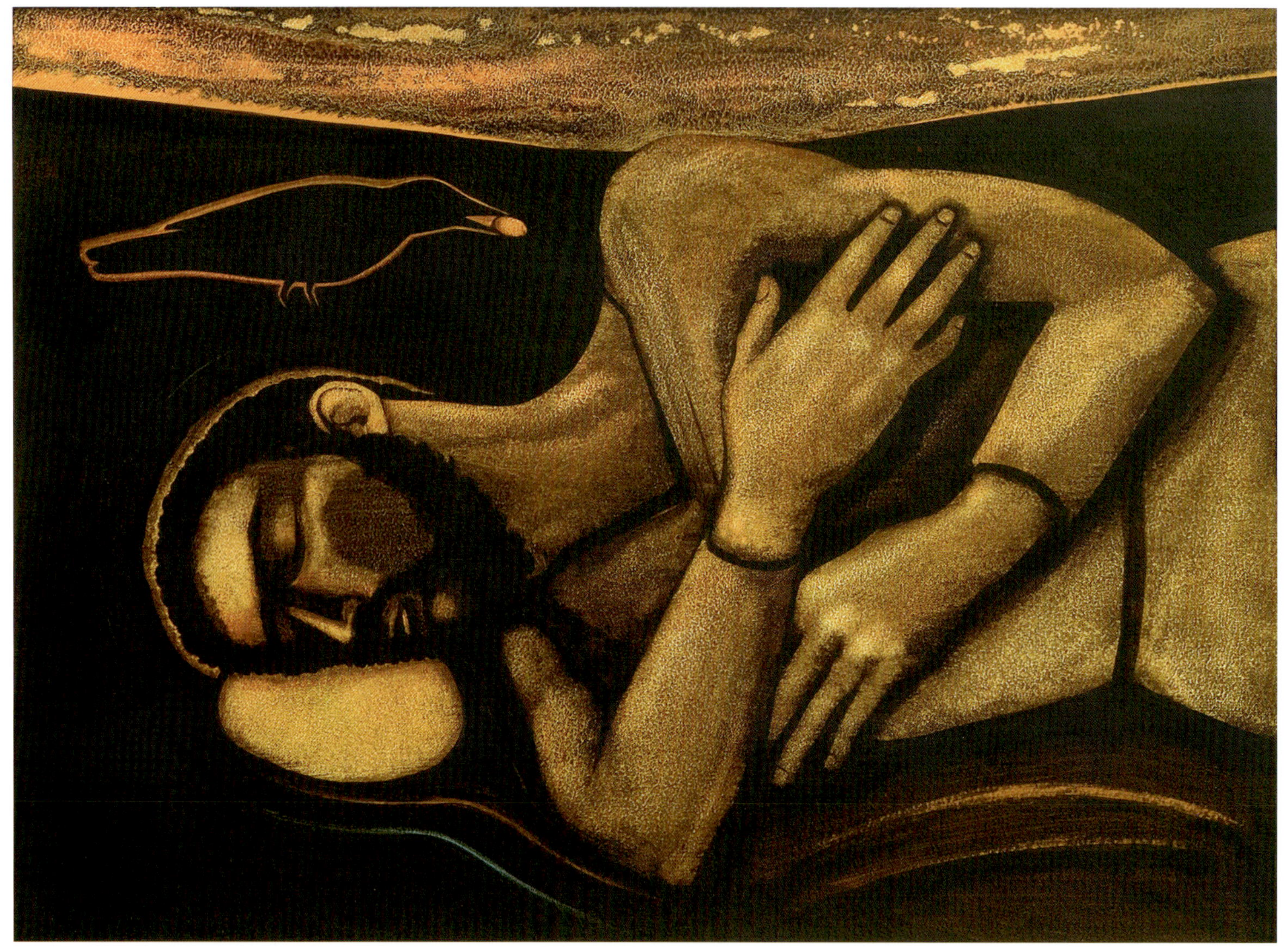

The Prophet Elijah, 2000

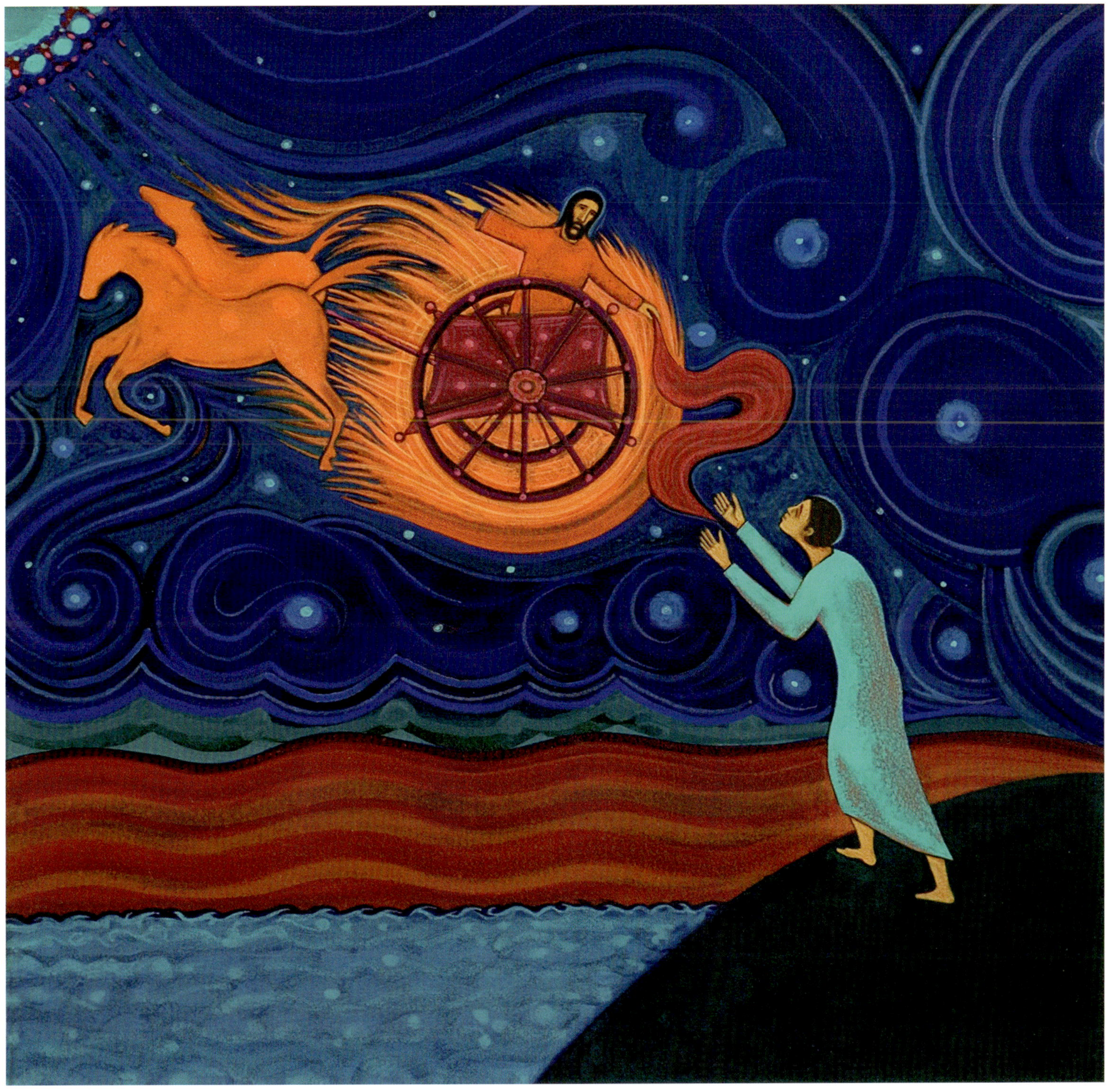

Elijah and Elisha, 2002

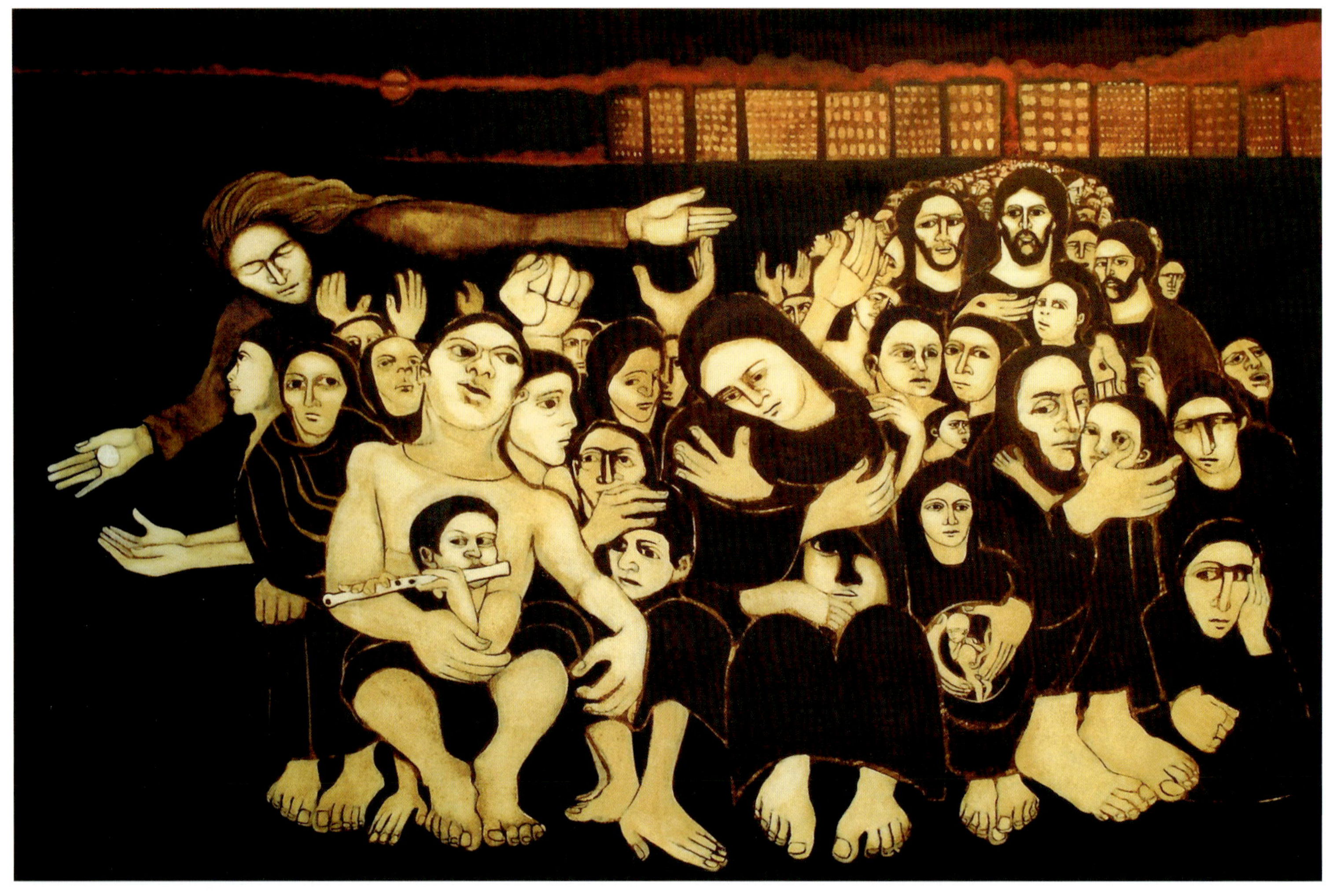

Exodus, 1982

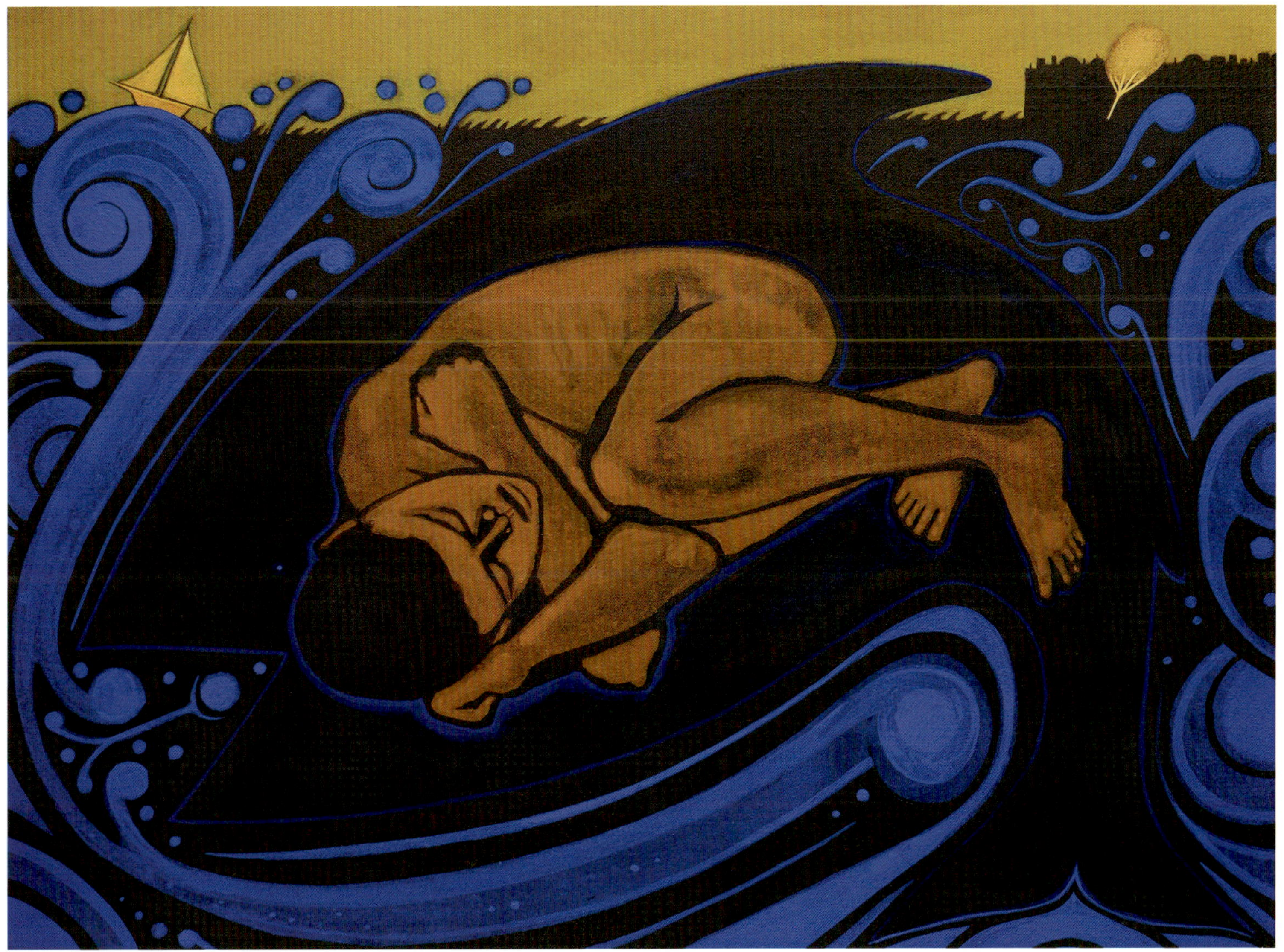

Jonah, 2001, 17 inches by 23 inches

78

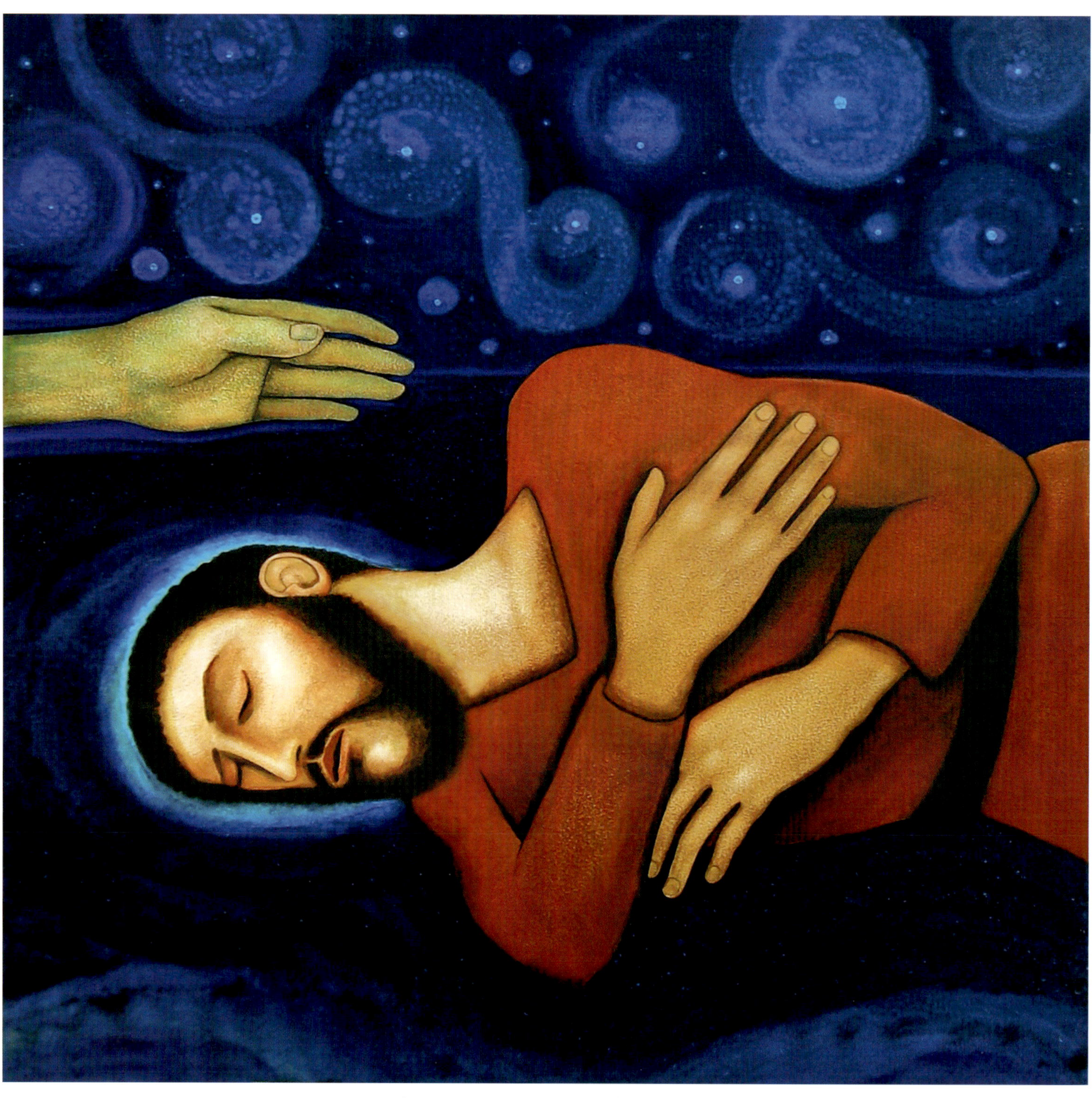

St. Joseph Dreaming, 2012, 22 inches by 22 inches

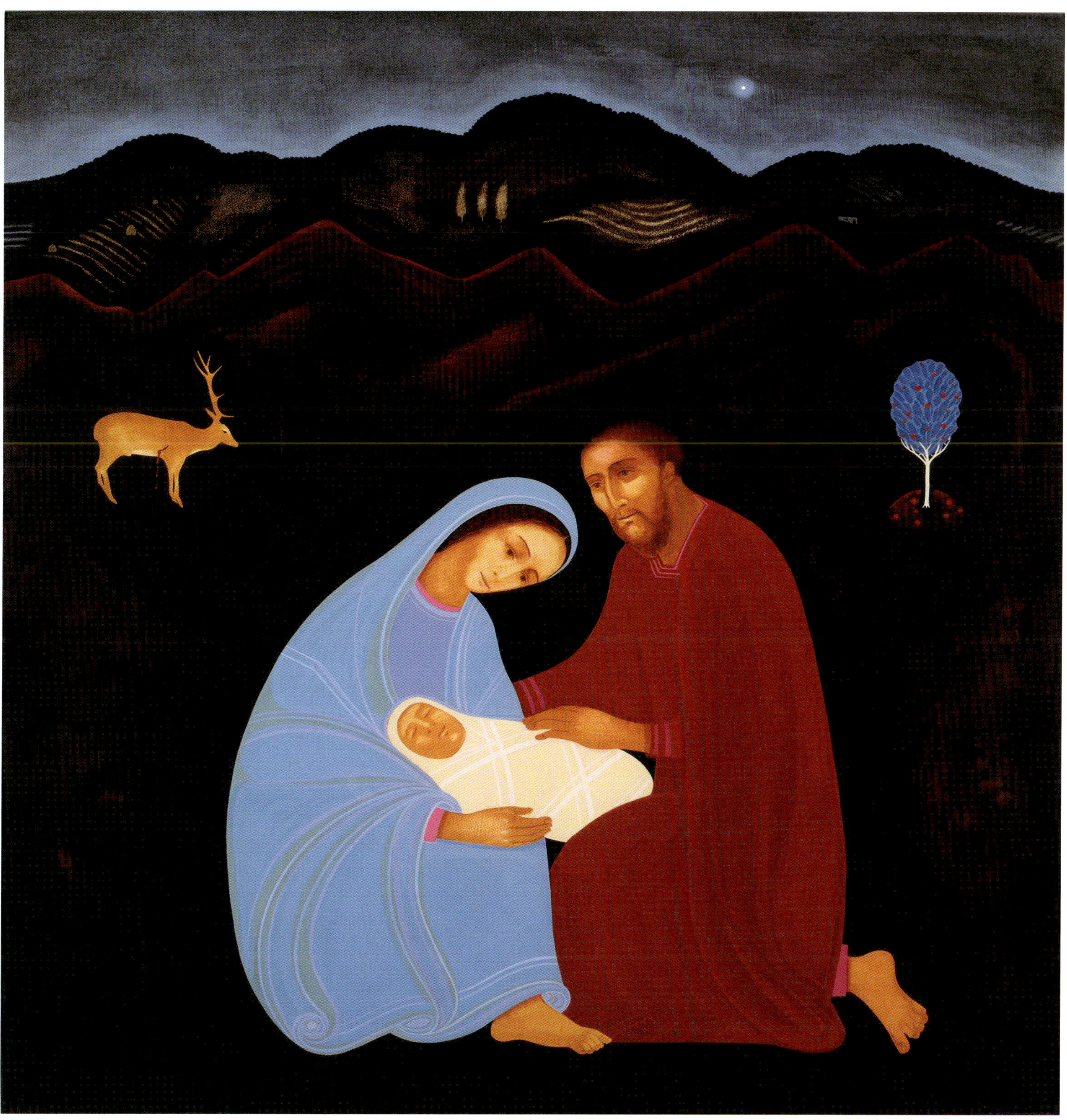

The Nativity, 1990–1991, 48 inches by 48 inches

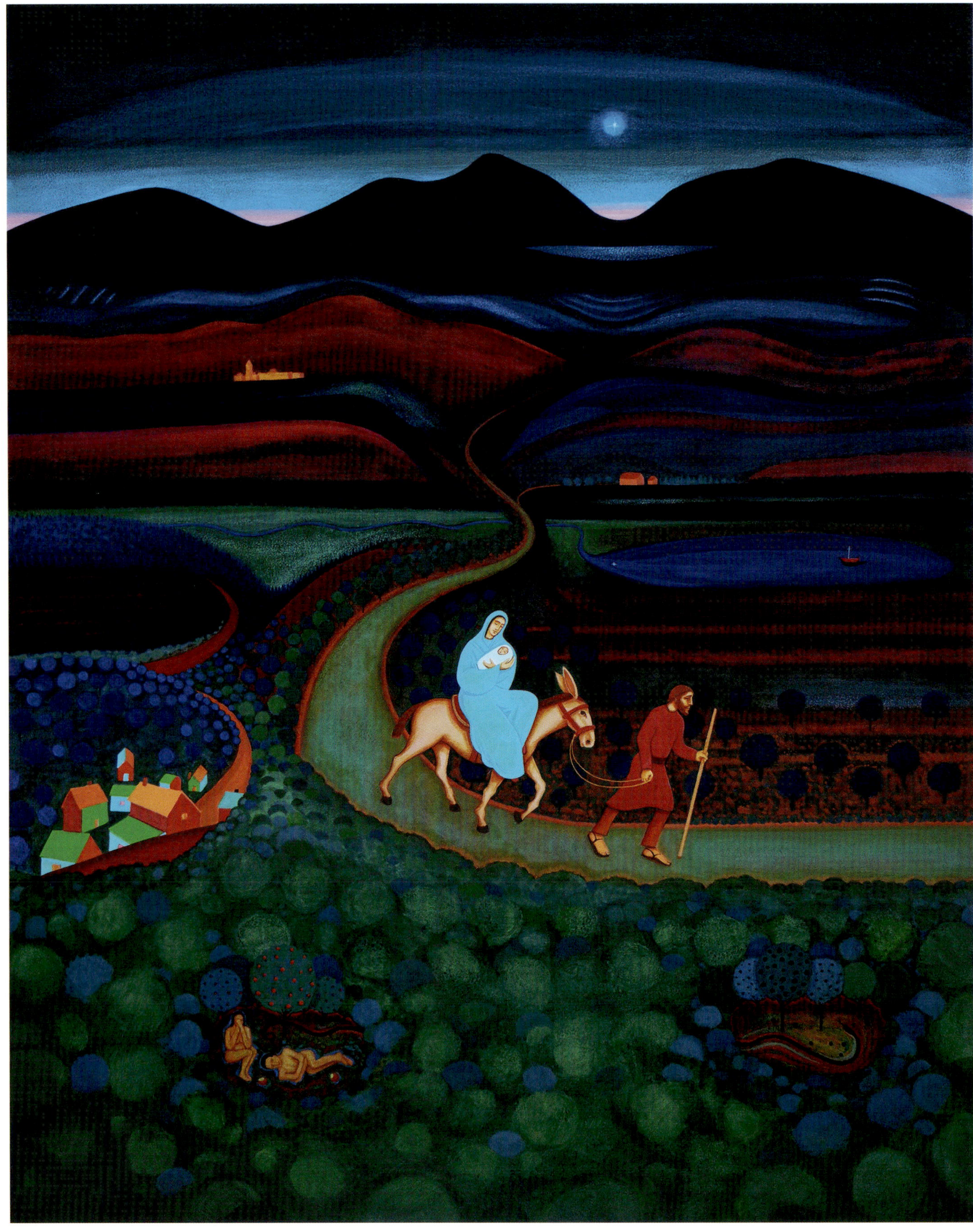

The Flight into Egypt, 2018, 30 inches by 38 inches

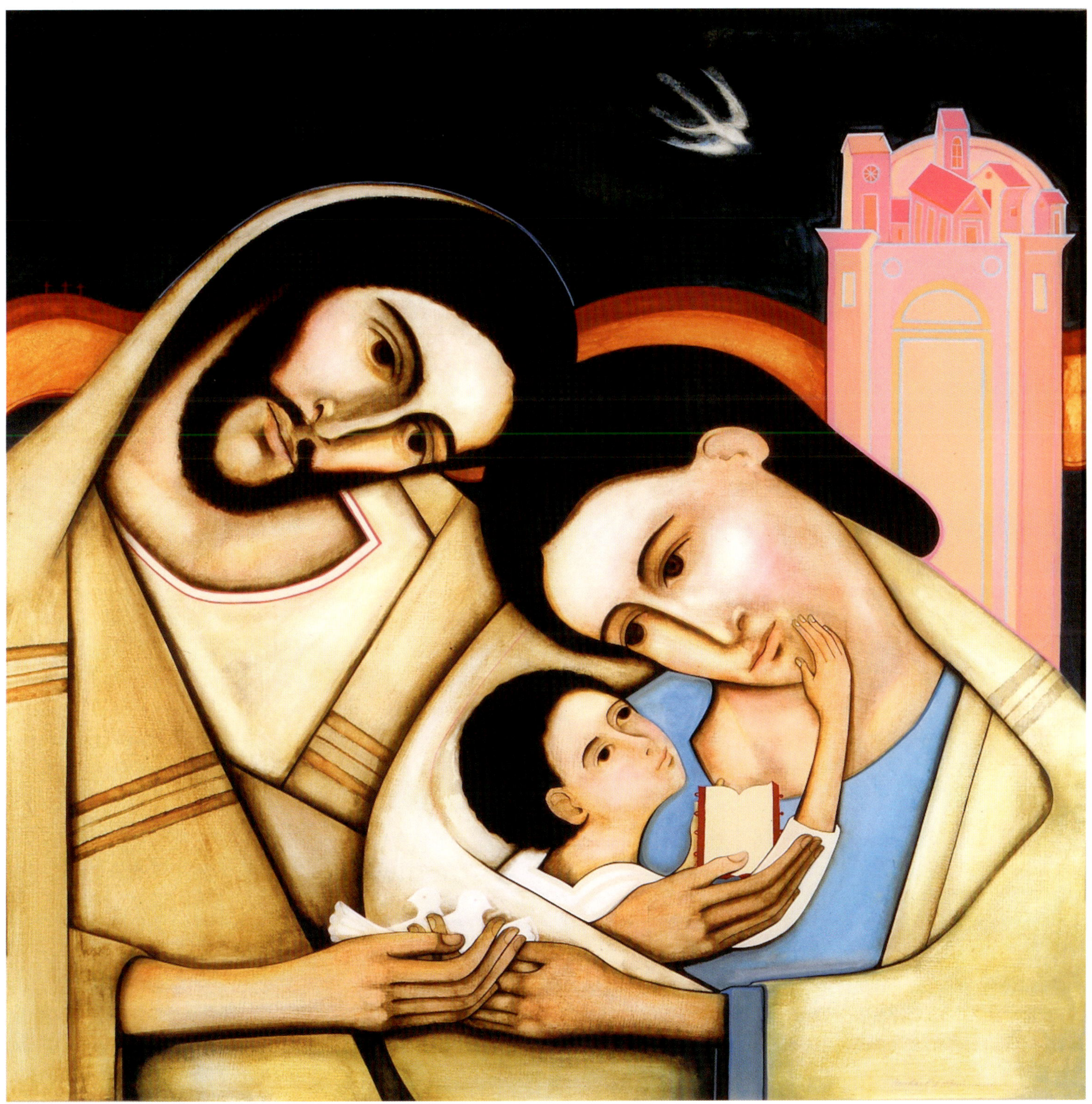

The Presentation, 1991, 48 inches by 48 inches

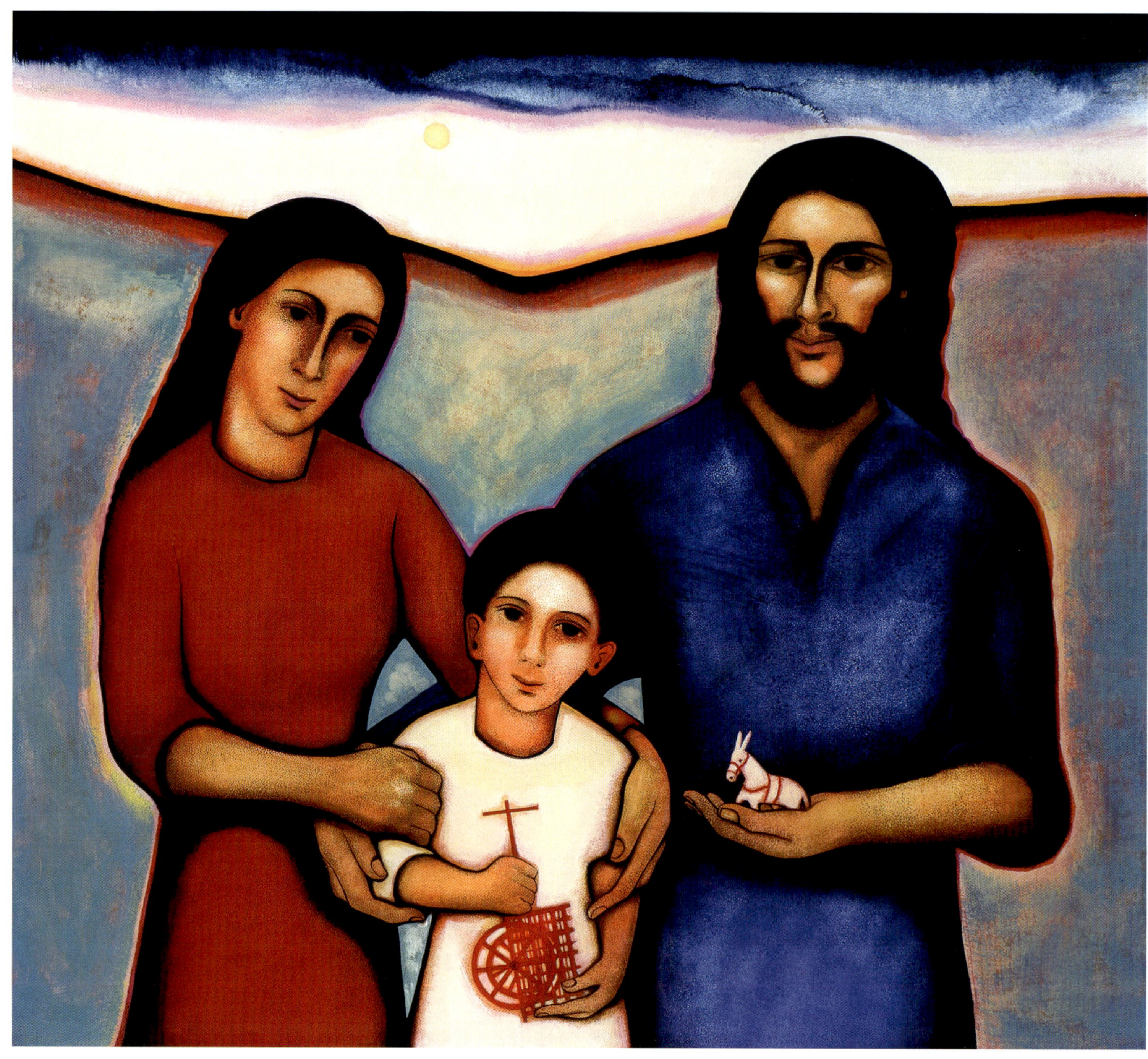

A Birthday in Nazareth, late 1970s

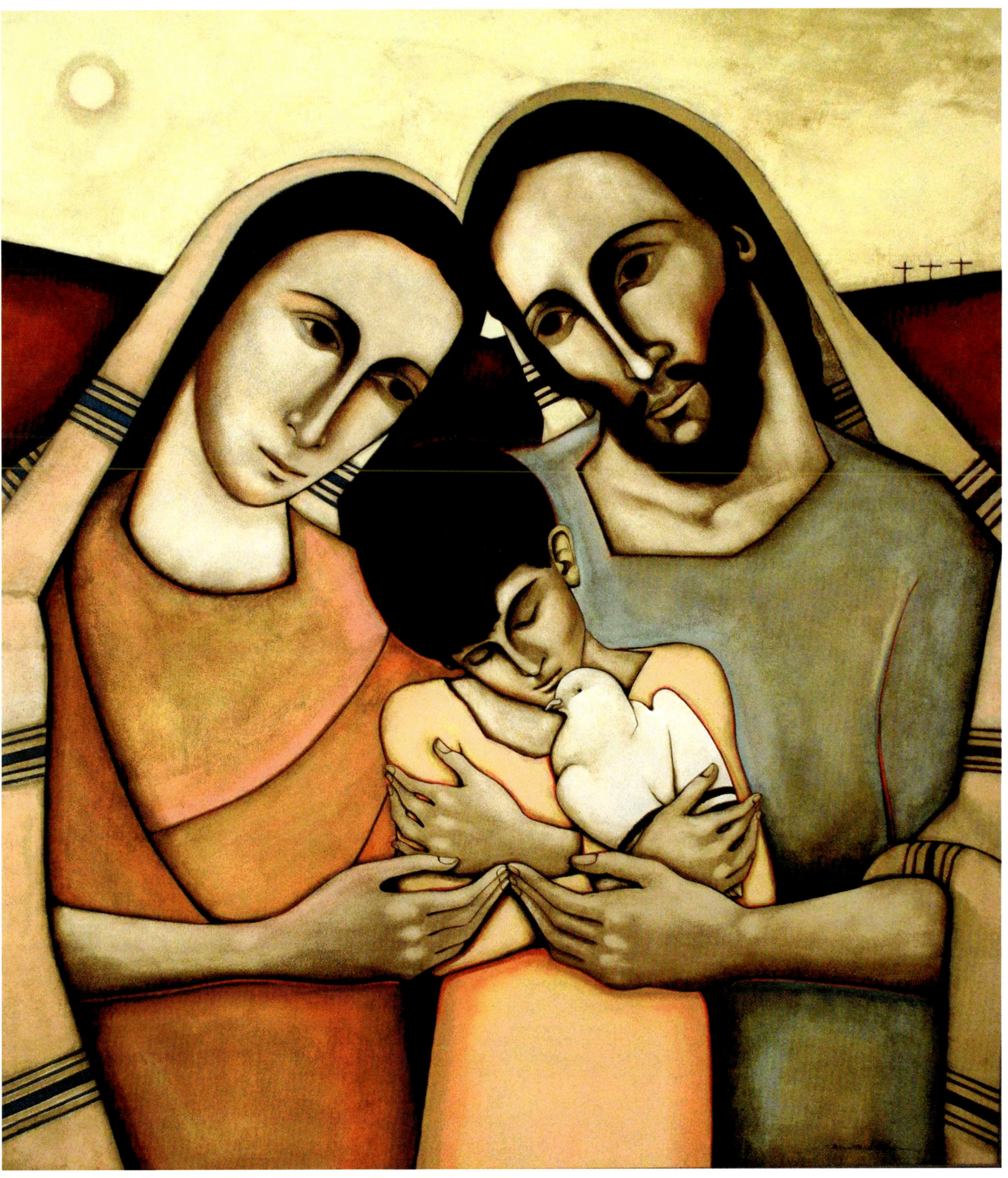

Nazareth, 1986, 24 inches by 24 inches

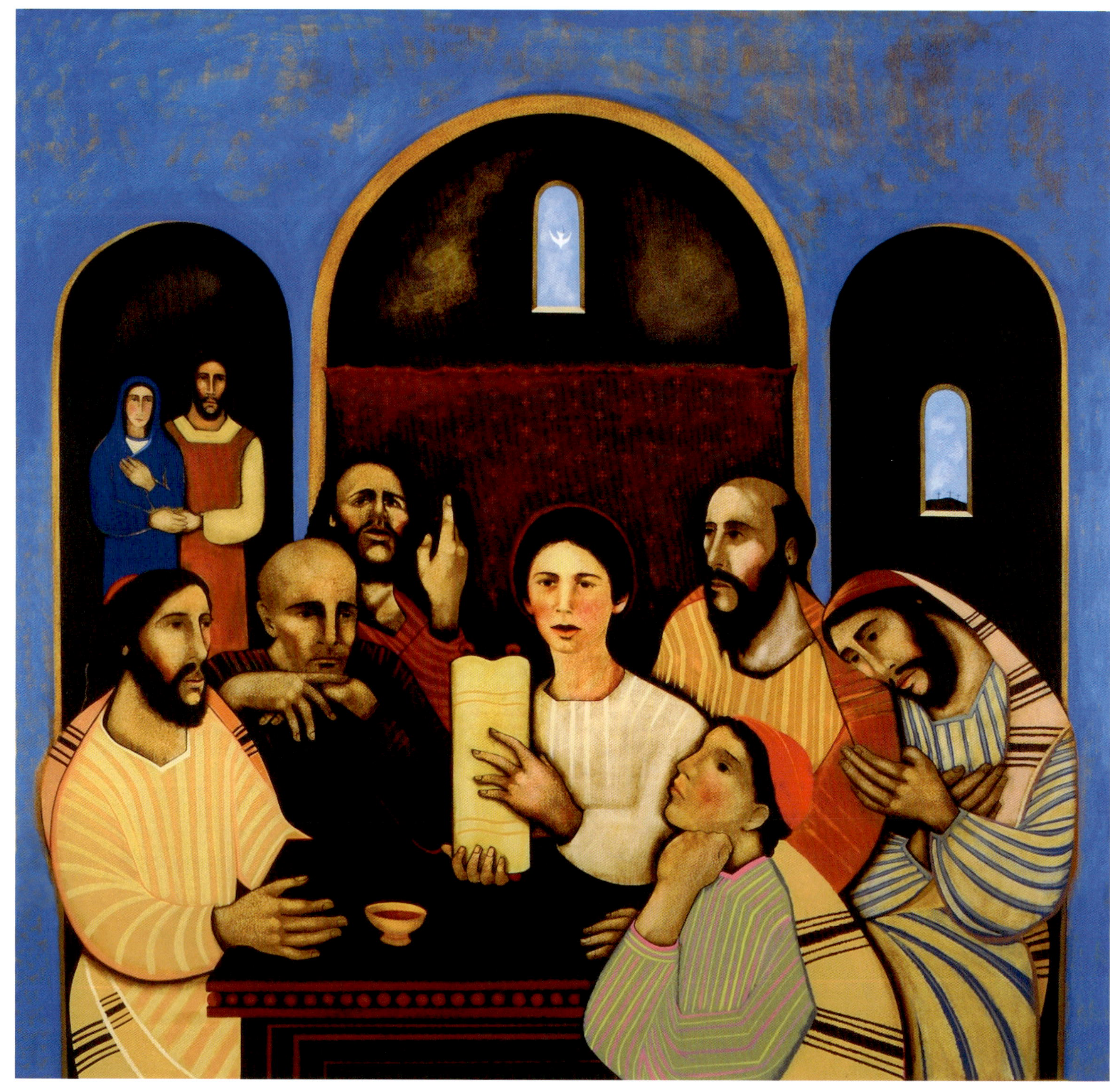

The Finding in the Temple, 1990, 48 inches by 48 inches

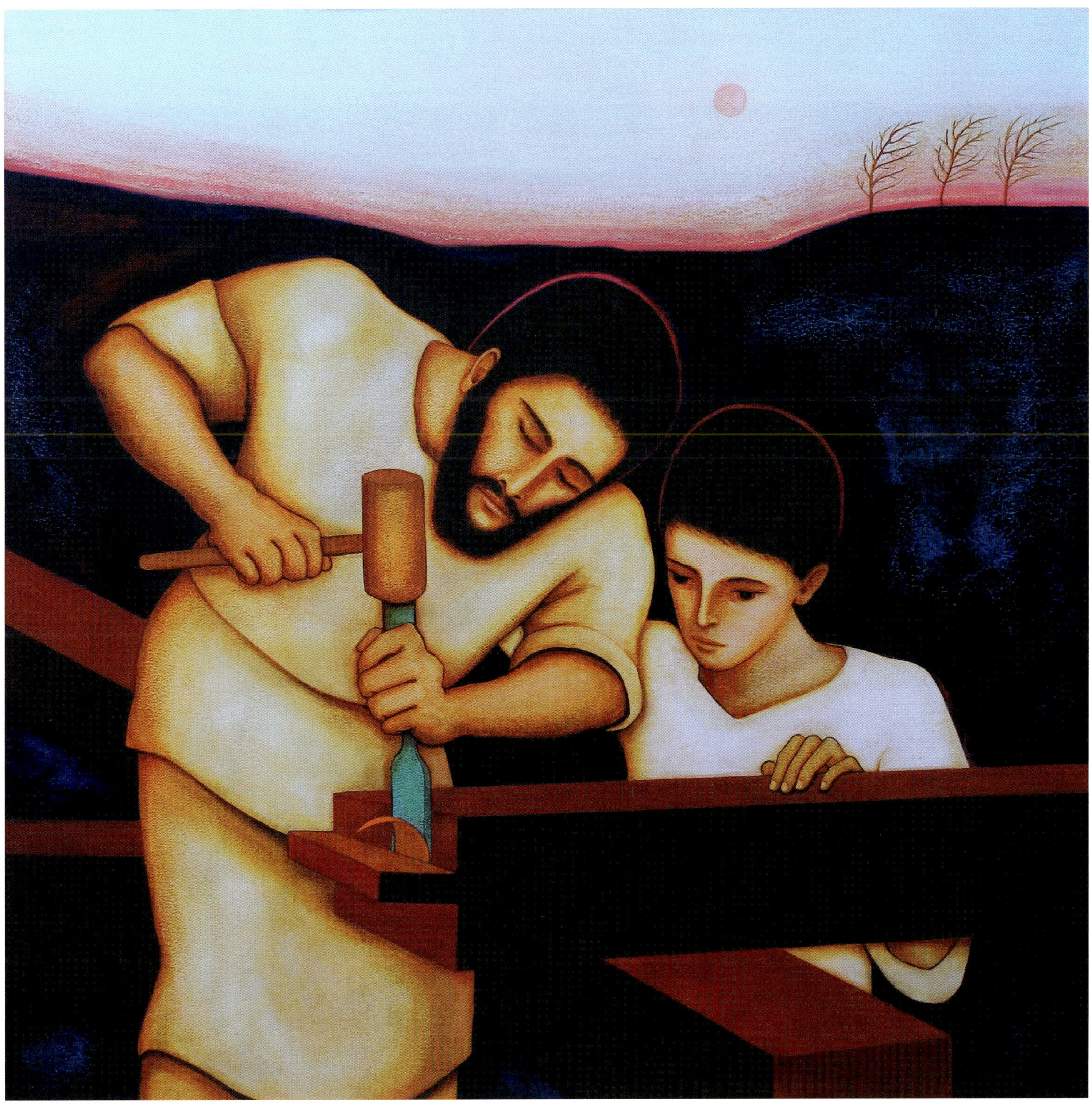

St. Joseph the Worker, 2006, 24 inches by 24 inches

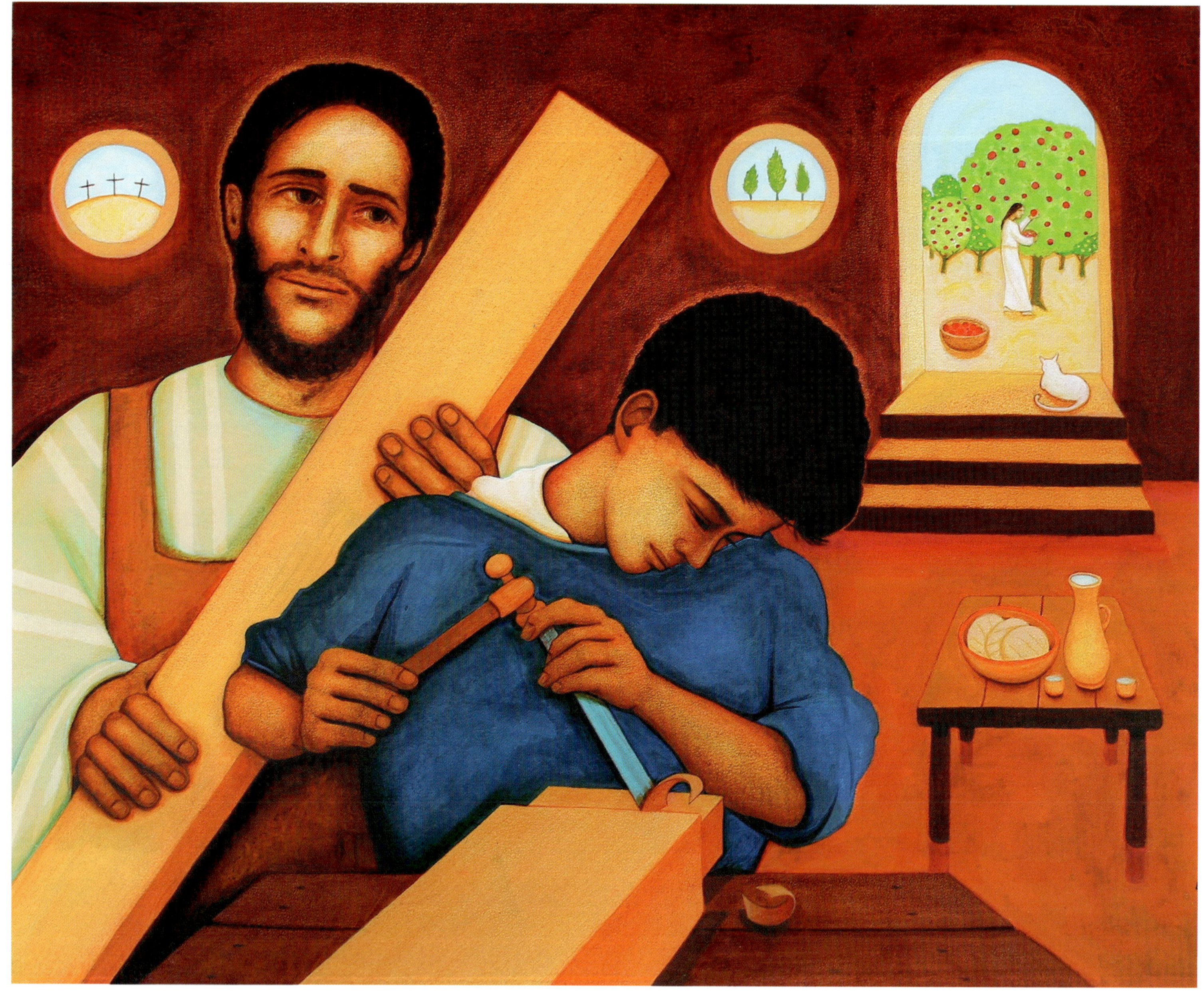

A Workshop in Nazareth, 2016

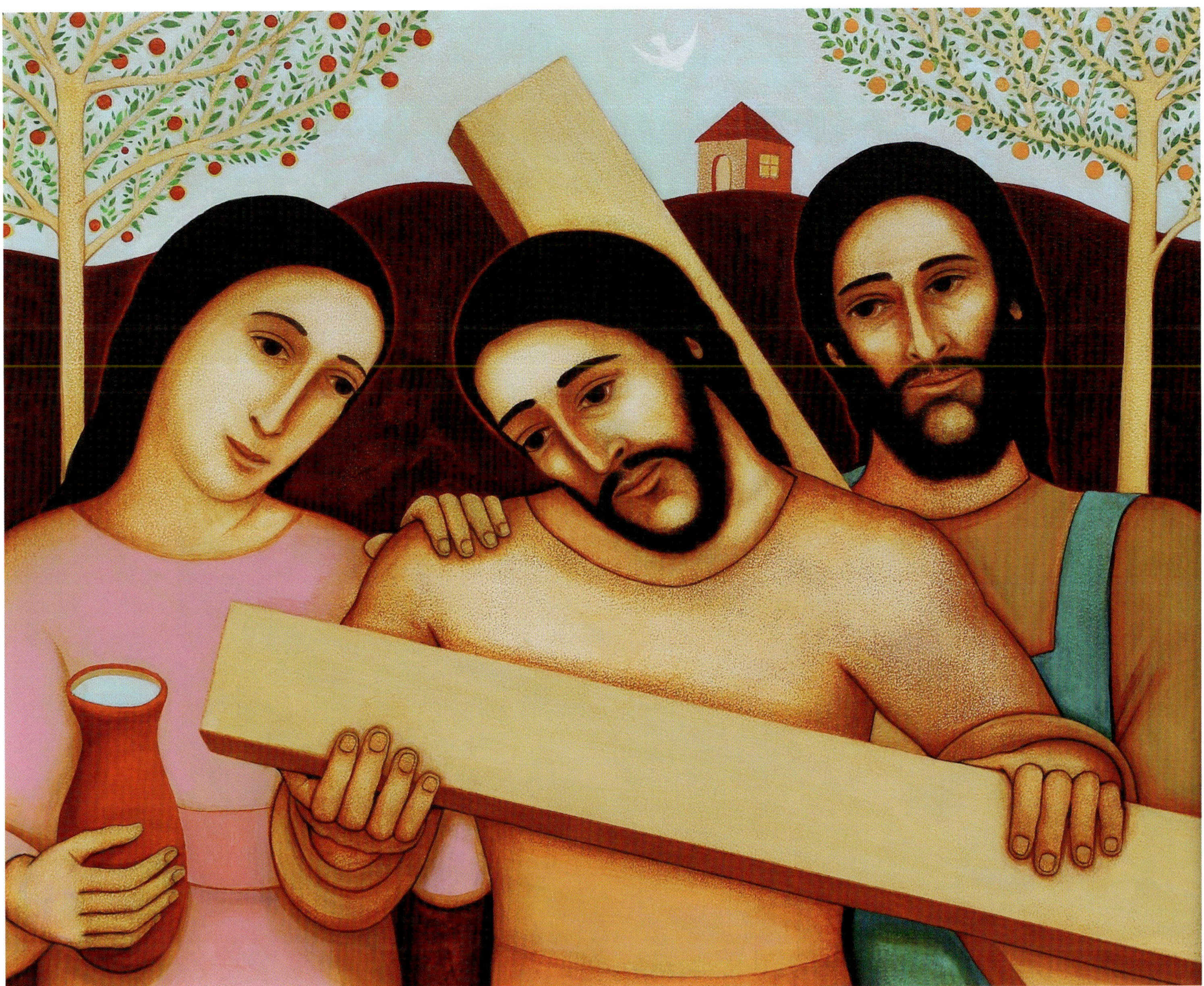

The Hidden Years of Nazareth, 2017, 19 inches by 24 inches

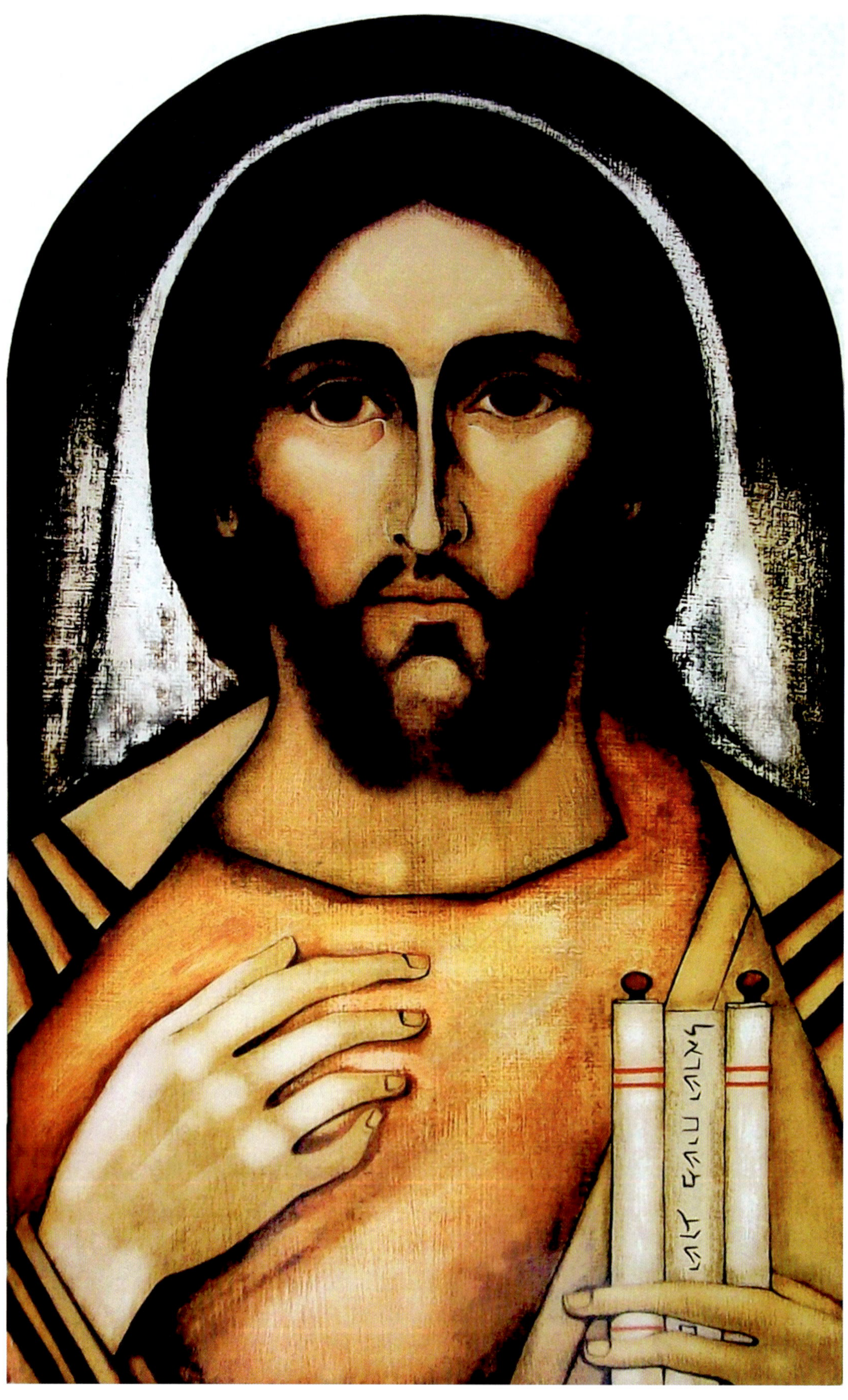

Jesus Christ the Word of Life, 1986

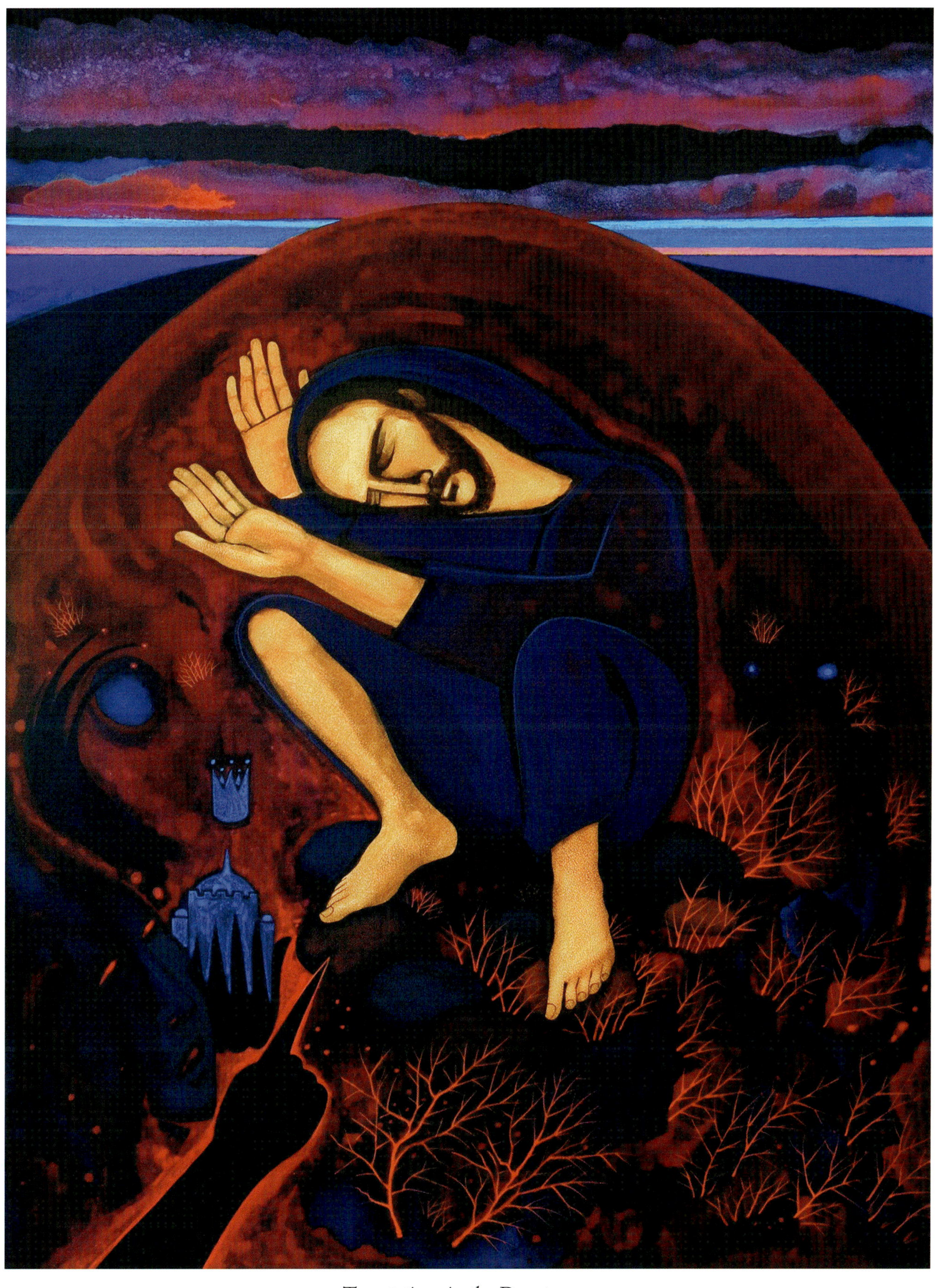

Temptations in the Desert, 2002

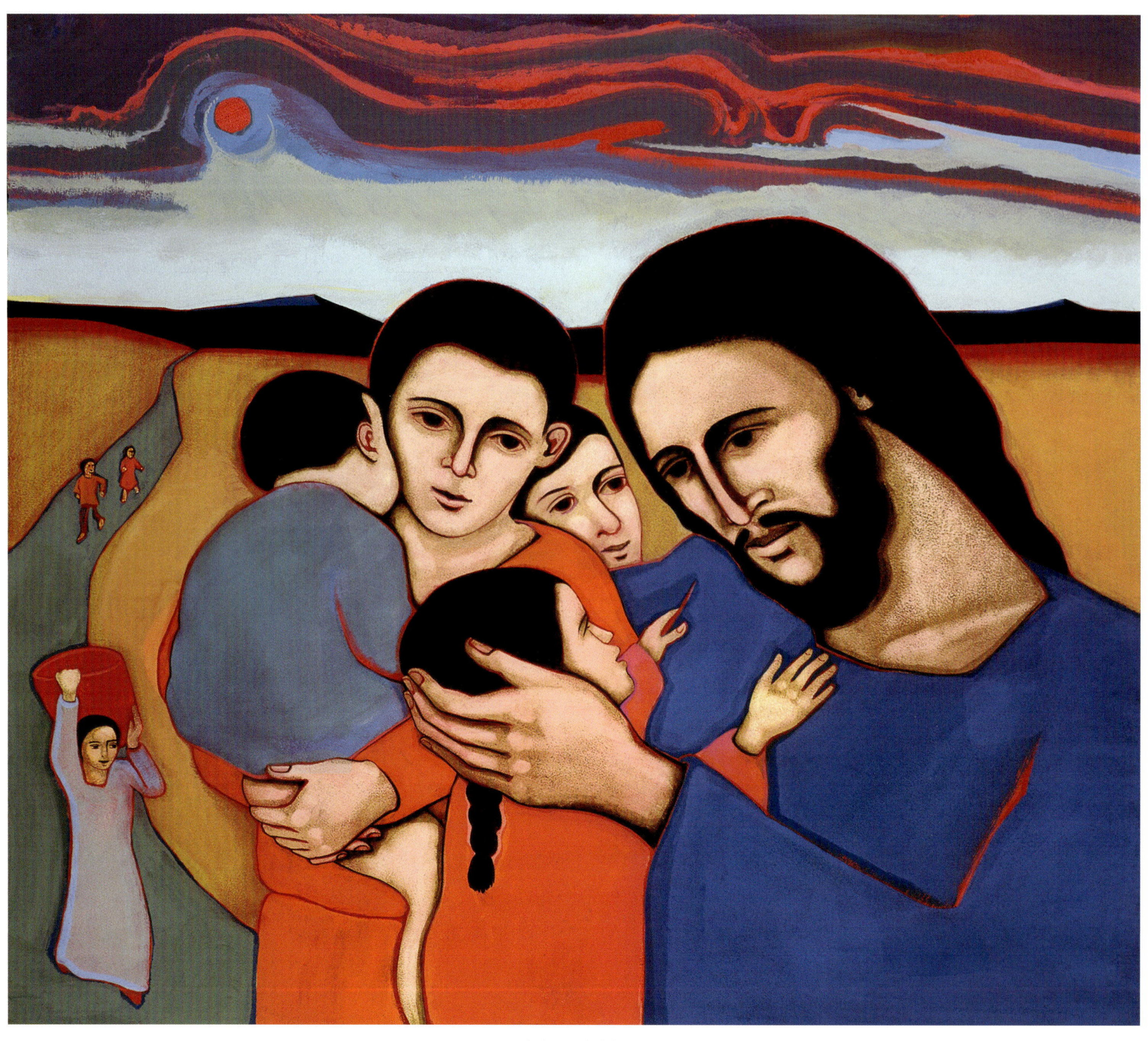

Jesus and the Children, 1988

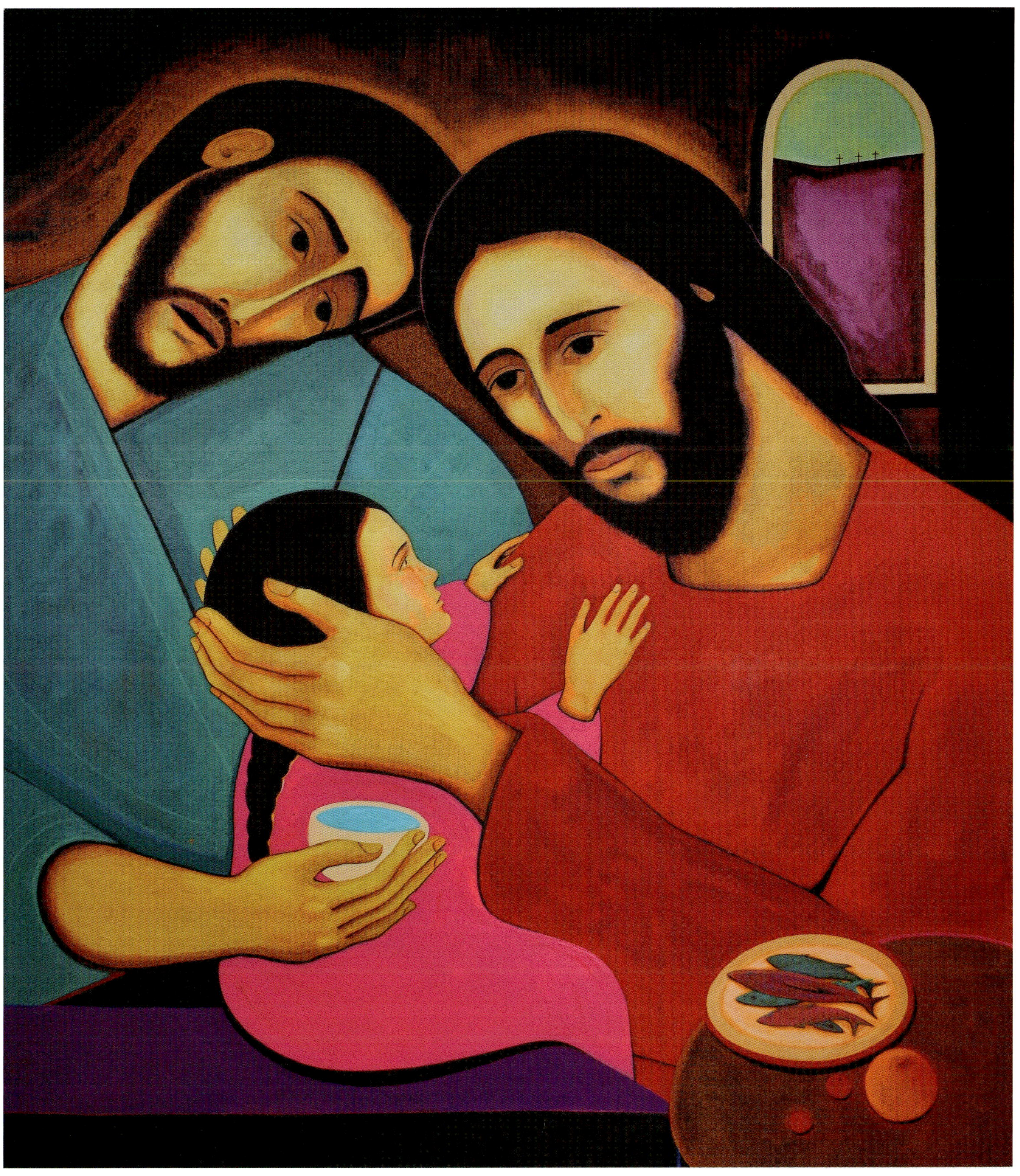

The Raising of Jairus' Daughter, 2001

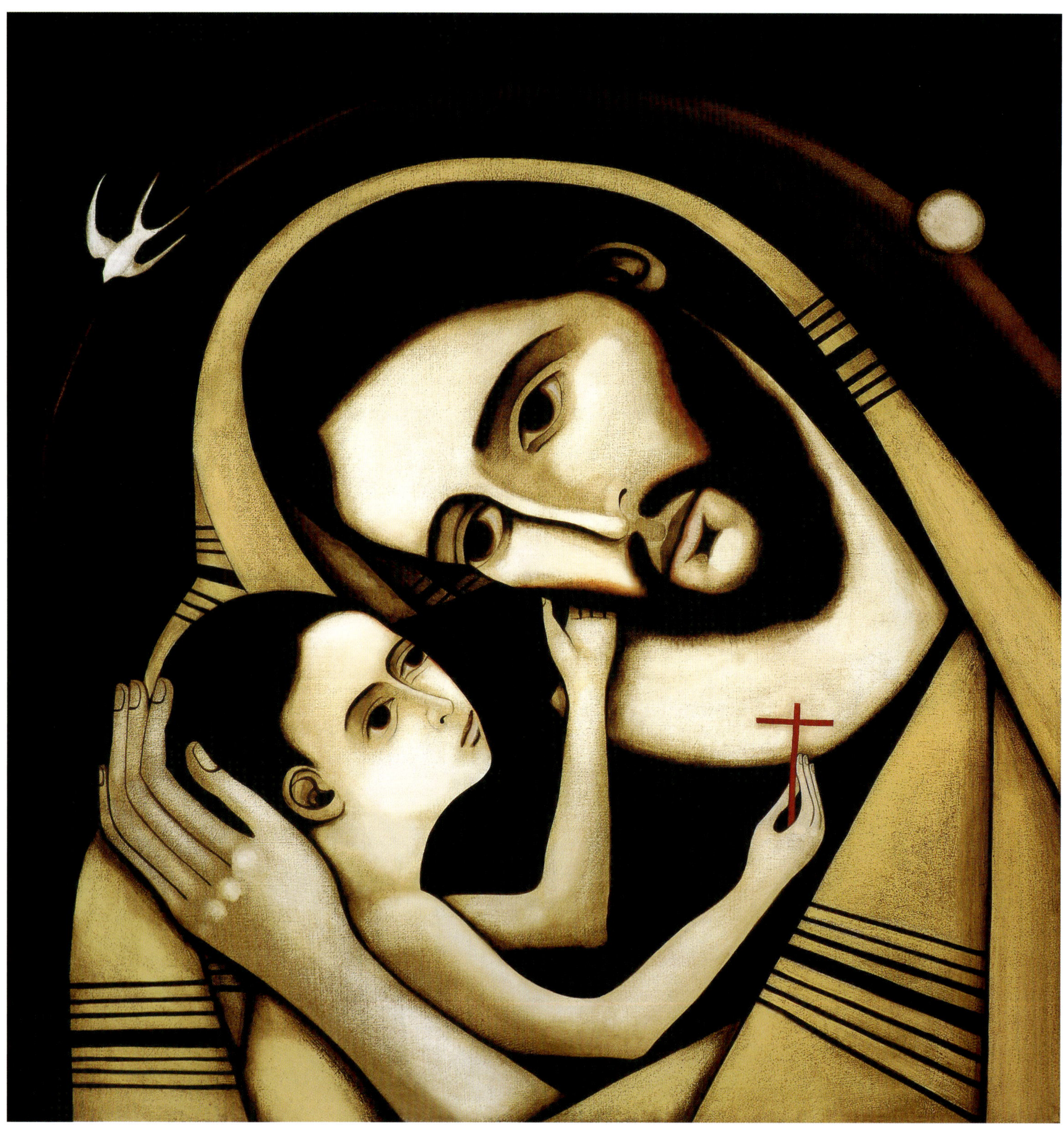

St. Joseph and the Christ Child, 1986, 22 inches by 22 inches

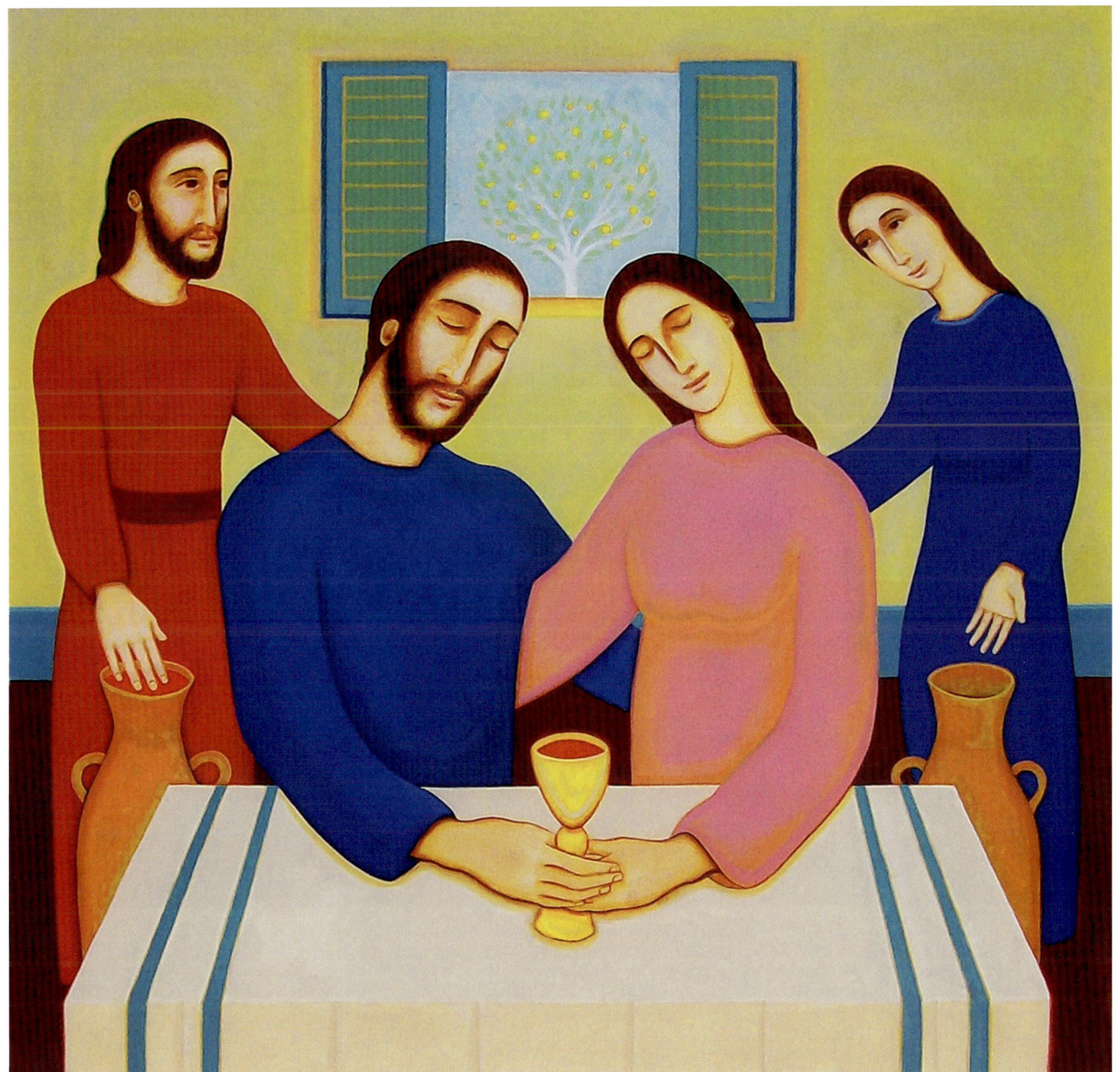

The Wedding Feast at Cana, 2012, 24 inches by 24 inches

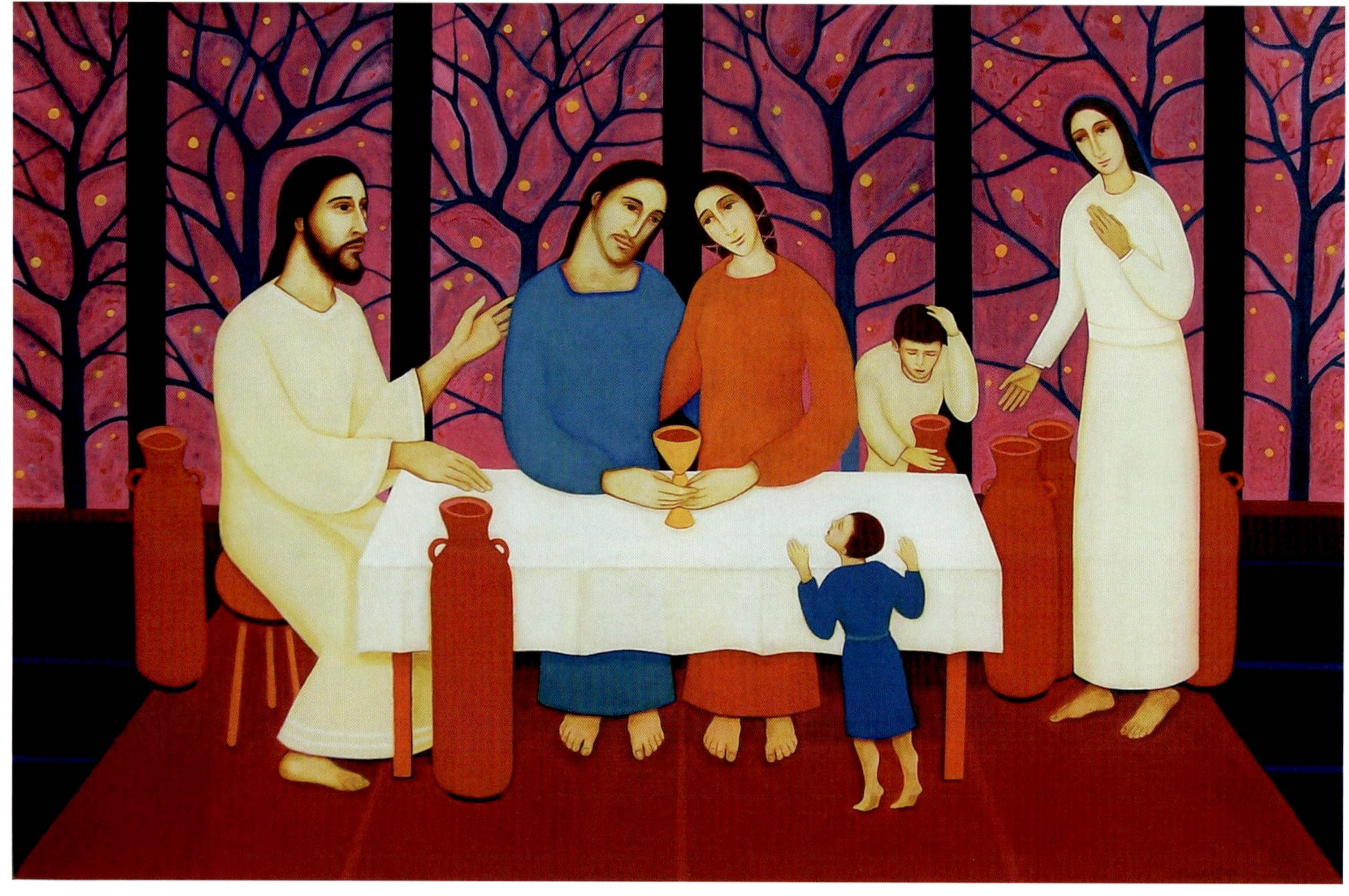

The Wedding Feast at Cana, 2010

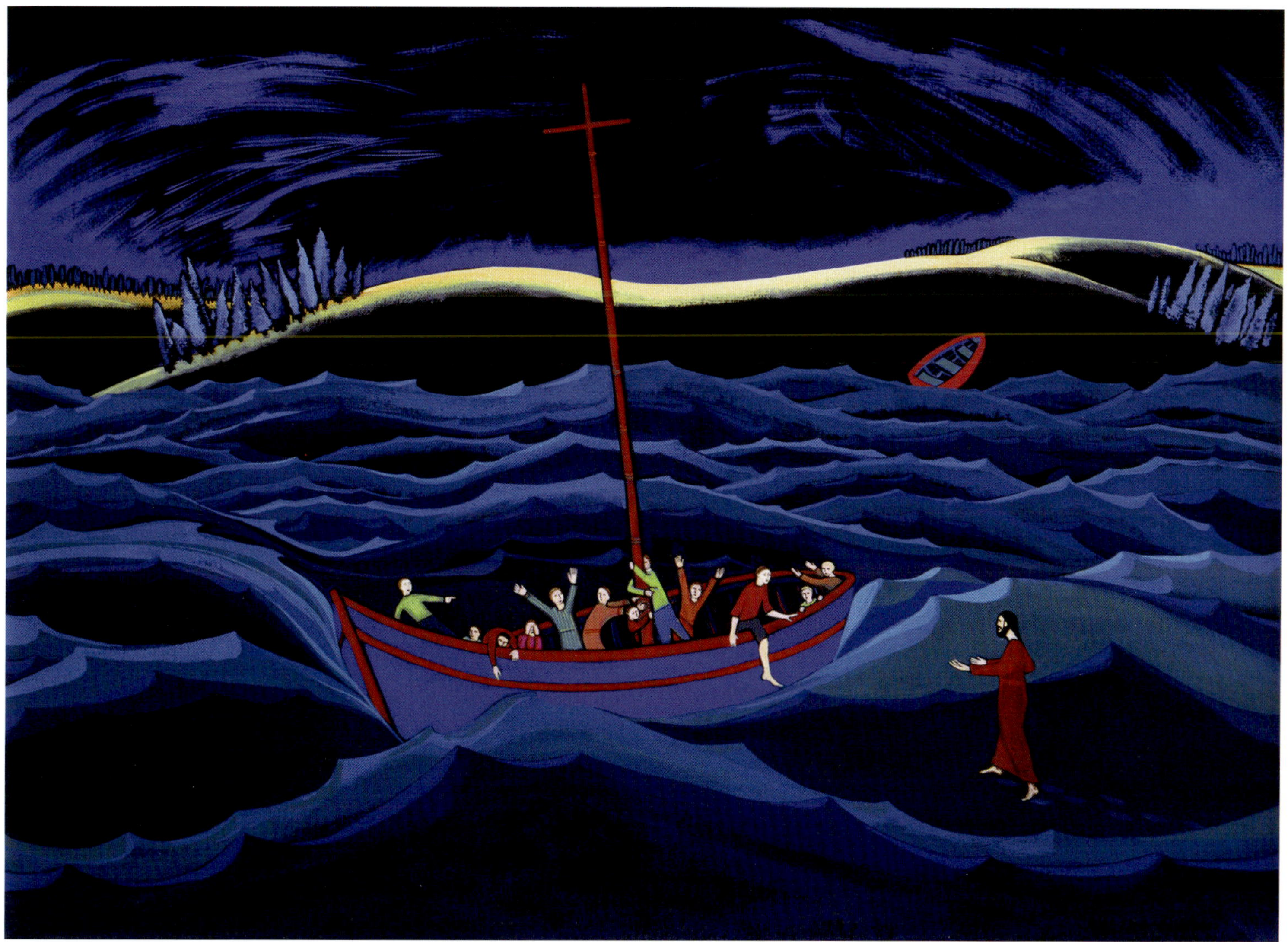

Jesus Walking on the Water, 1991, 23.5 inches by 32 inches

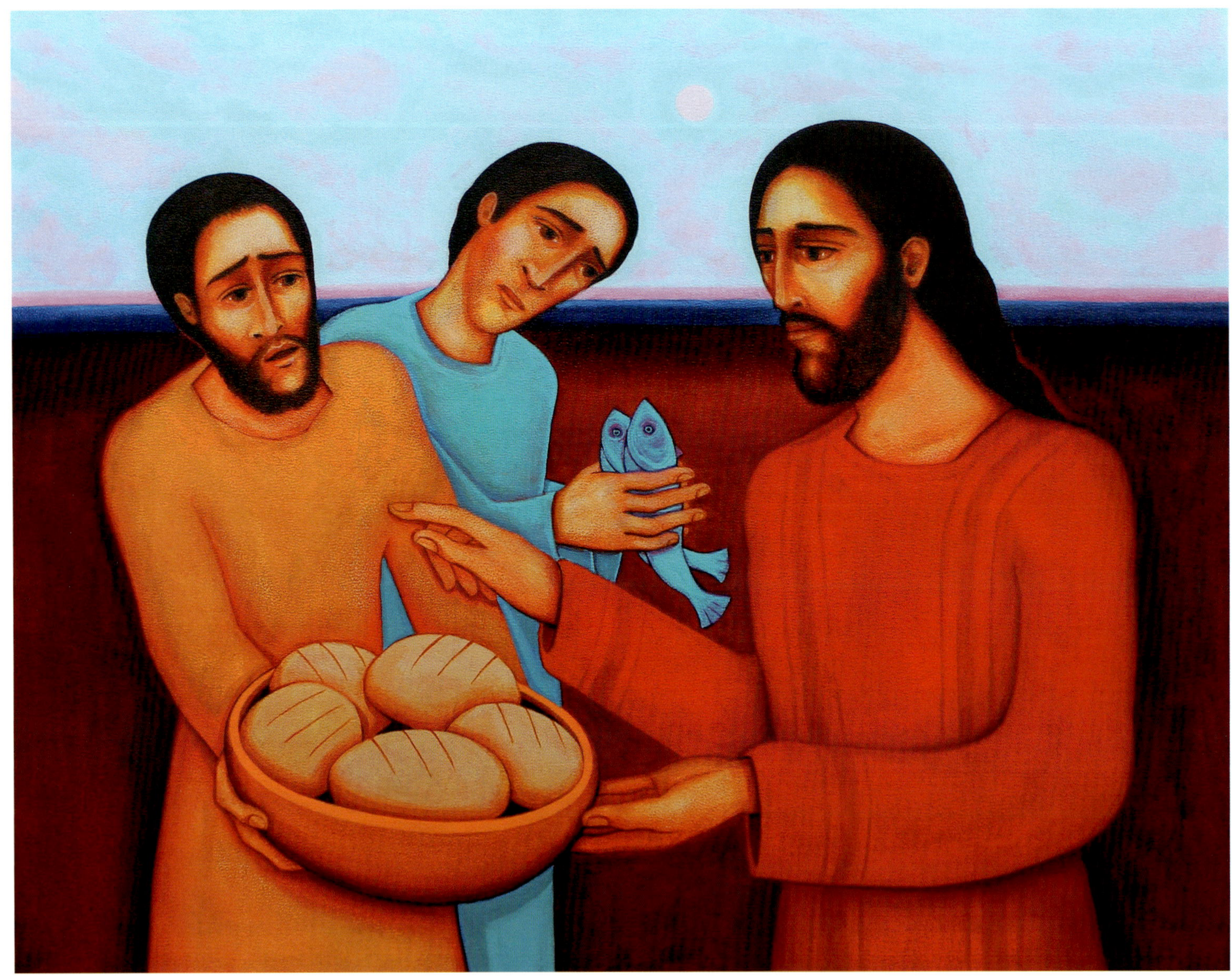

Loaves and Fishes, 2019, 22 inches by 27.5 inches

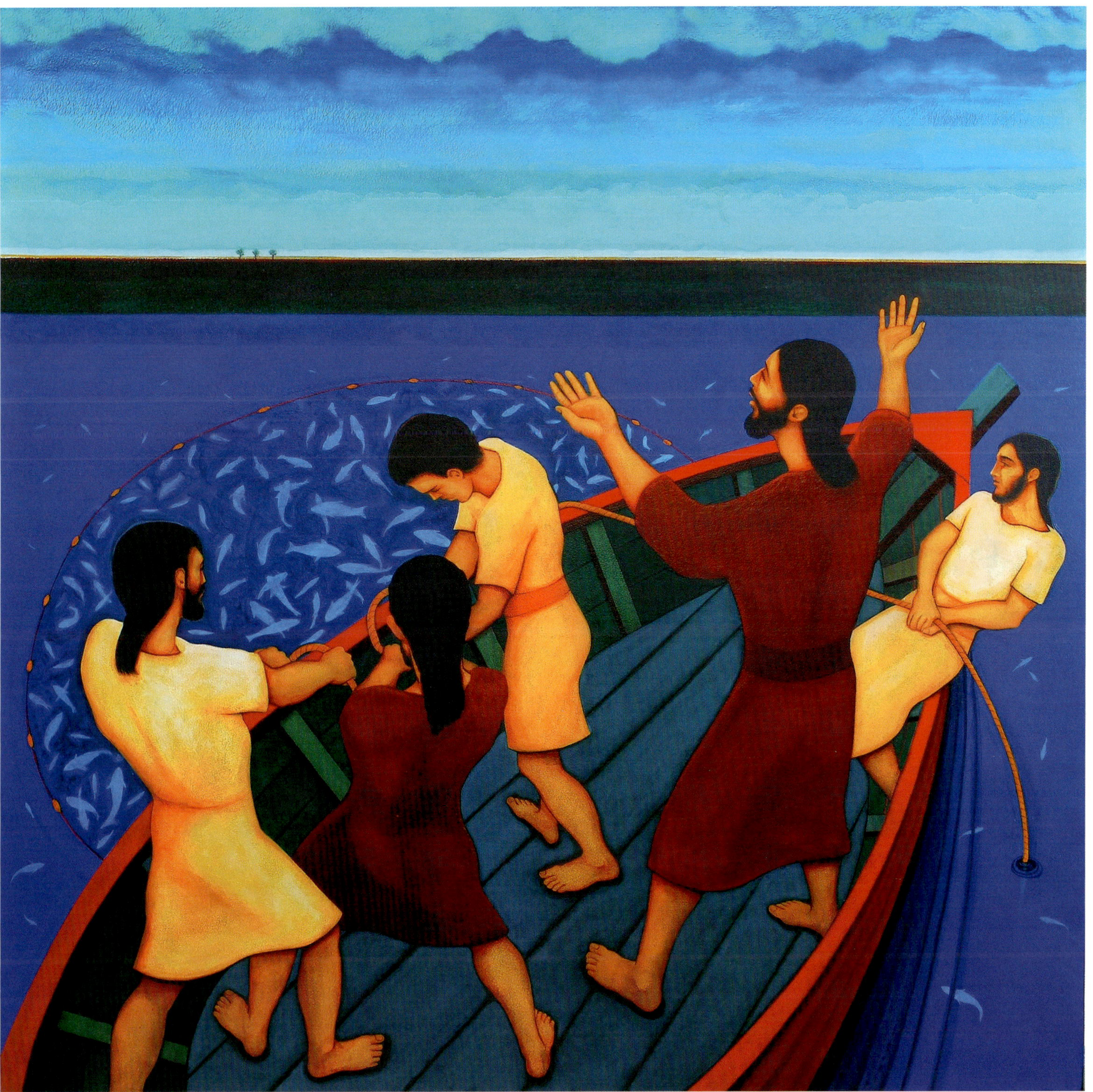

The Miraculous Catch of Fishes, 2016, 48 inches by 48 inches

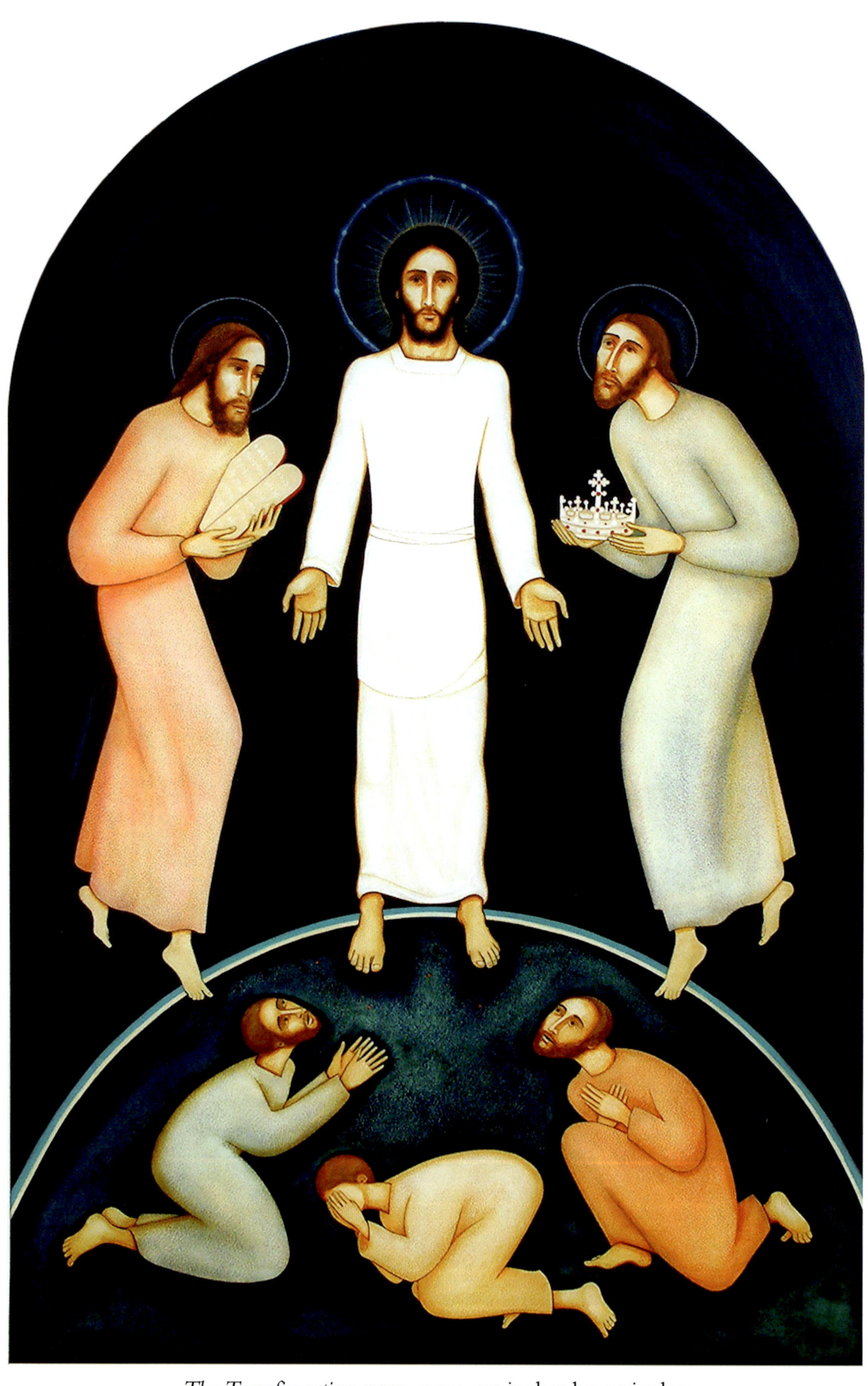

The Transfiguration, 2003–2004, 29 inches by 45 inches

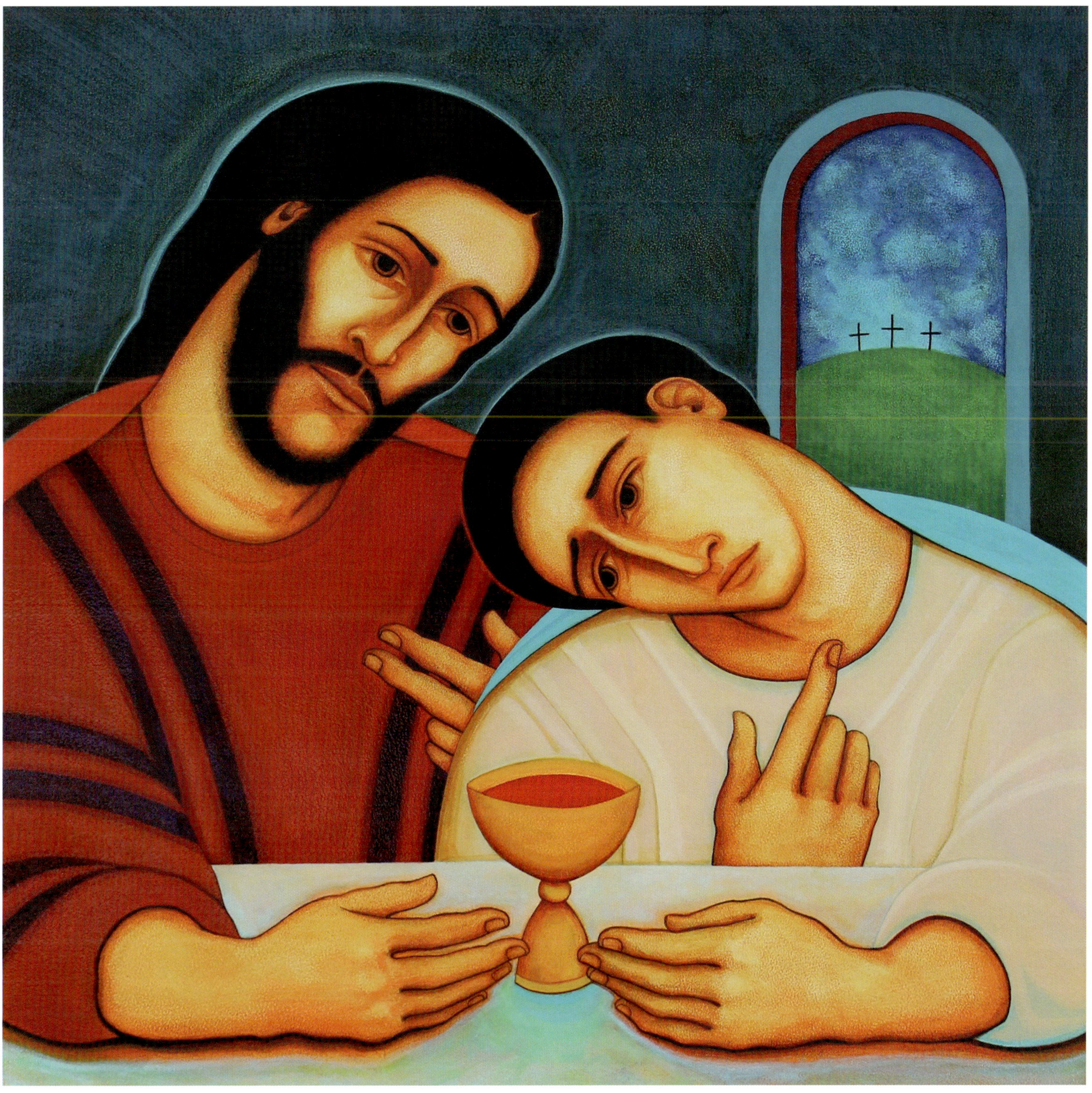

The Institution of the Holy Eucharist, 2016, 24 inches by 24 inches

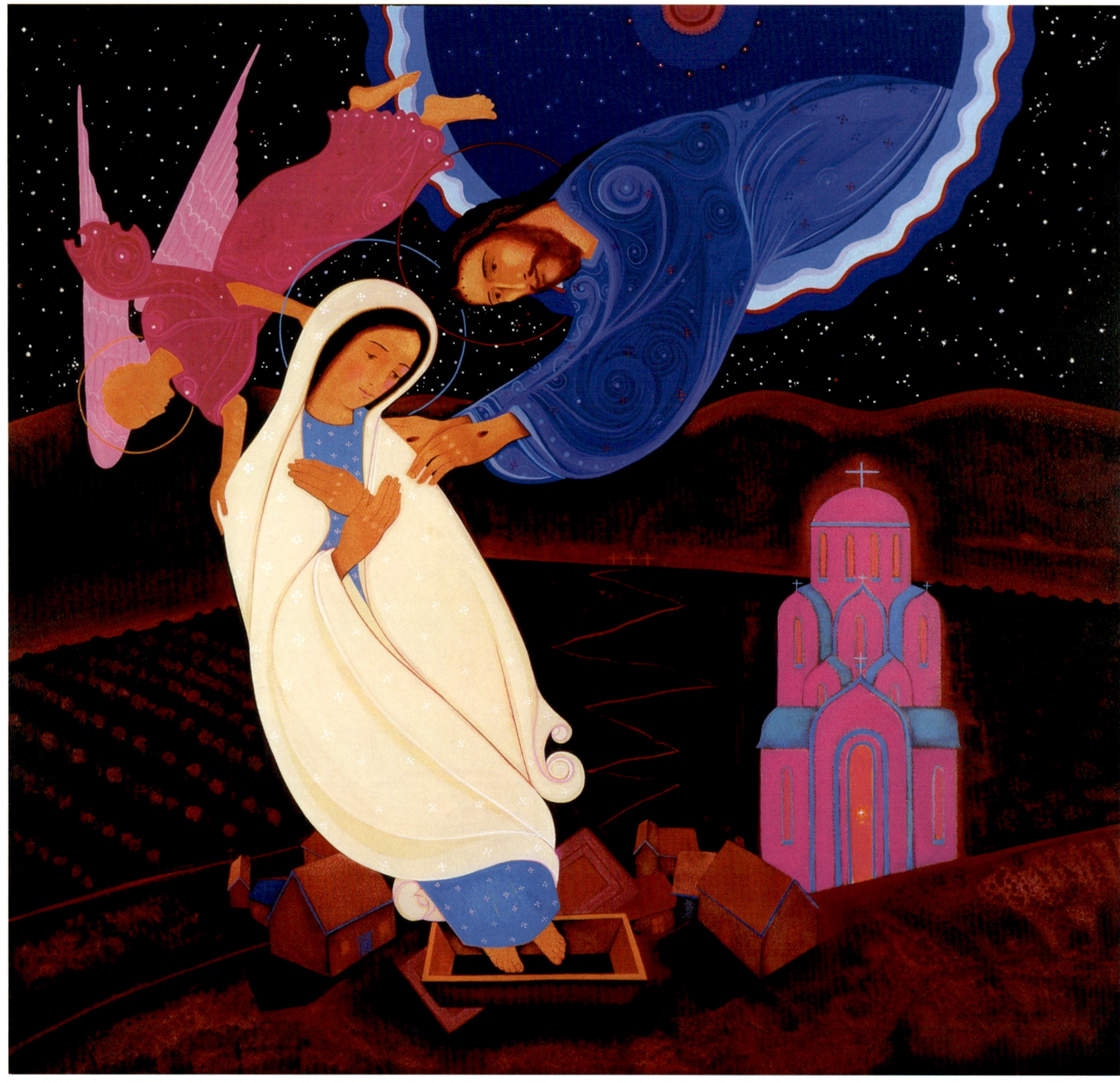

The Assumption of the Blessed Virgin Mary, 1990–1991, 48 inches by 48 inches

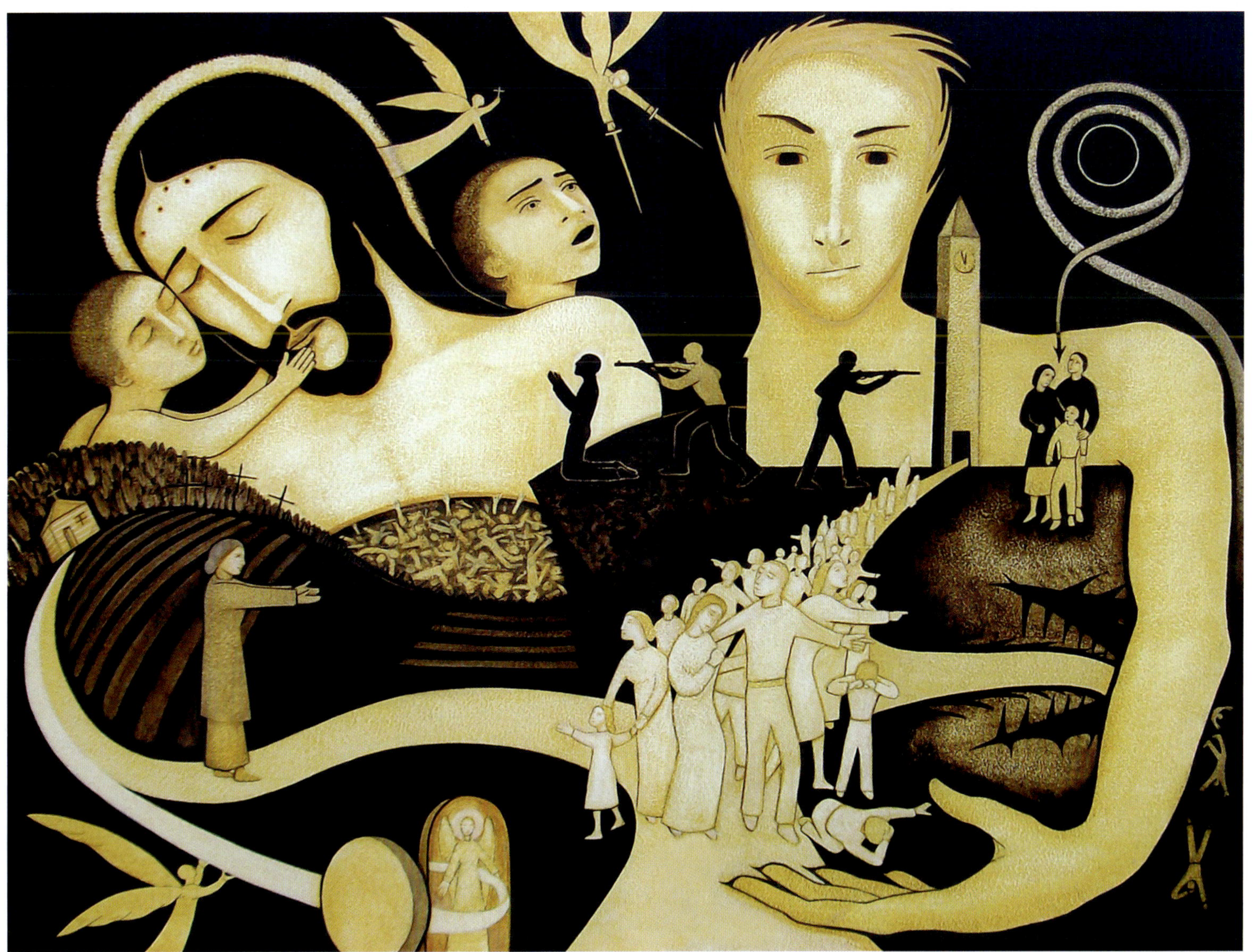

The Two Deaths, 2000

Saints

The saints are our beloved friends, our brothers and sisters who have gone before us on the way of the Cross—their lives unique and manifesting the life of Christ in countless forms. More than models on the path of faith, they are living presences, always regarding us with great love and yearning for us to invoke their aid. I have painted their features in various styles, ranging from the symbolism of the Byzantine to the high realism made possible by the photographs of some saints who lived in the twentieth century. It is my hope that, in all of these paintings, the hidden face of divine love is made visible.

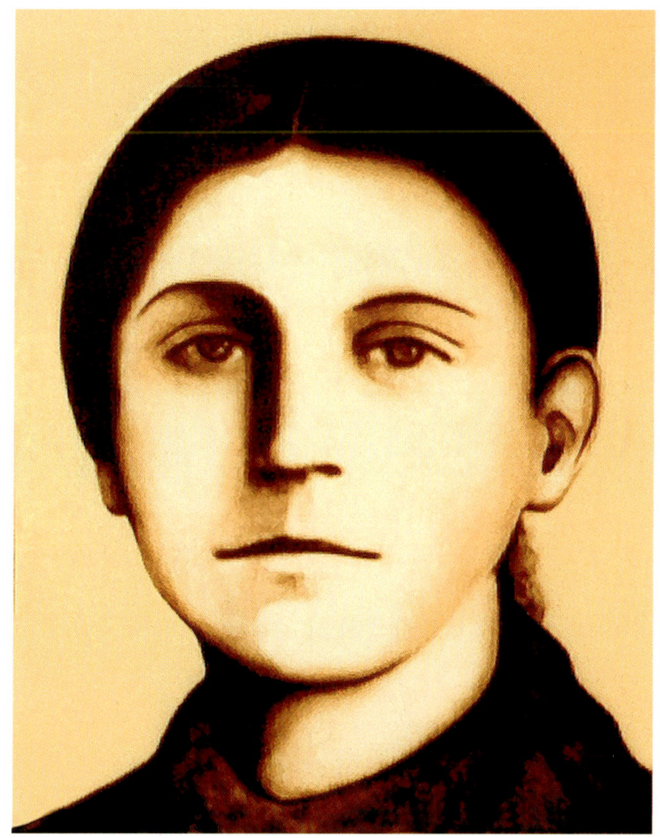

St. Gemma Galgani

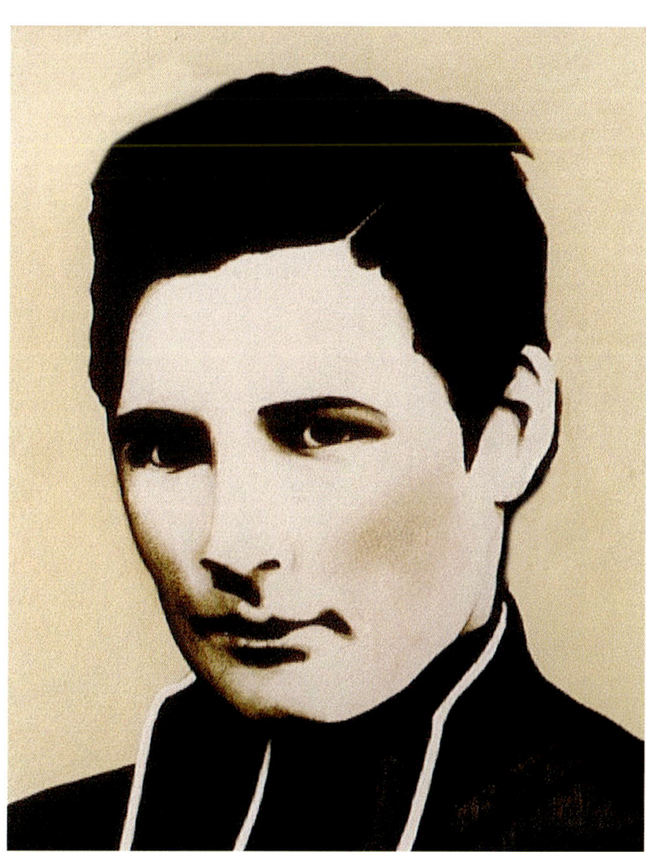

St. Théophane Venard

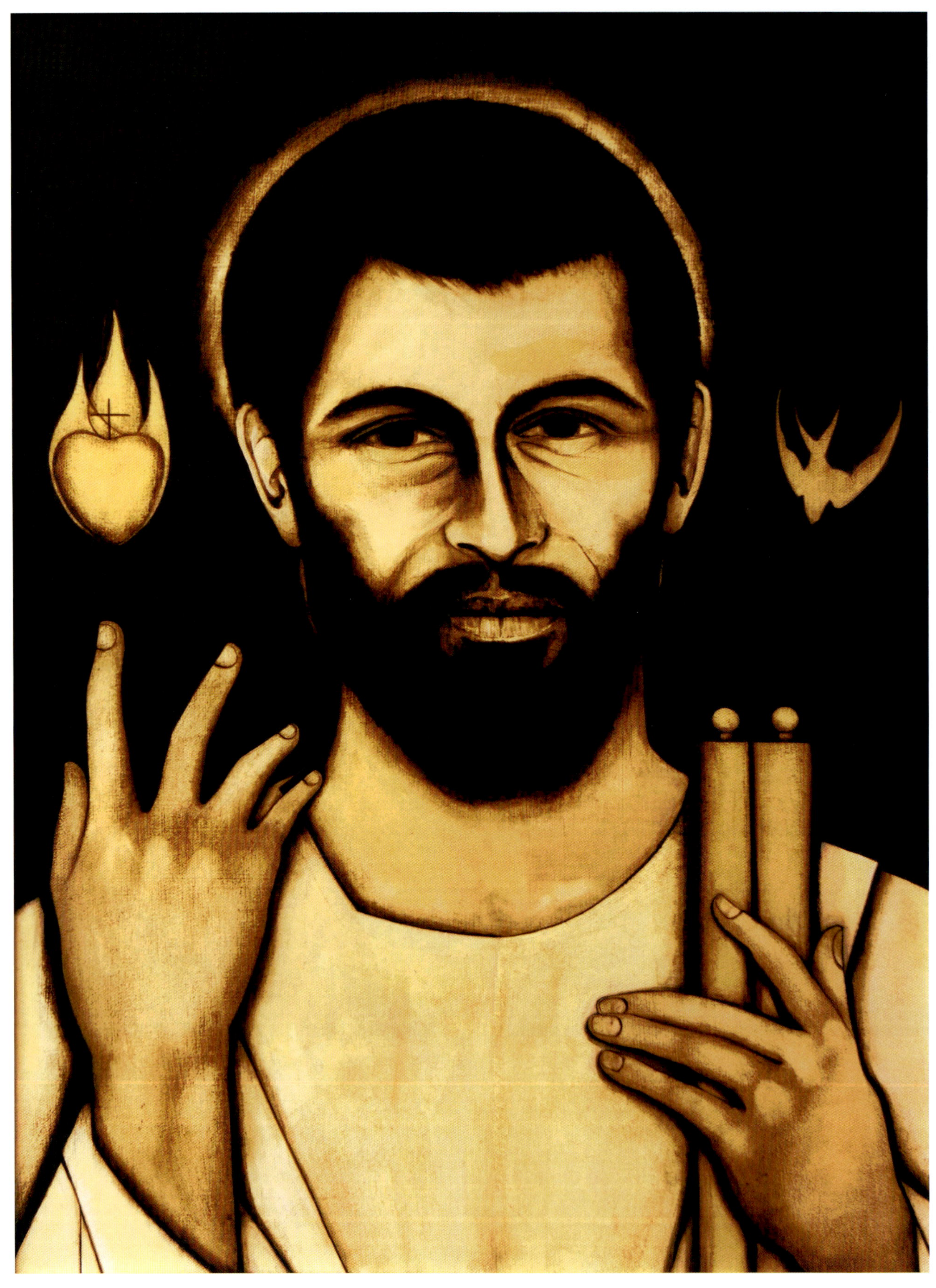

St. Augustine, 1987

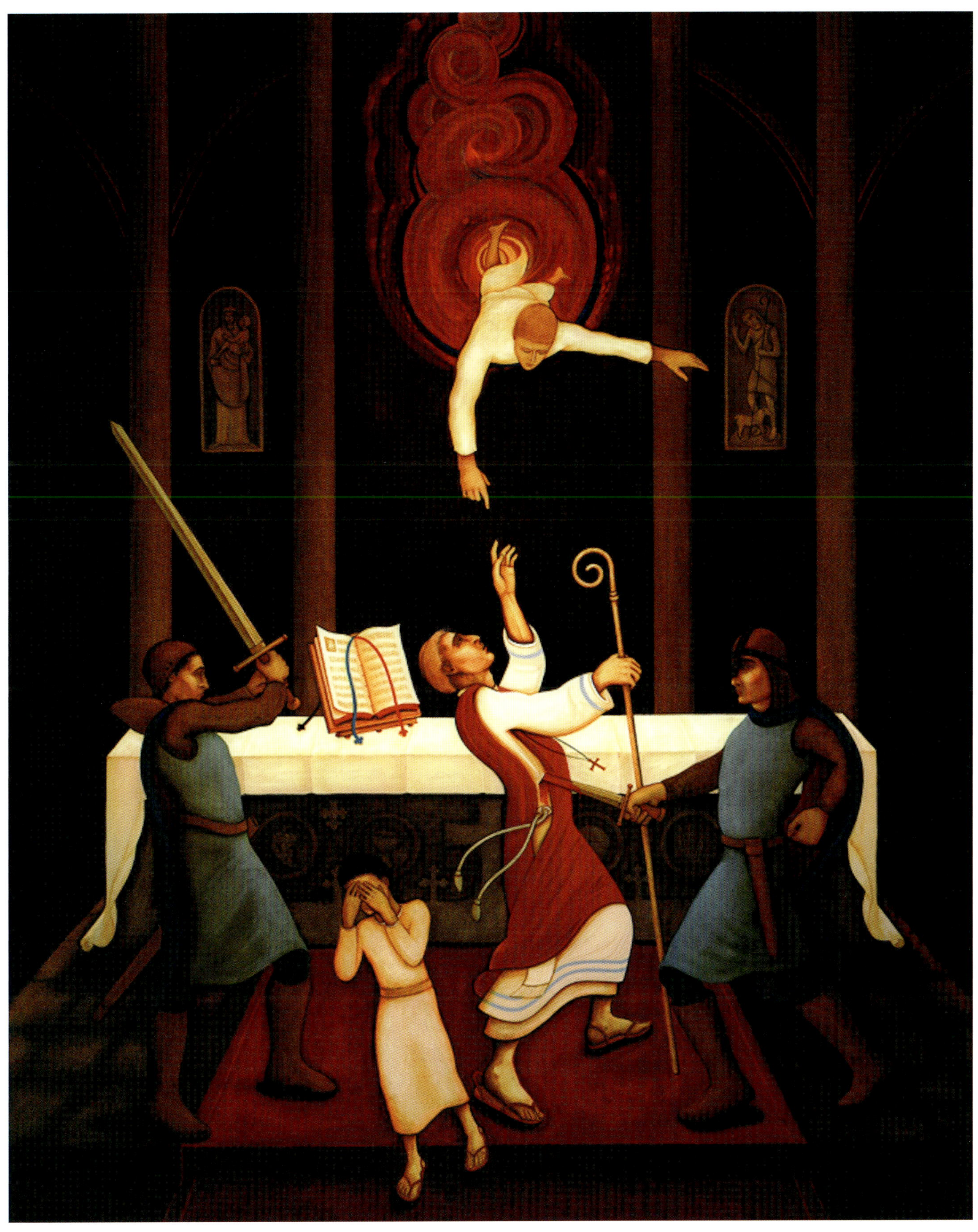

The Martyrdom of St. Thomas Becket, 2004

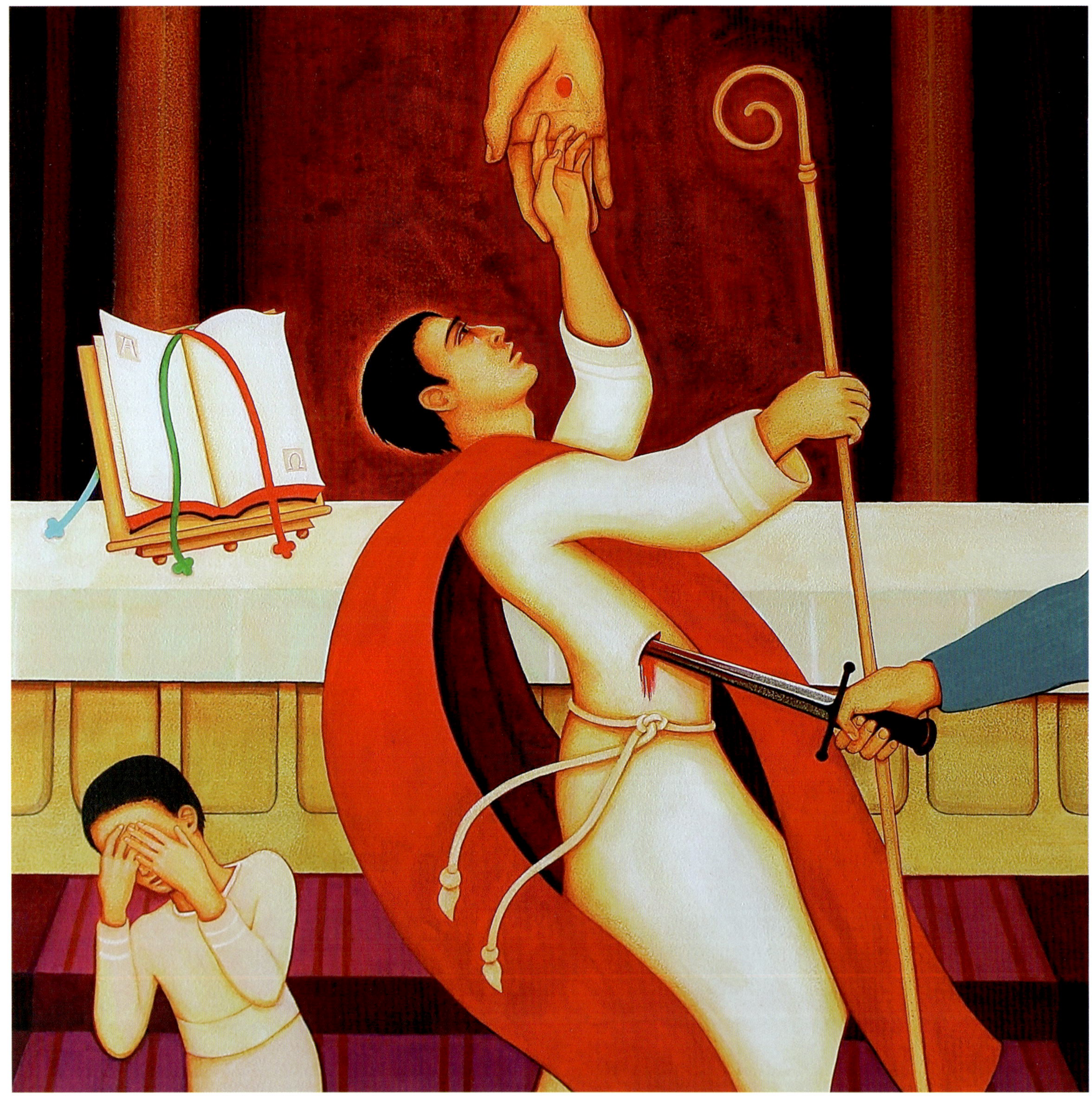

Martyrdom (study after *The Martyrdom of St. Thomas Becket*), 2015, 24 inches by 24 inches

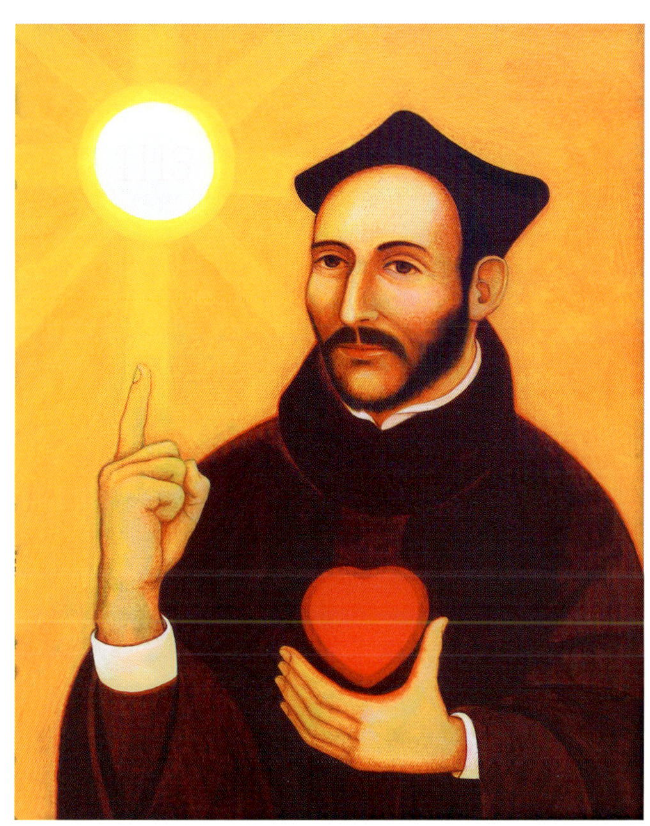

St. Ignatius of Loyola, 2017

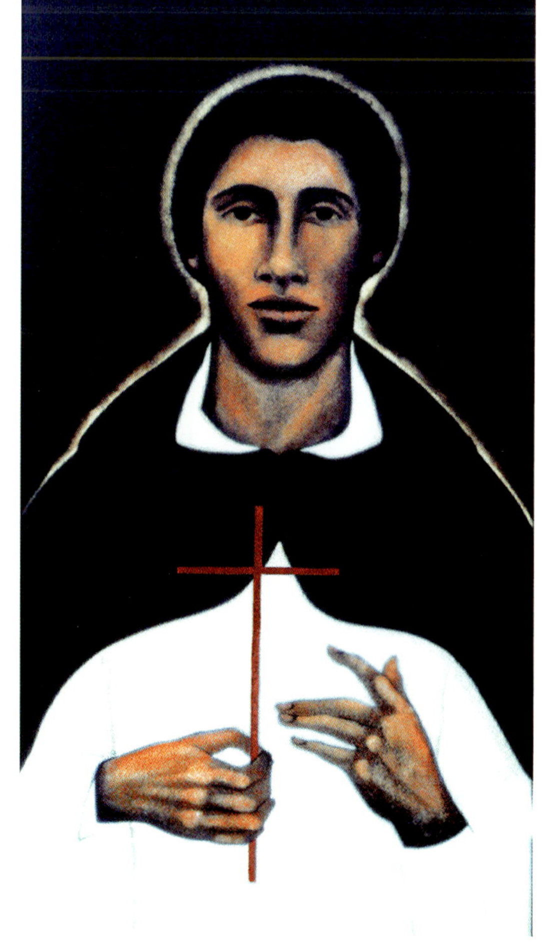

St. Martin de Porres, circa 1990

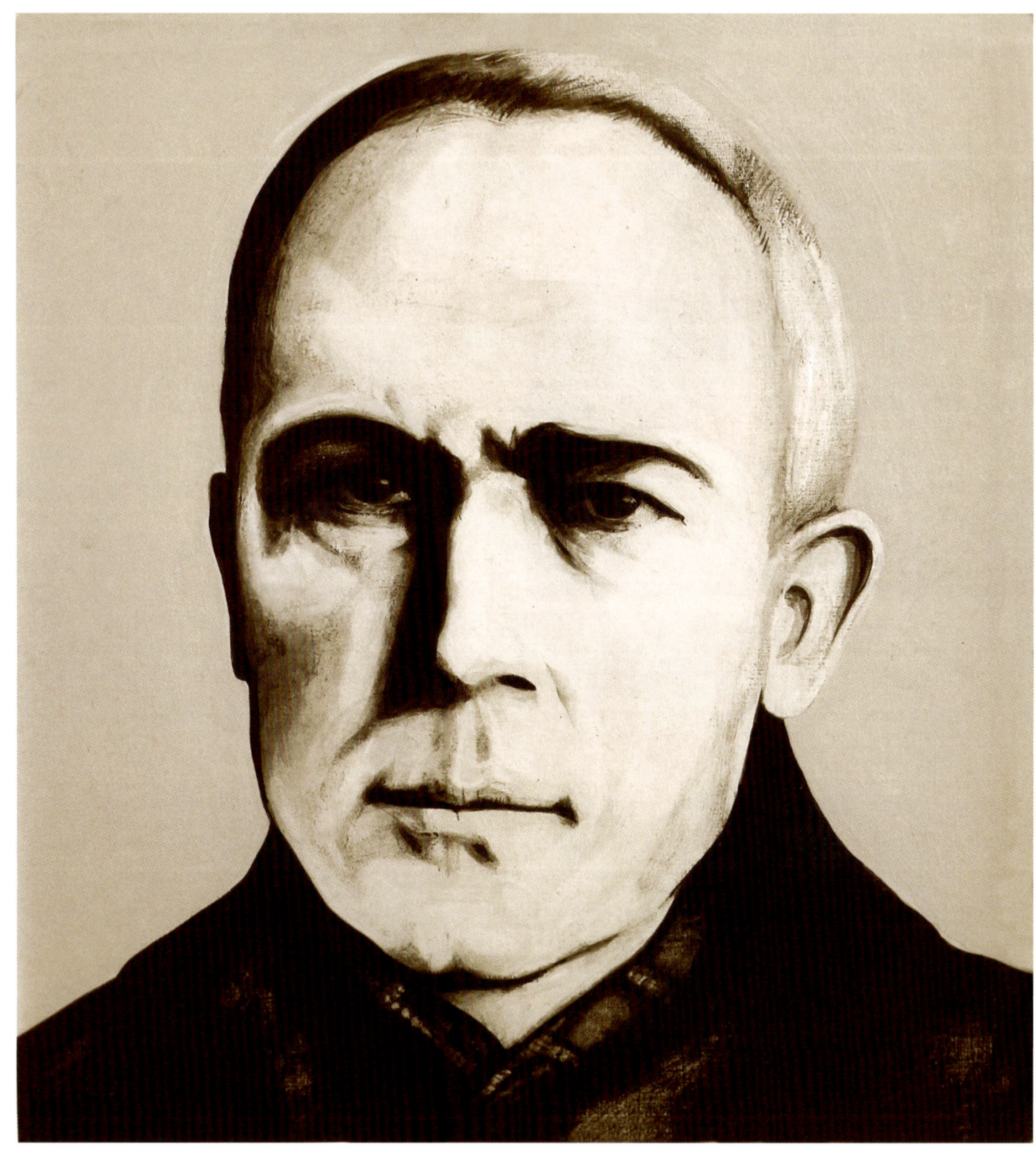

St. Maximilian Kolbe, 1988

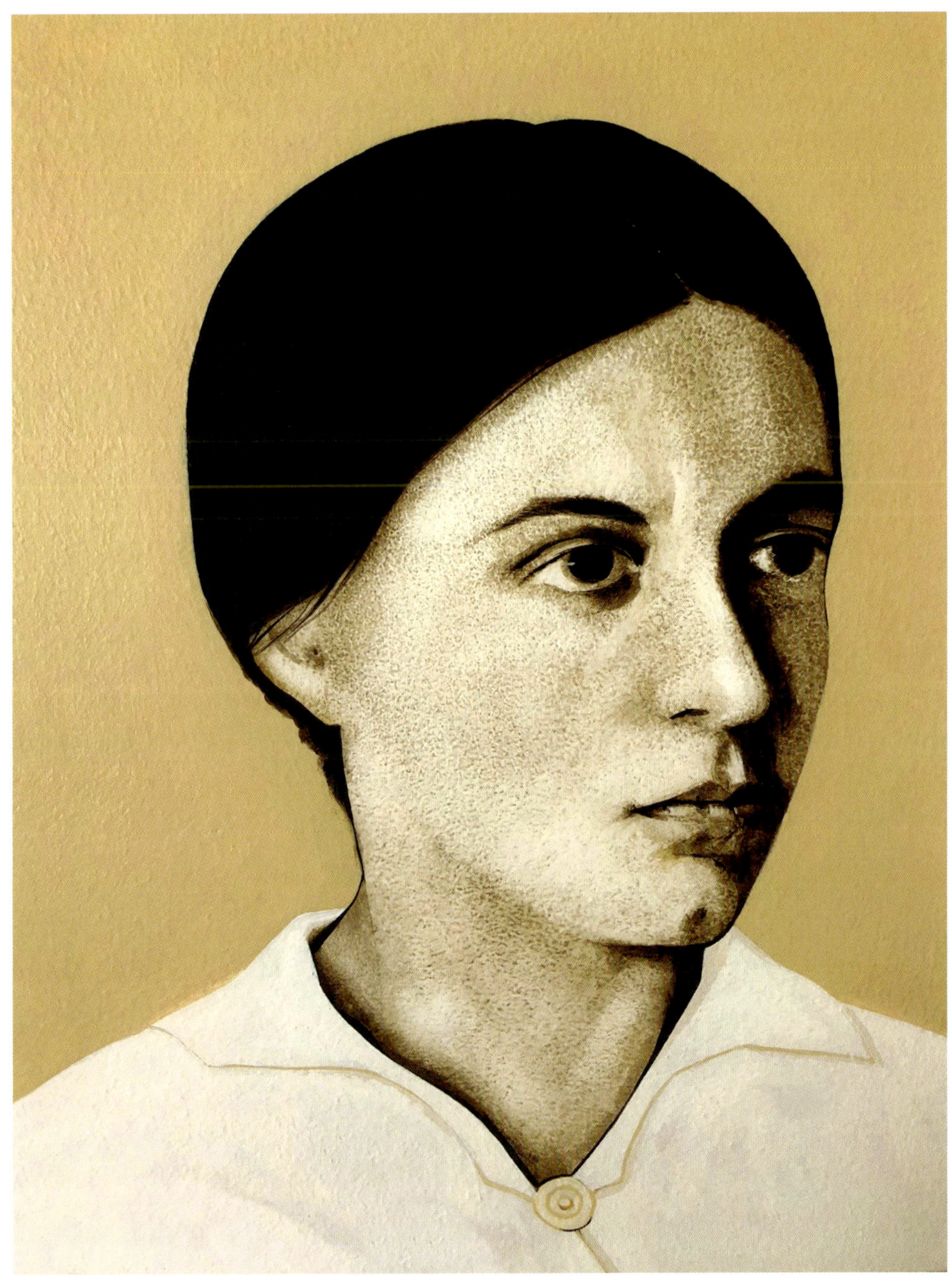

St. Teresa Benedicta (Edith Stein), 1992

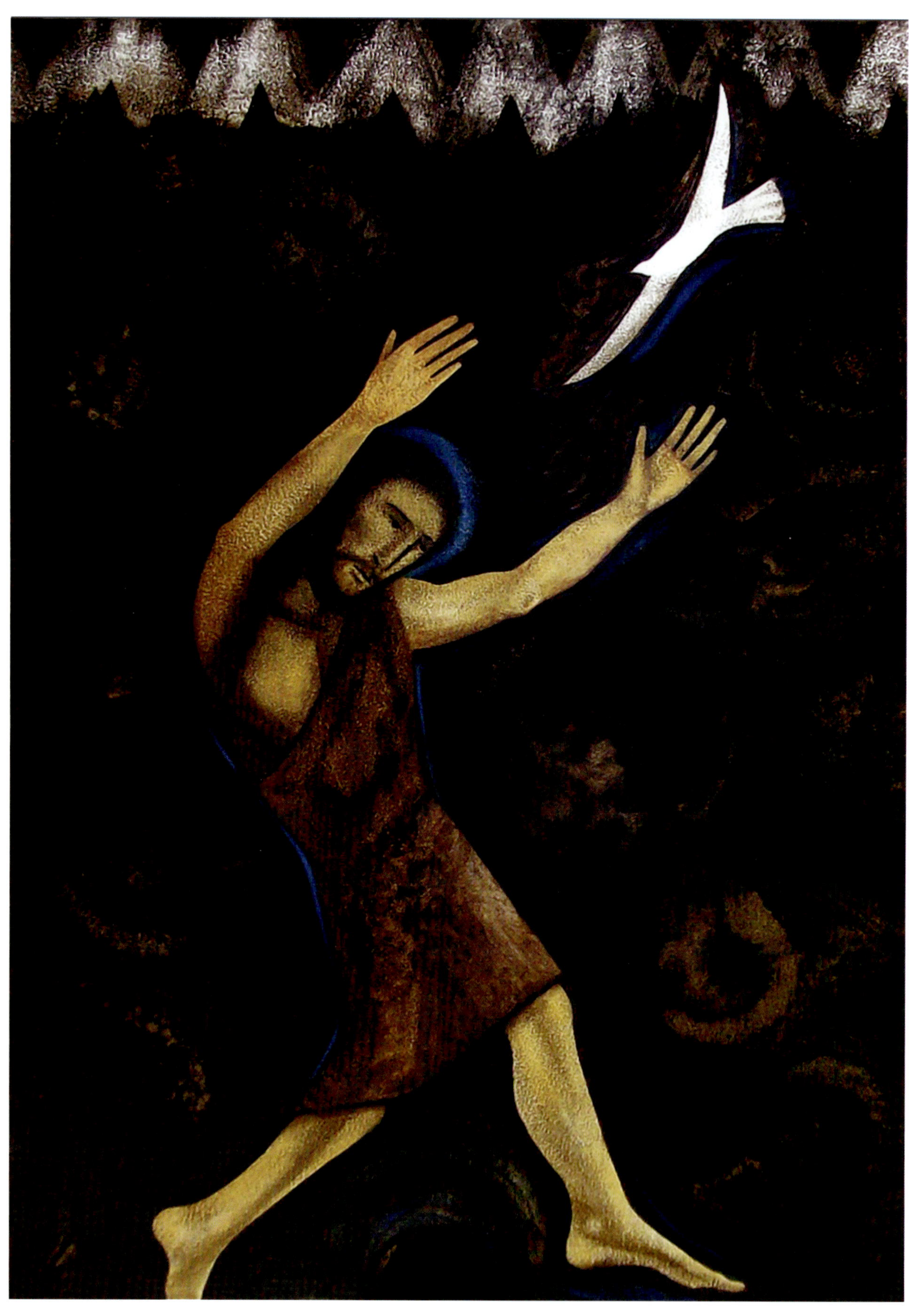

St. John the Baptist in Prison, 2001

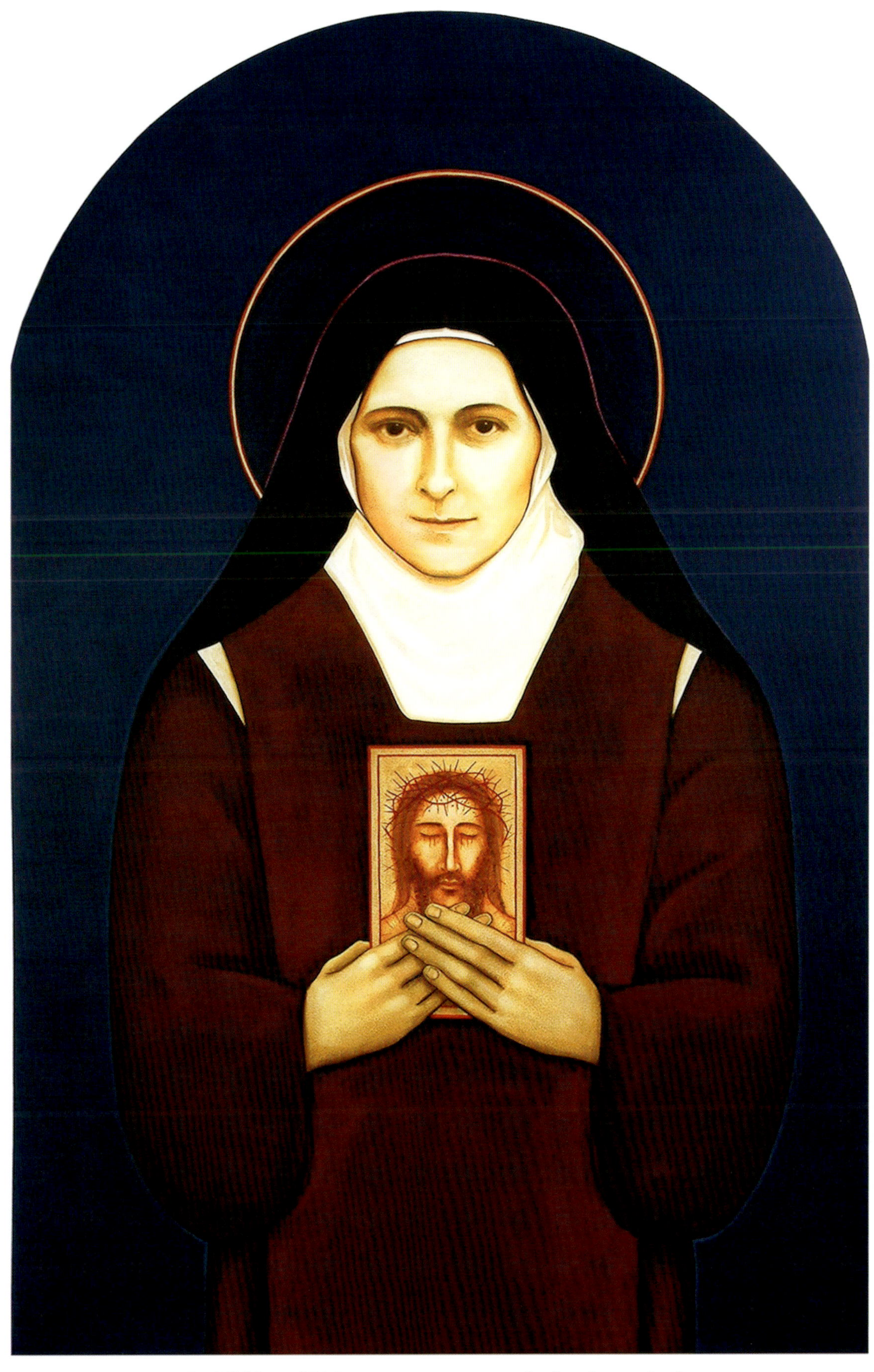

St. Thérèse of Lisieux, 2003–2004, 29 inches by 45 inches

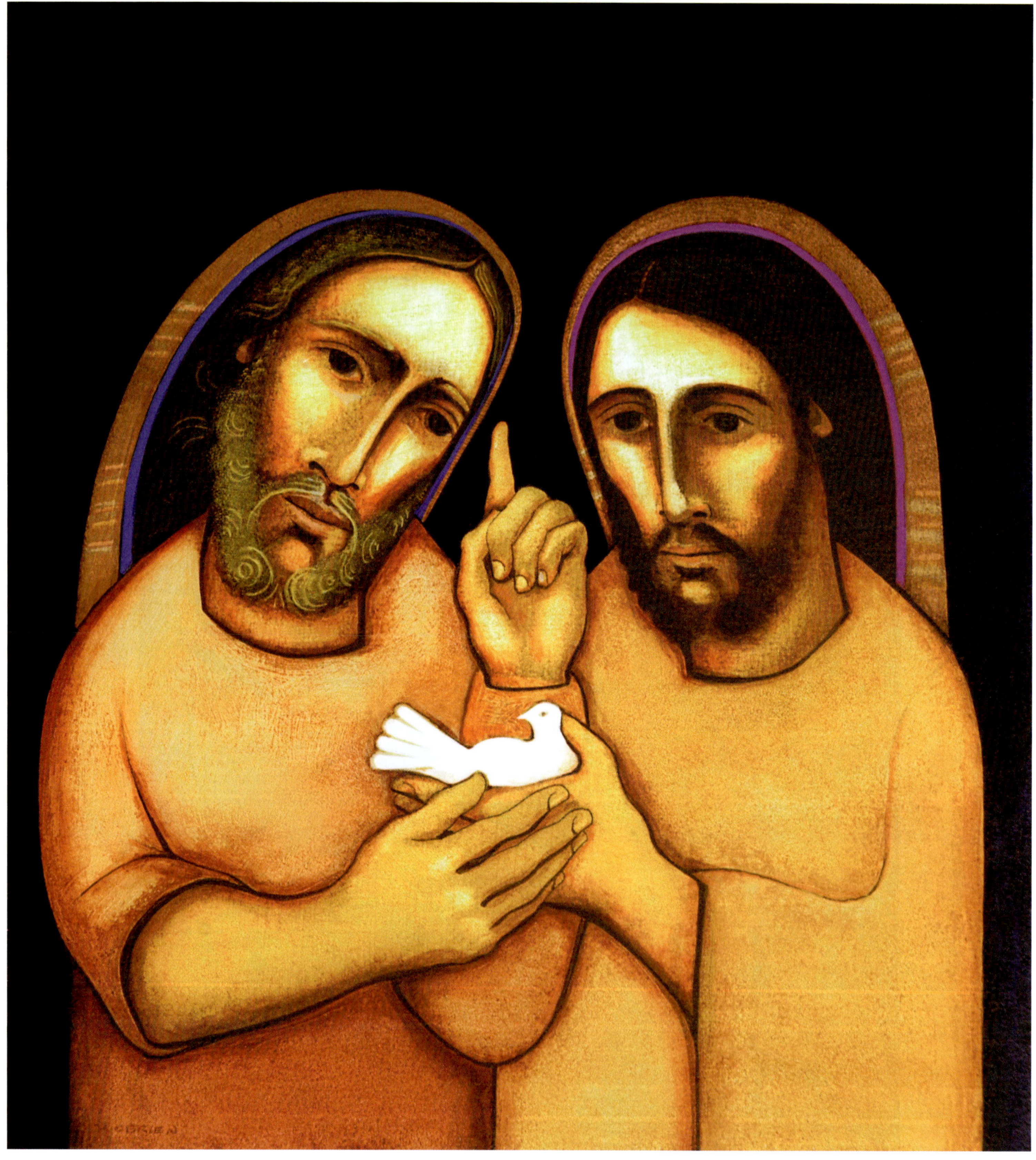

St. Joachim Entrusting the Blessed Virgin Mary to St. Joseph, 2000

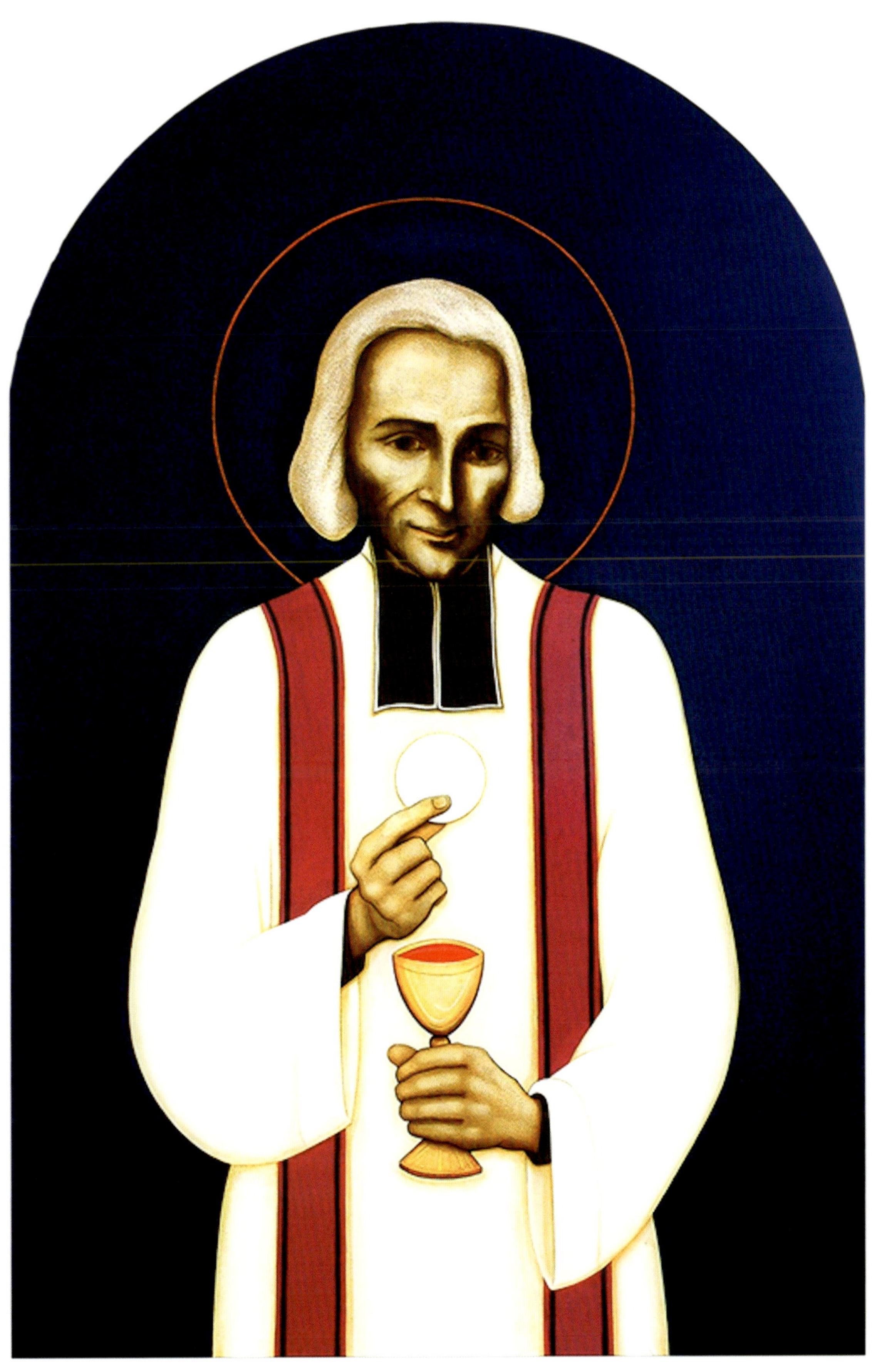

St. Jean Vianney, 2003–2004, 29 inches by 45 inches

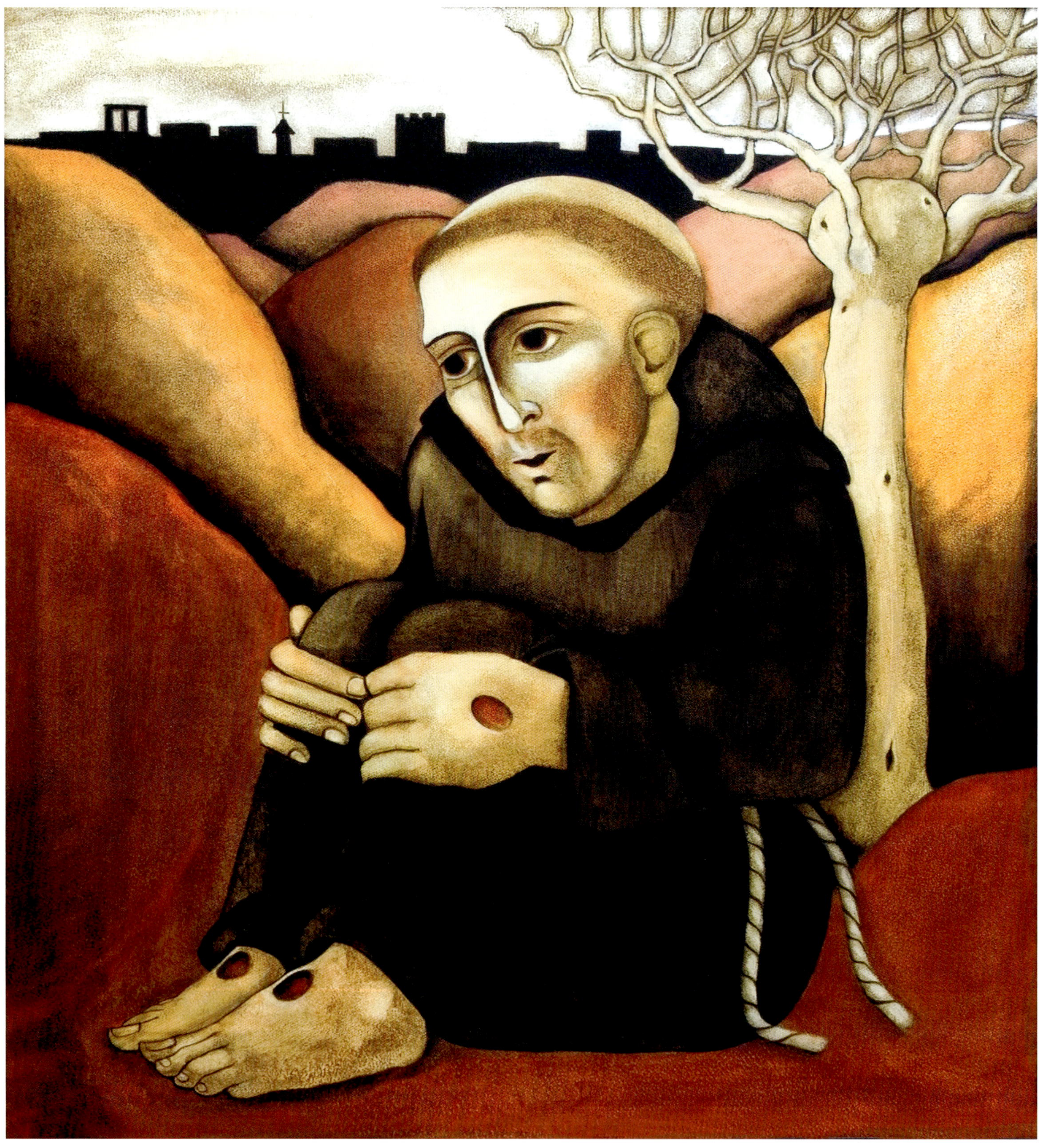

St. Francis Contemplating His Wounds, 1984, 24 inches by 24 inches

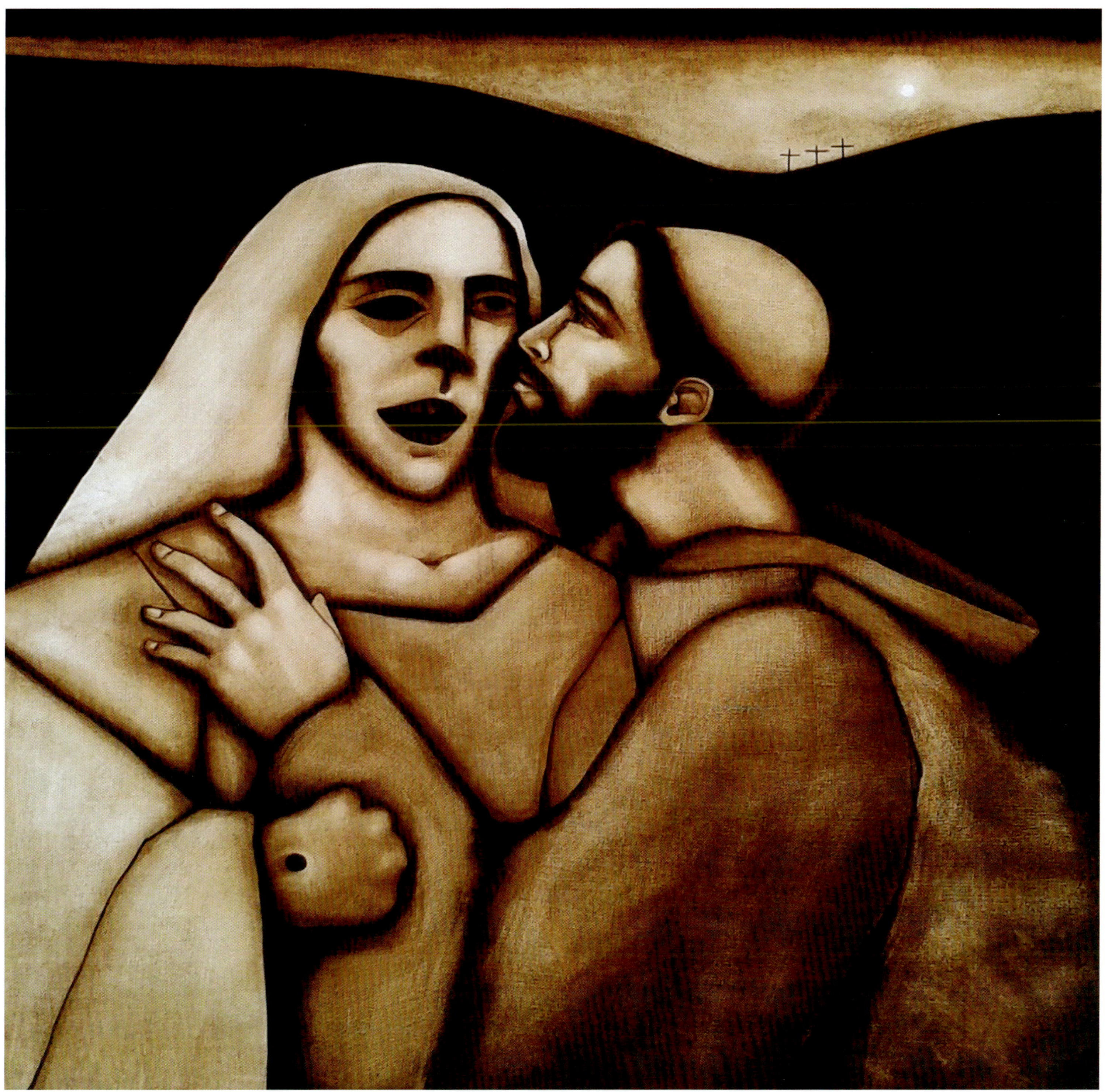

St. Francis Embracing the Leper, 1988

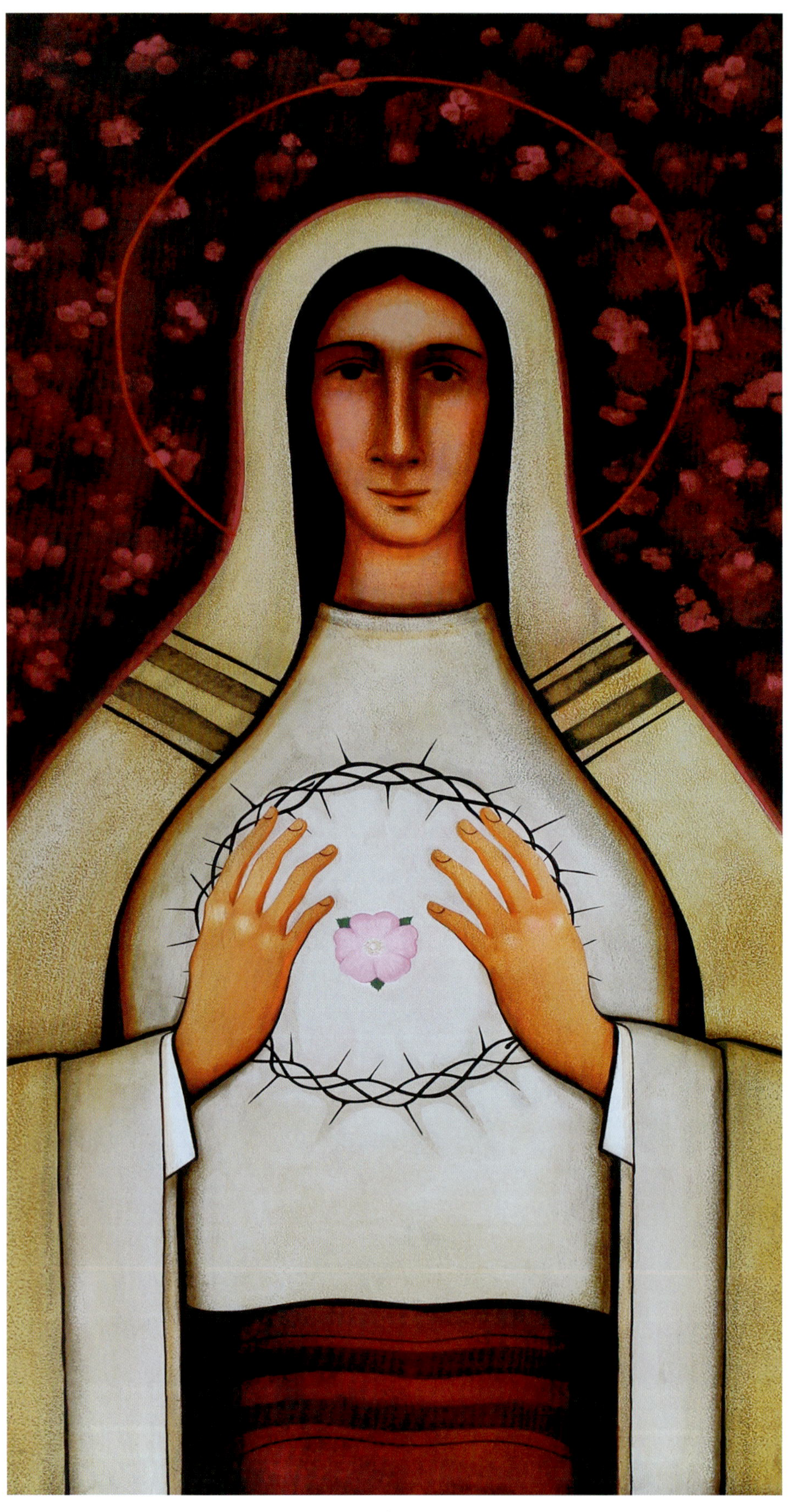

St. Rose of Lima, 1993

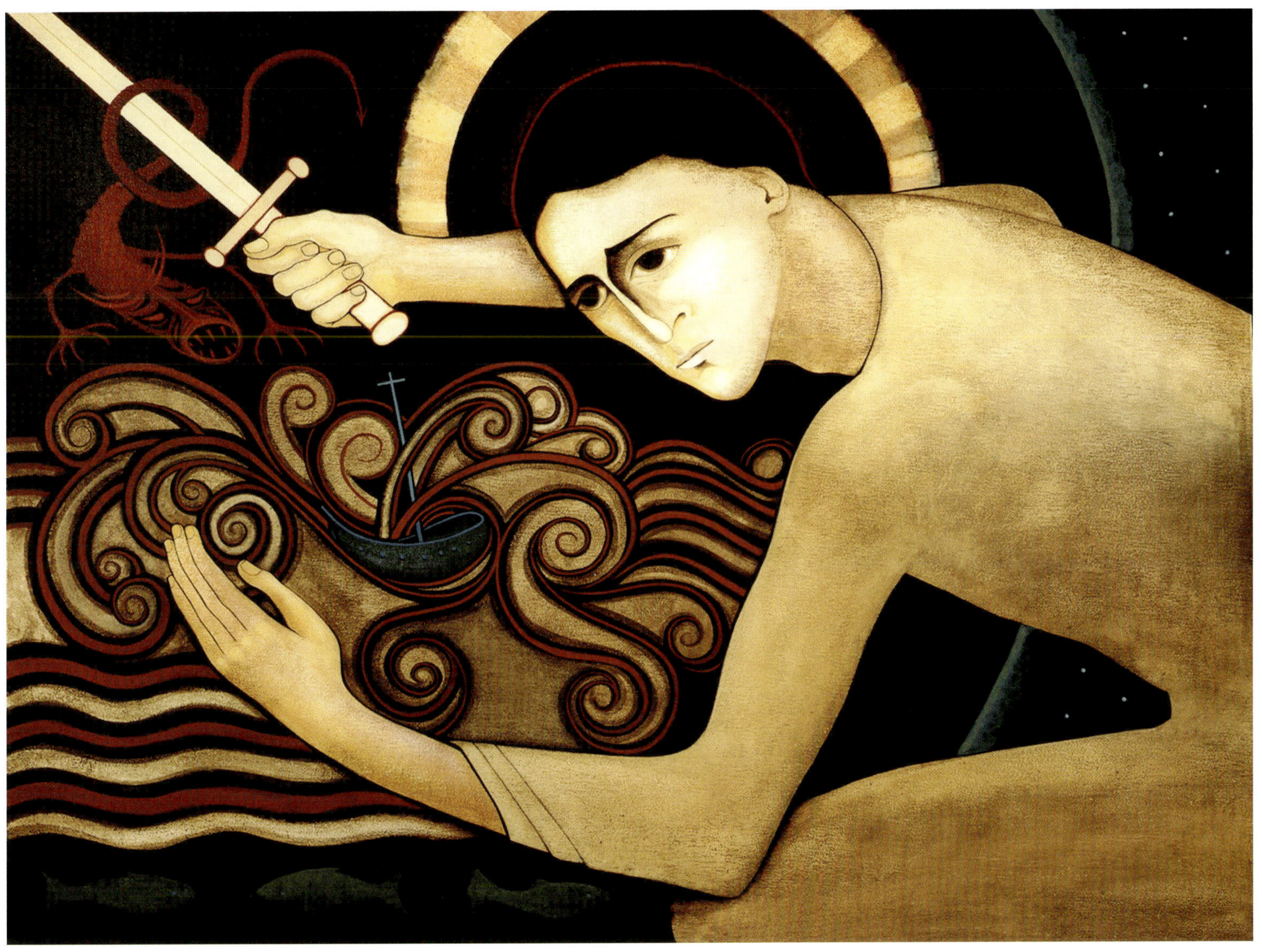

St. Michael Protecting the Church, 1991

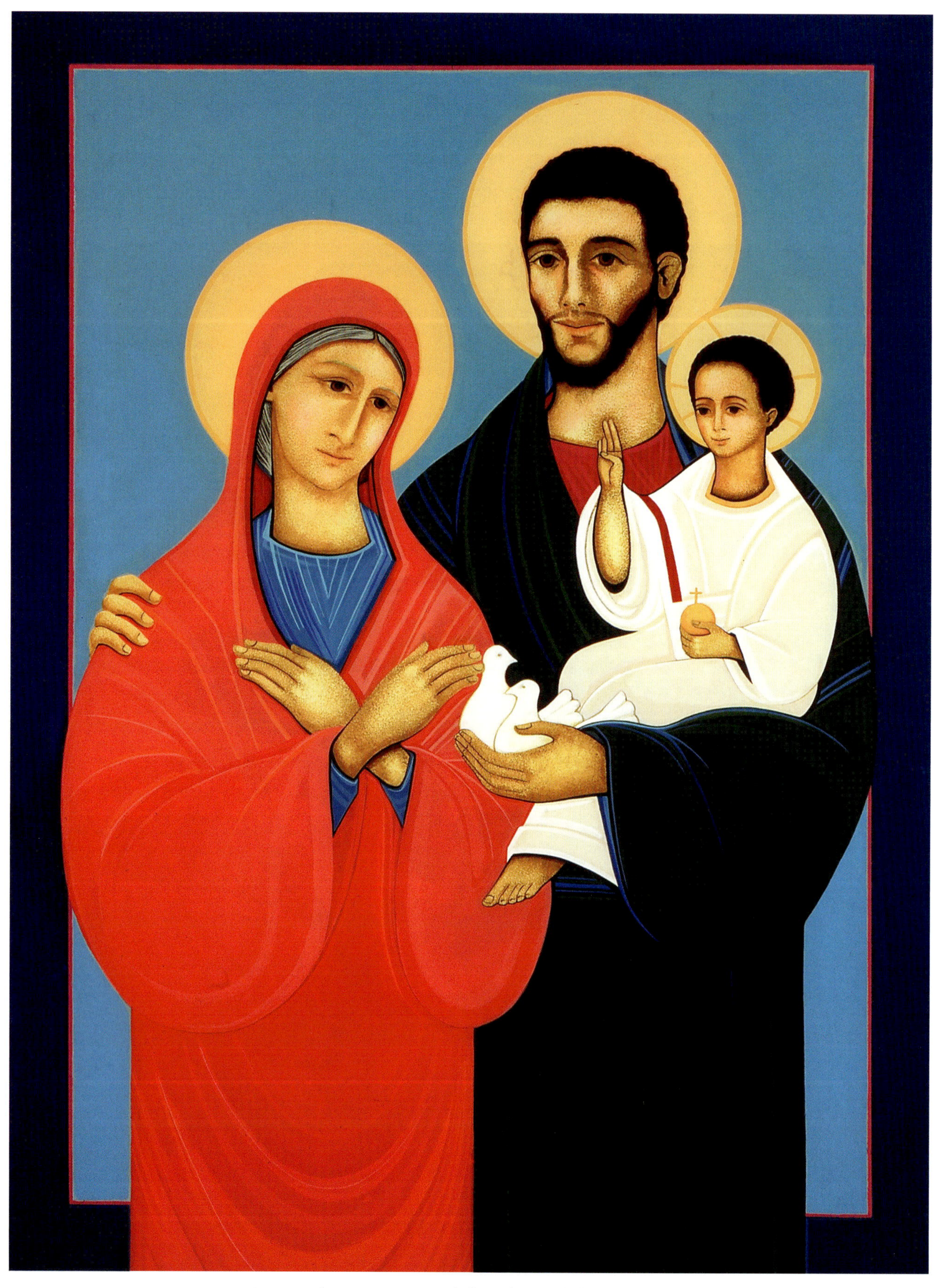

St. Joseph, St. Anne, and the Christ Child, late 1980s

Implicitness

There is a stream in my work that is not overtly religious yet offers reflections on the deepest questions in man's heart. Implicitly religious, these paintings range across several decades of creative work.

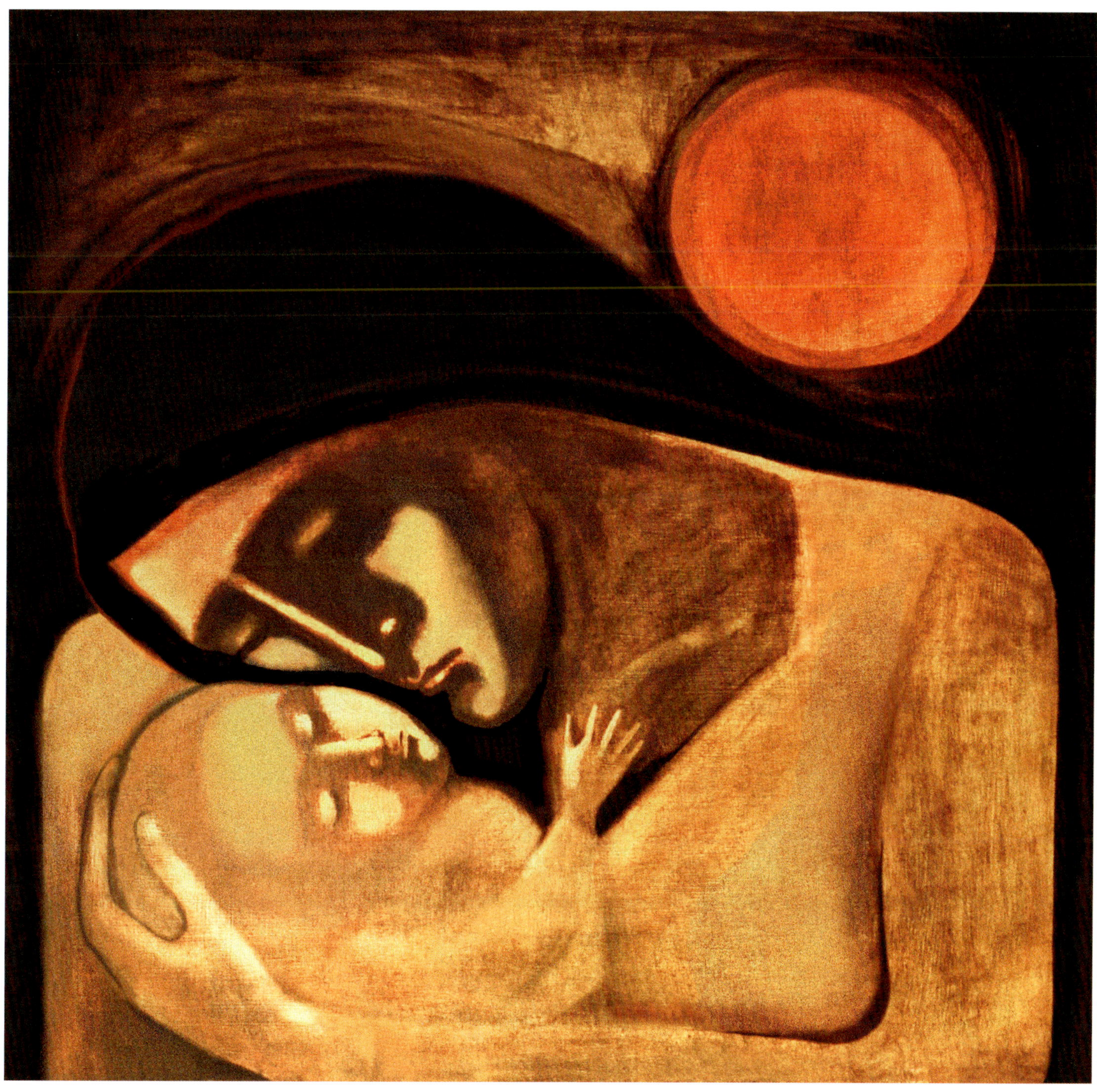

Creation, 1978, 24 by 24 inches

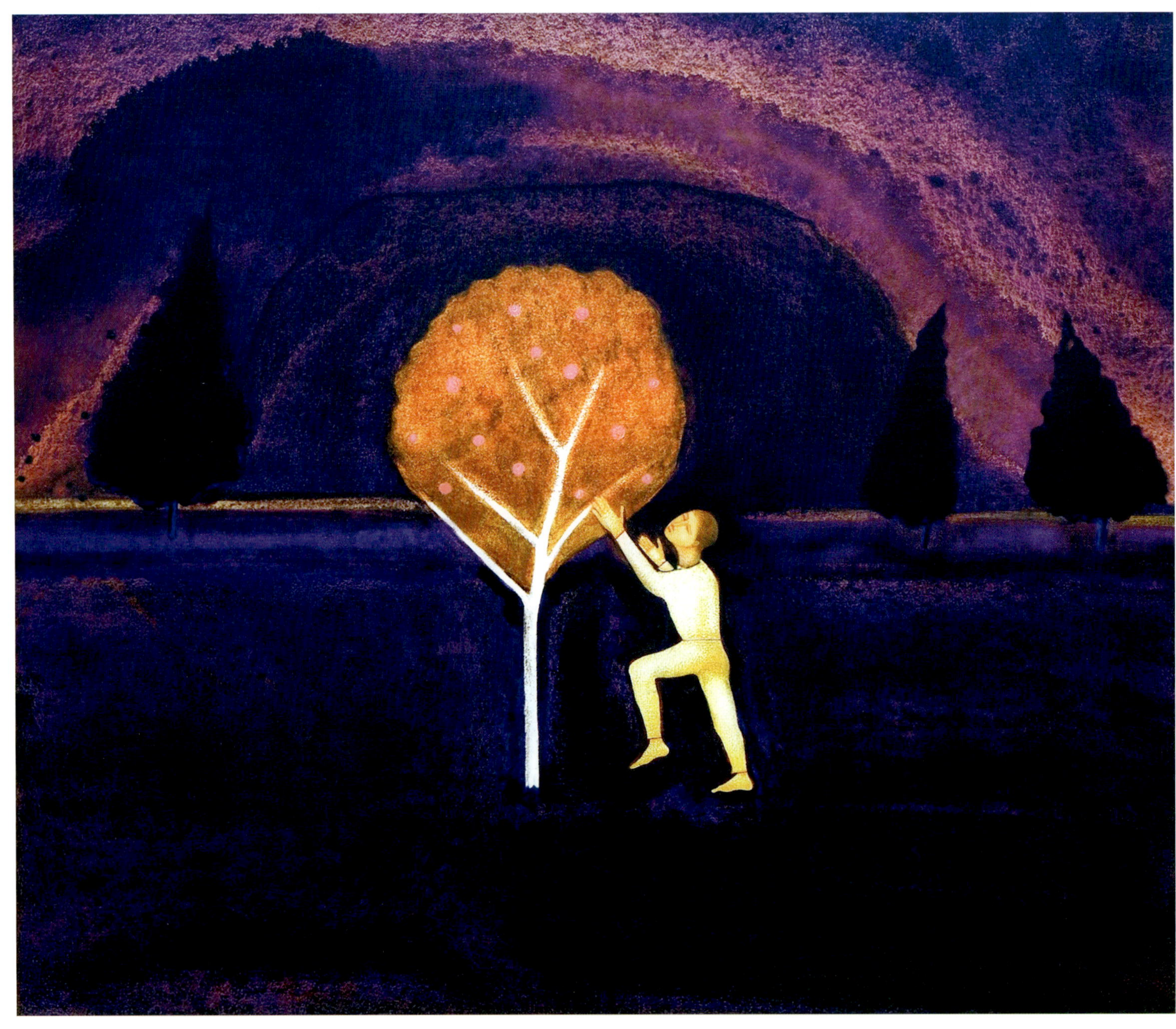

Boy and Tree, 2003

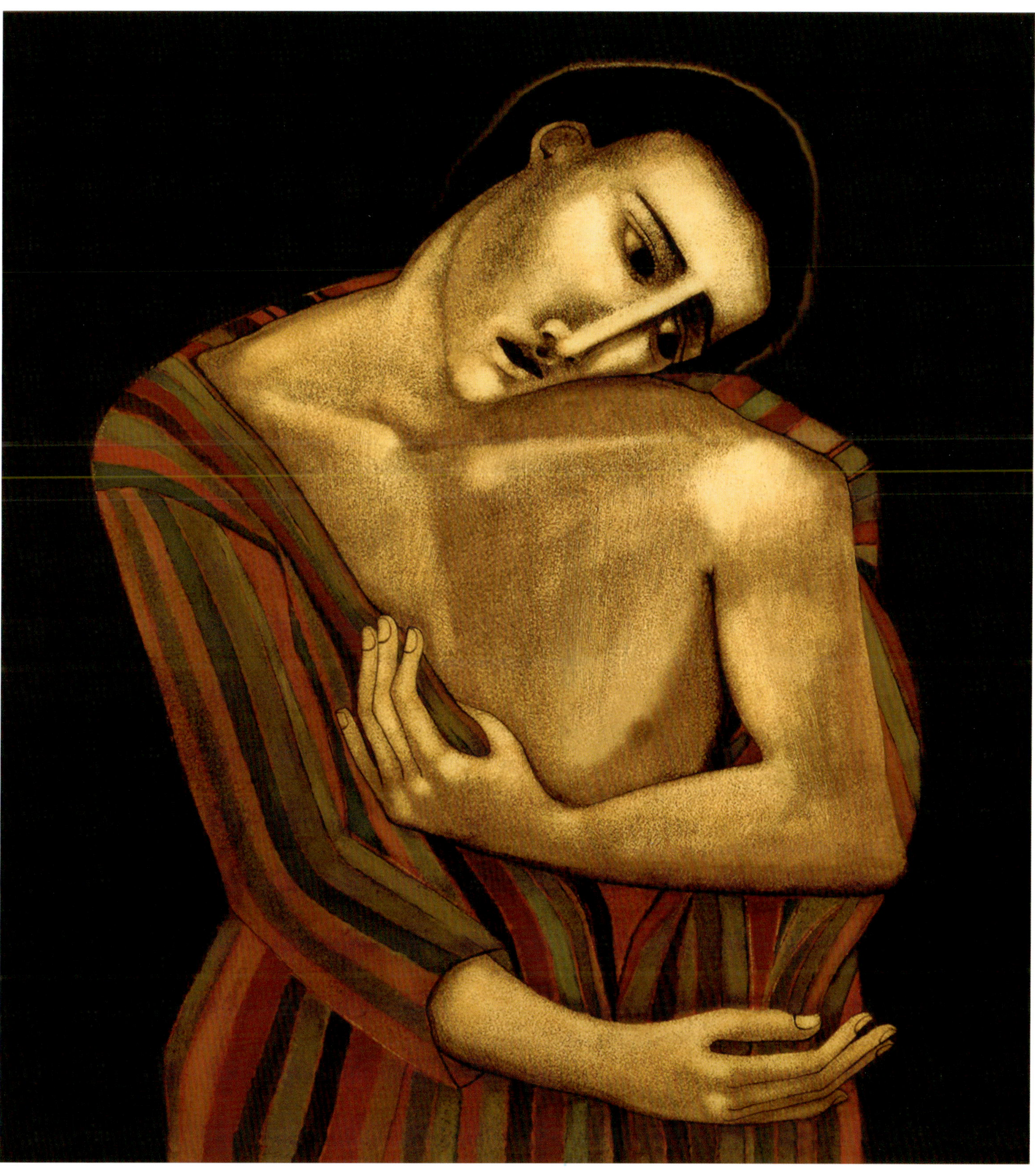

Coat of Many Colors, 1984

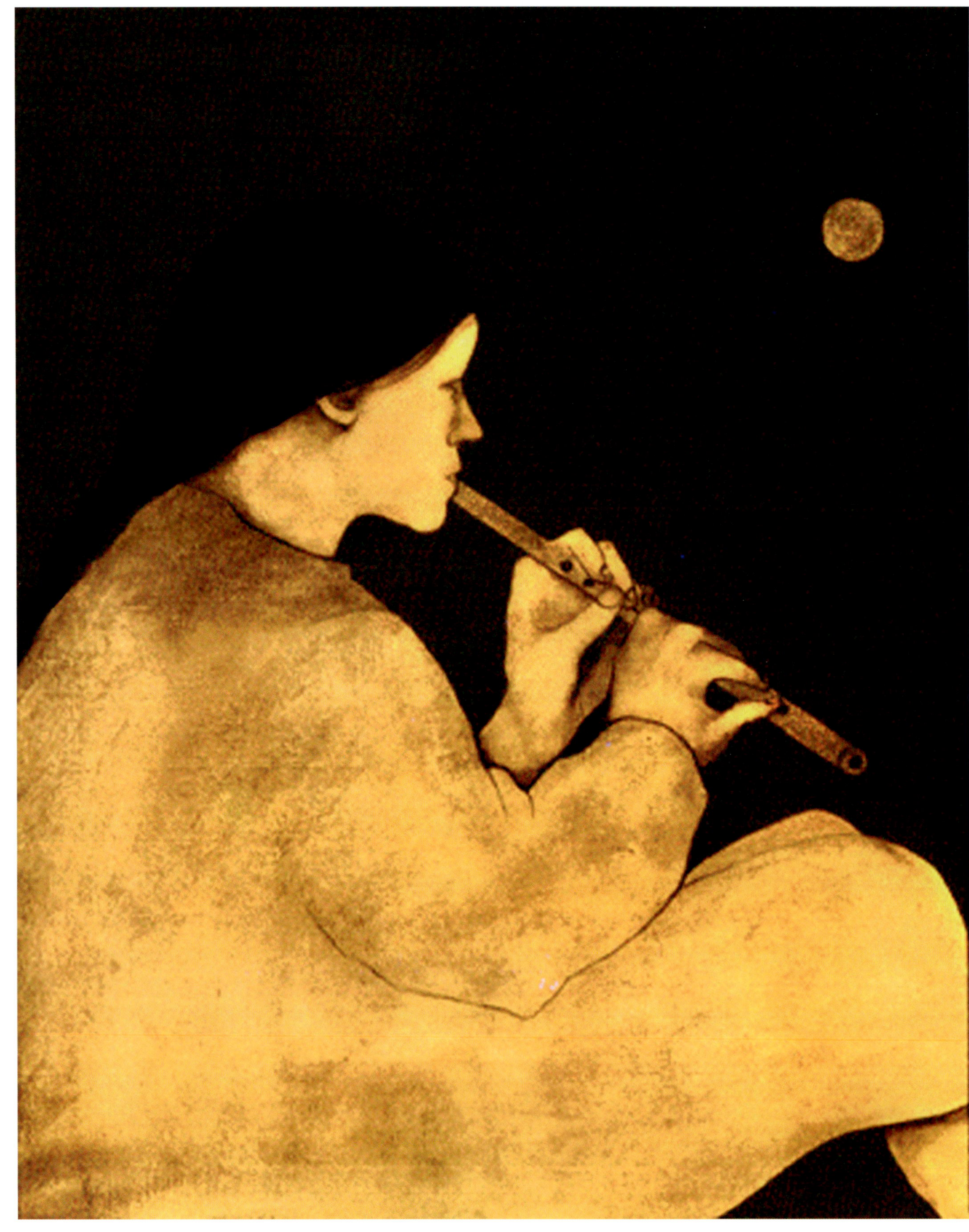

Girl and Flute, mid-1980s

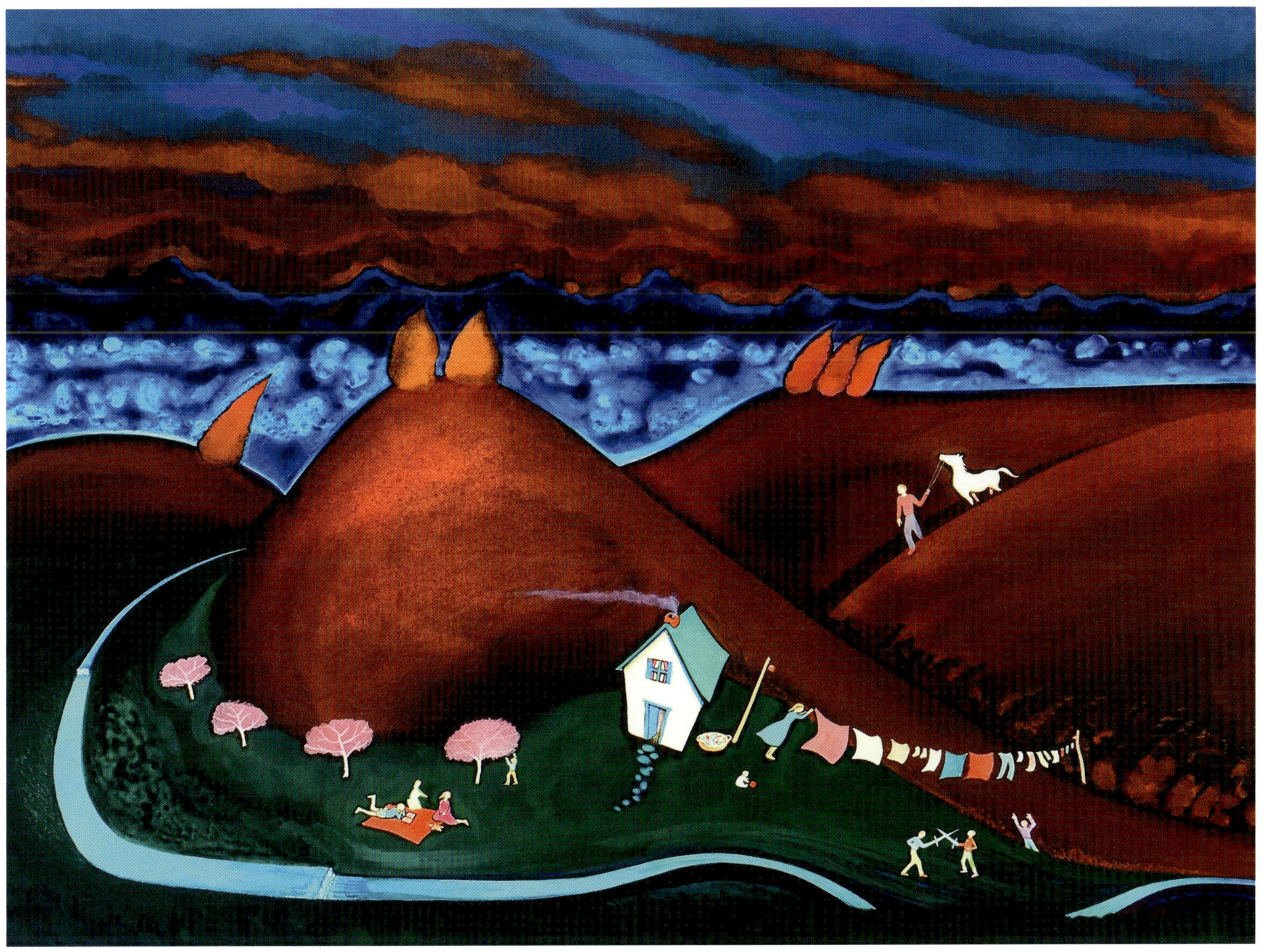

Homecoming, 2004

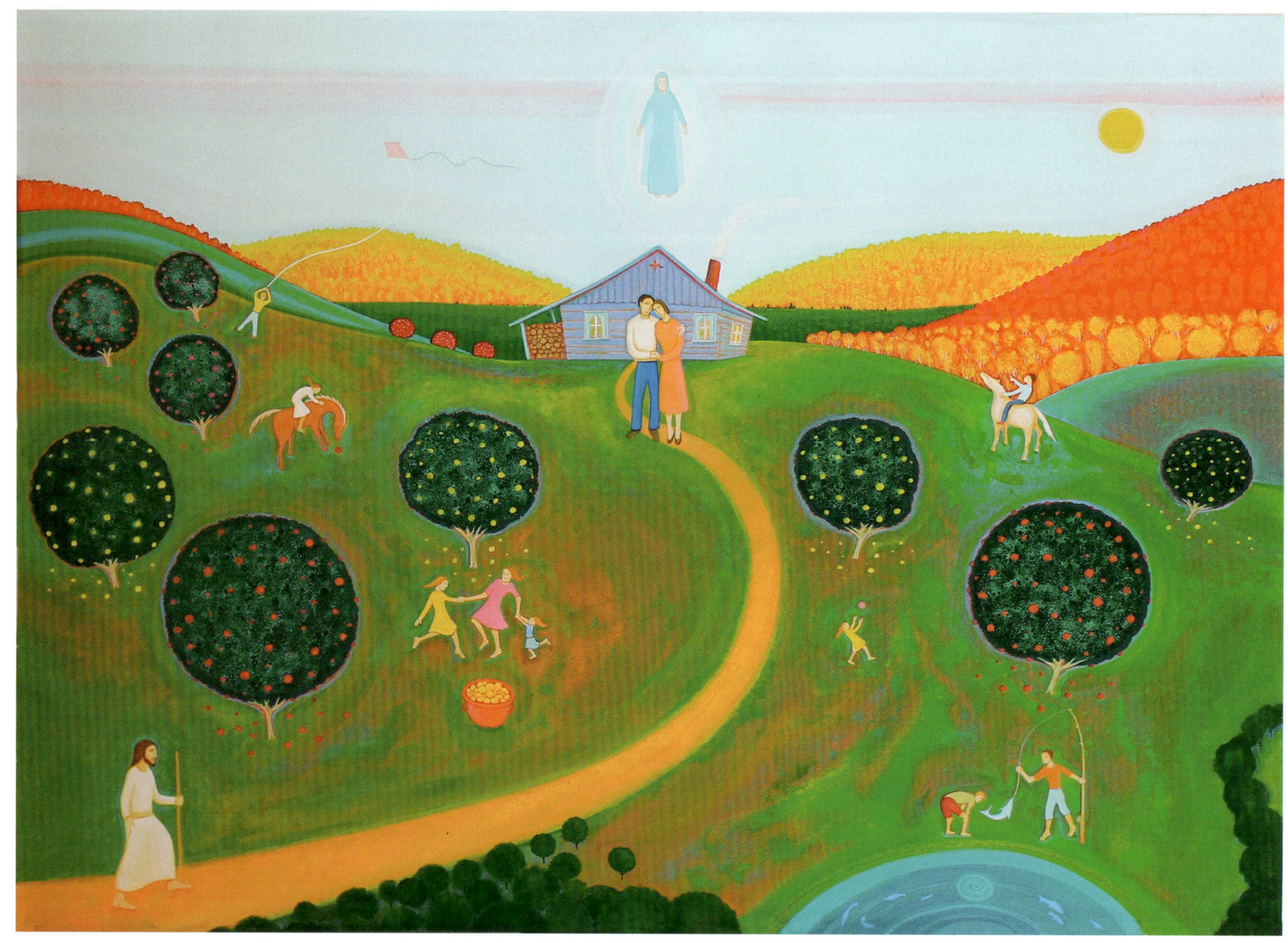

Sanctuary of the Heart, 2010, 24 inches by 32 inches

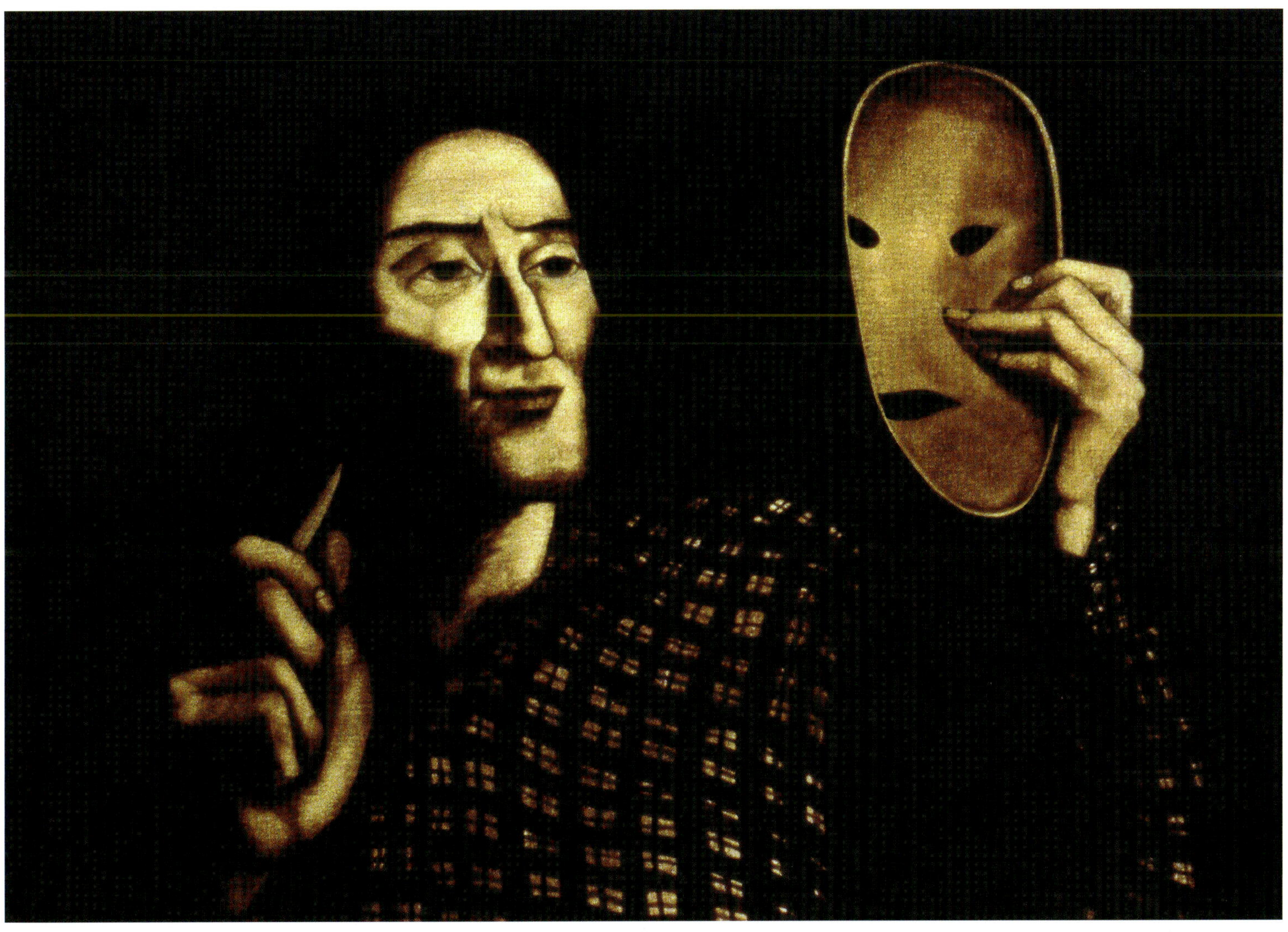

The Mask, 1978

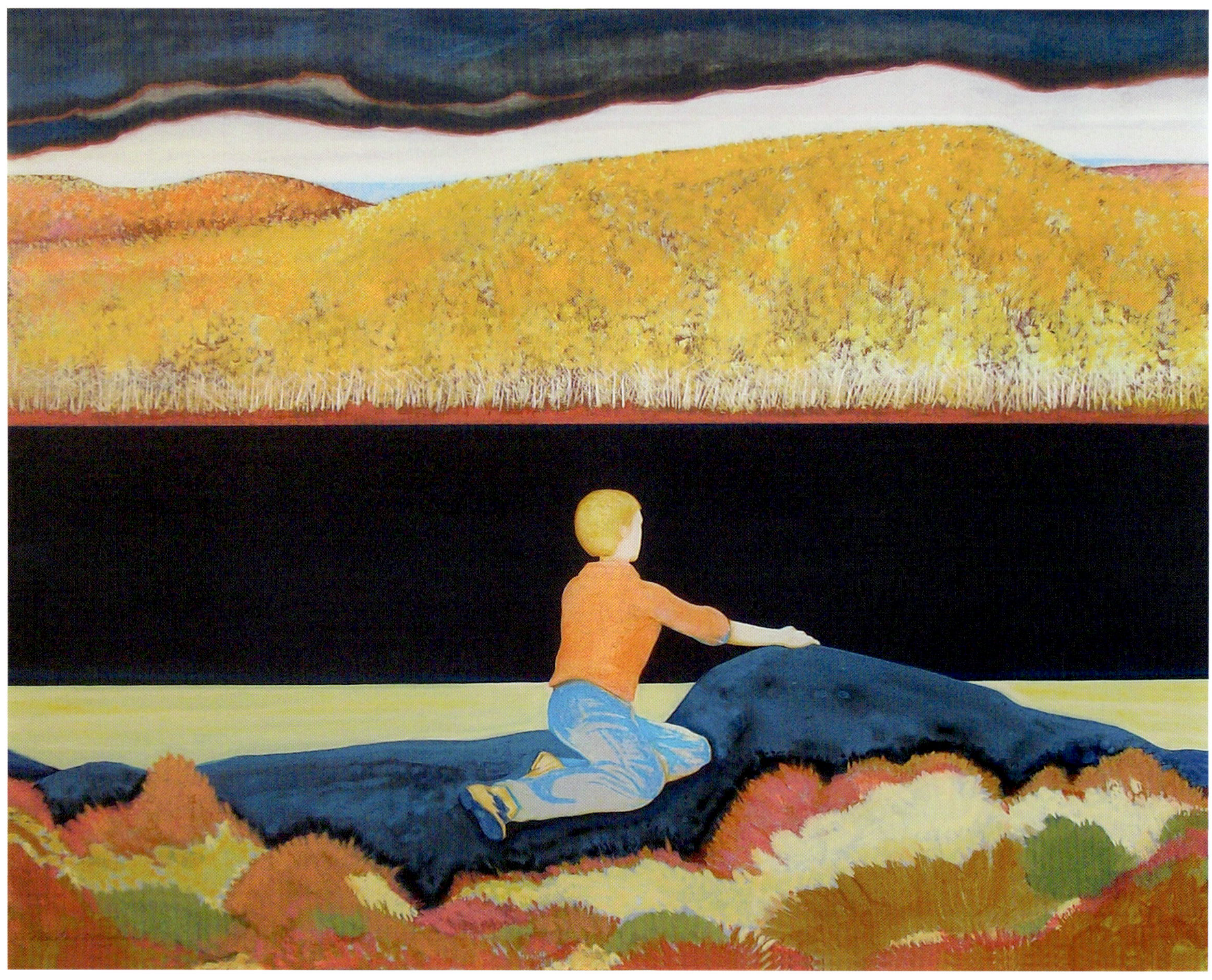

The Distant Shore, 2007

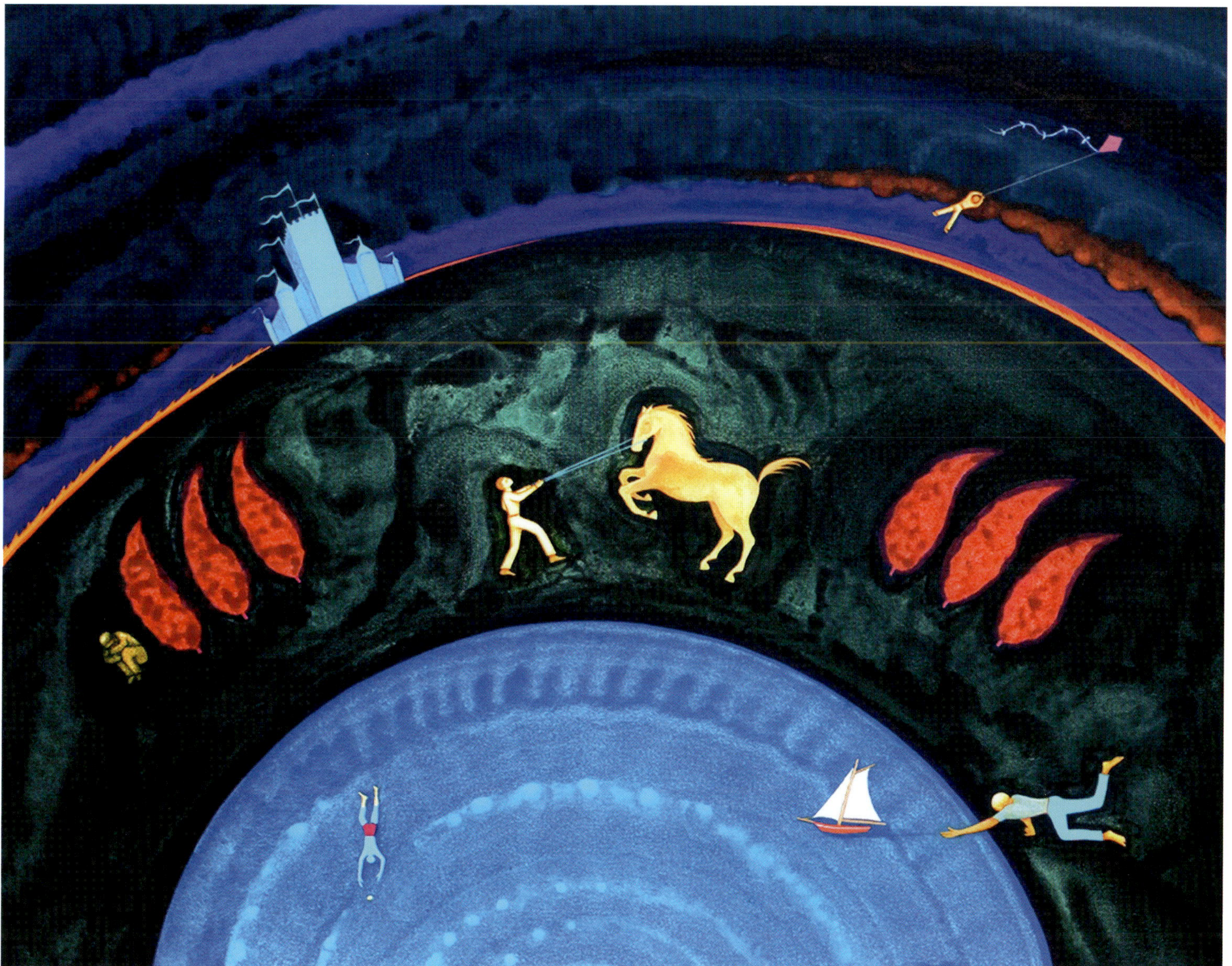

Allegory on Seeking and Striving, 2002

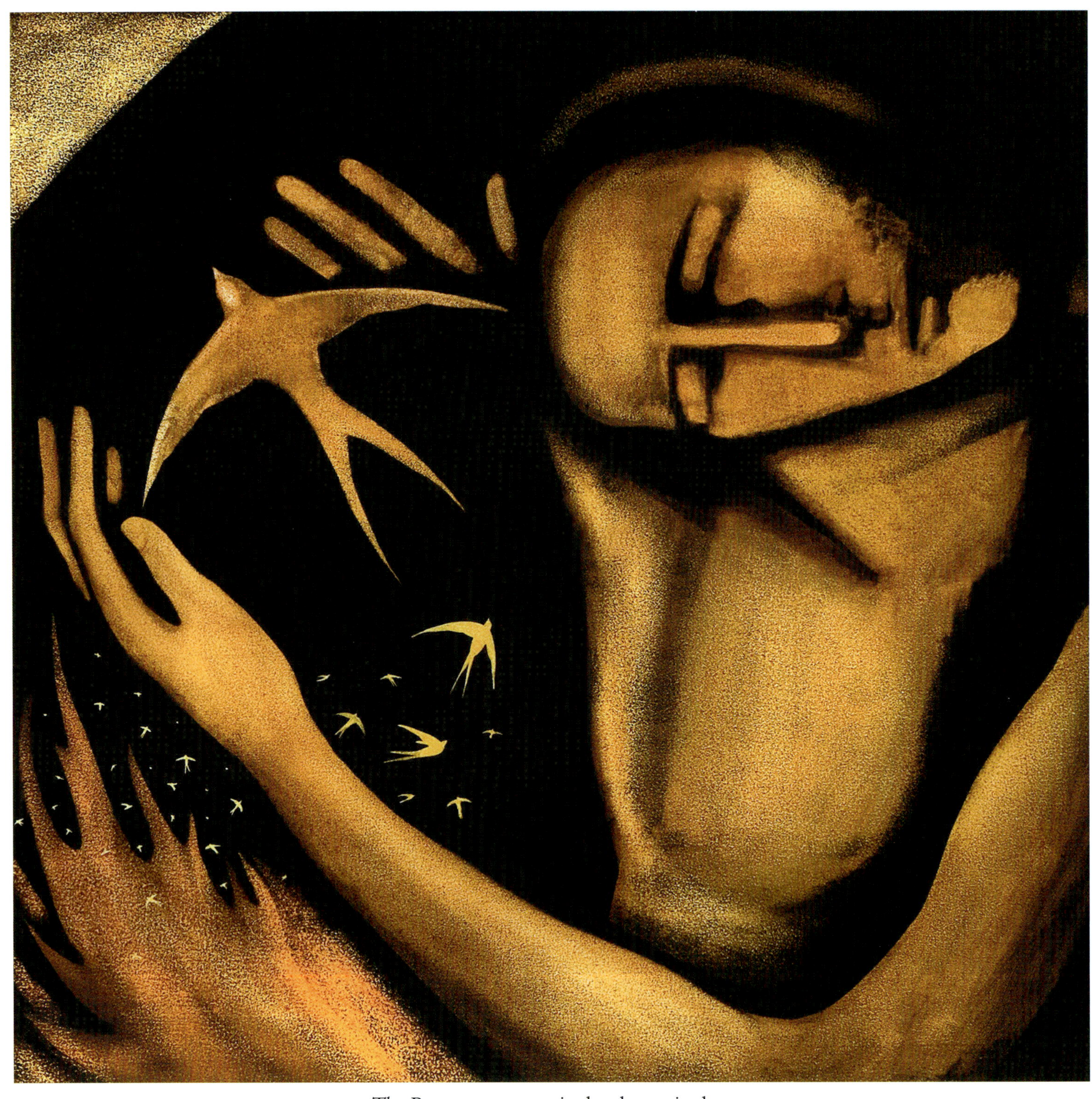

The Rescuer, 2003, 24 inches by 24 inches

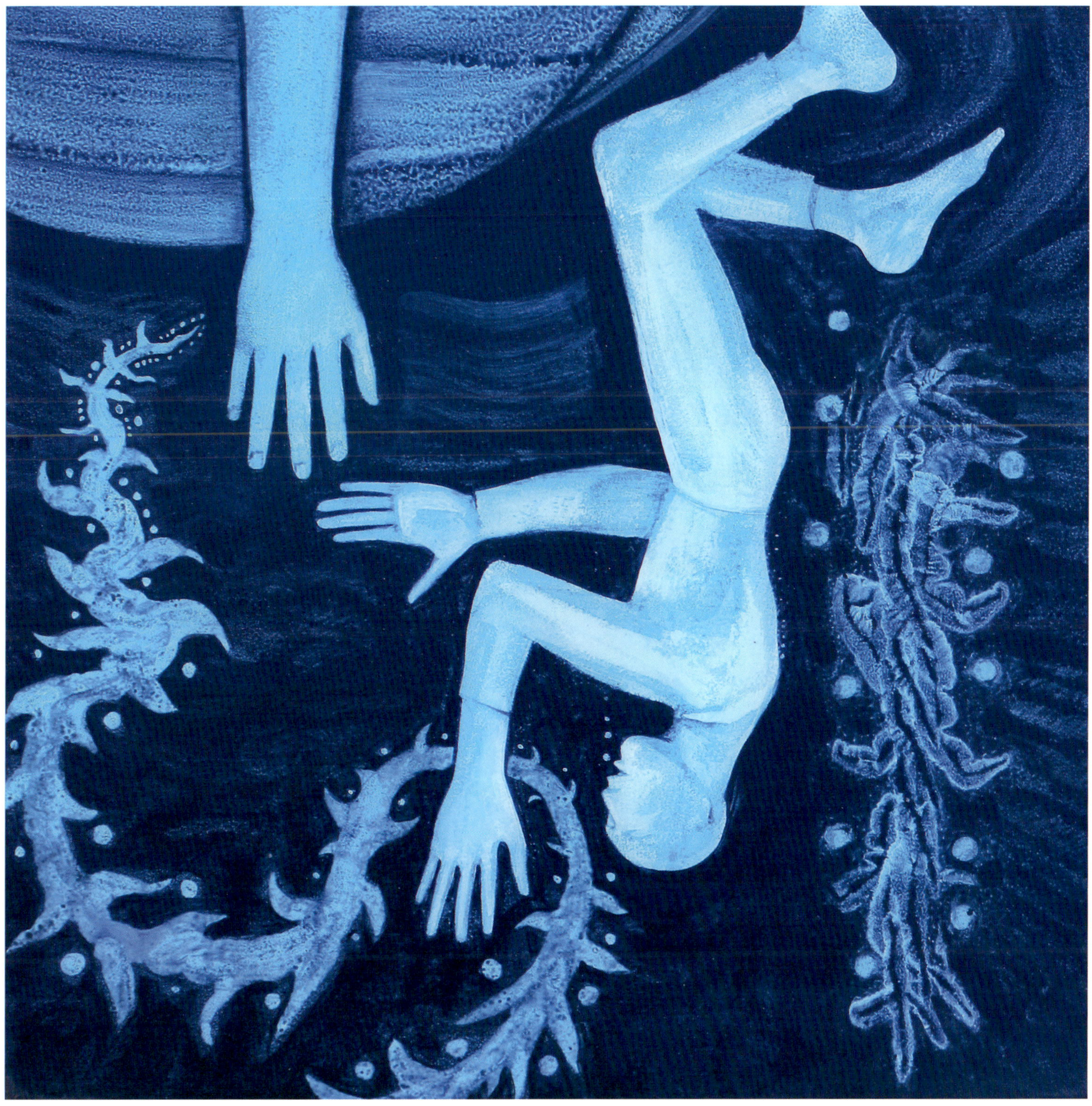

Hope of the Drowning, 2005, 18 inches by 18 inches

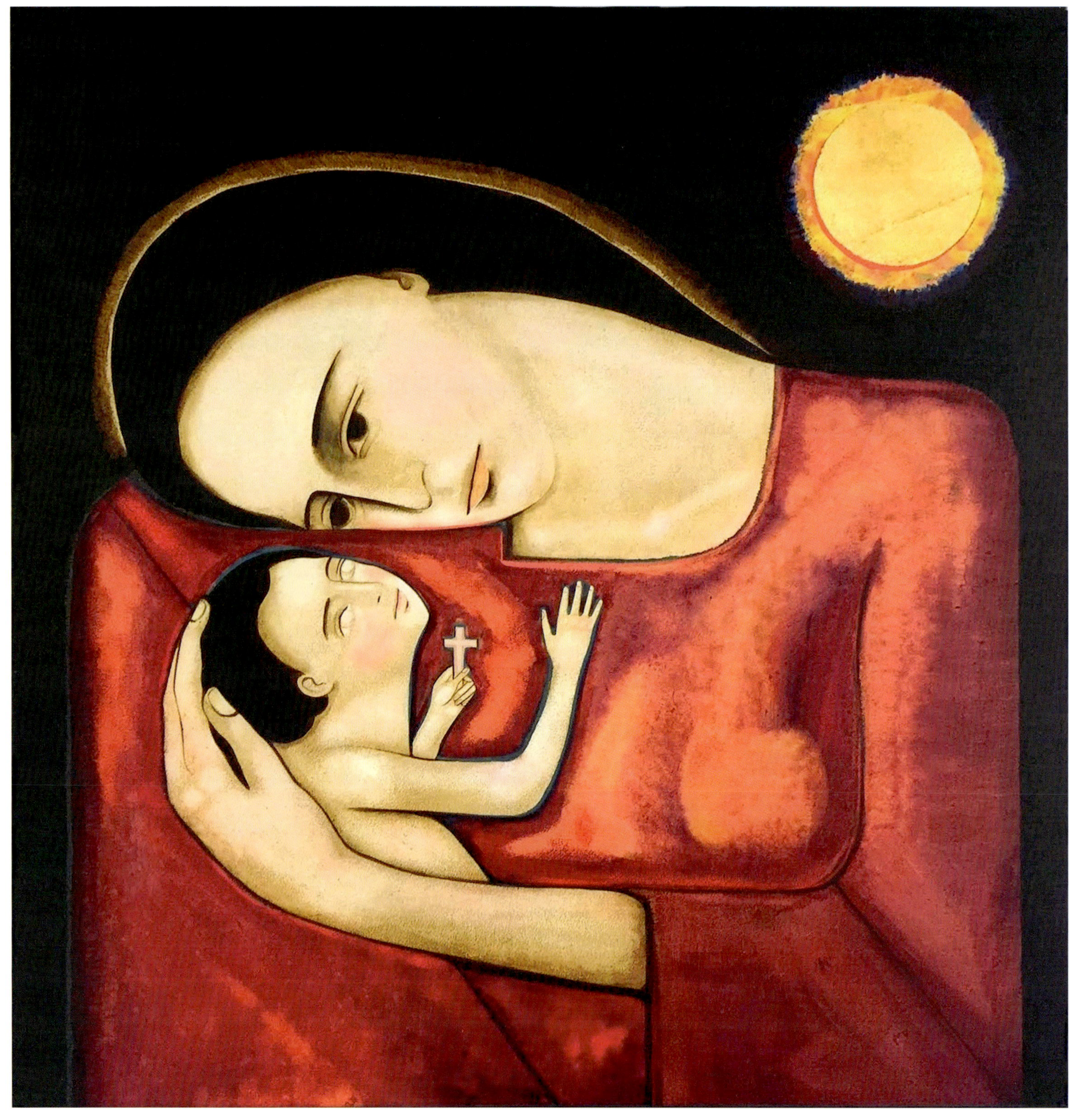

Genshi Bakudan ("Original Child Bomb", the Japanese name for the atomic bomb), early 1980s

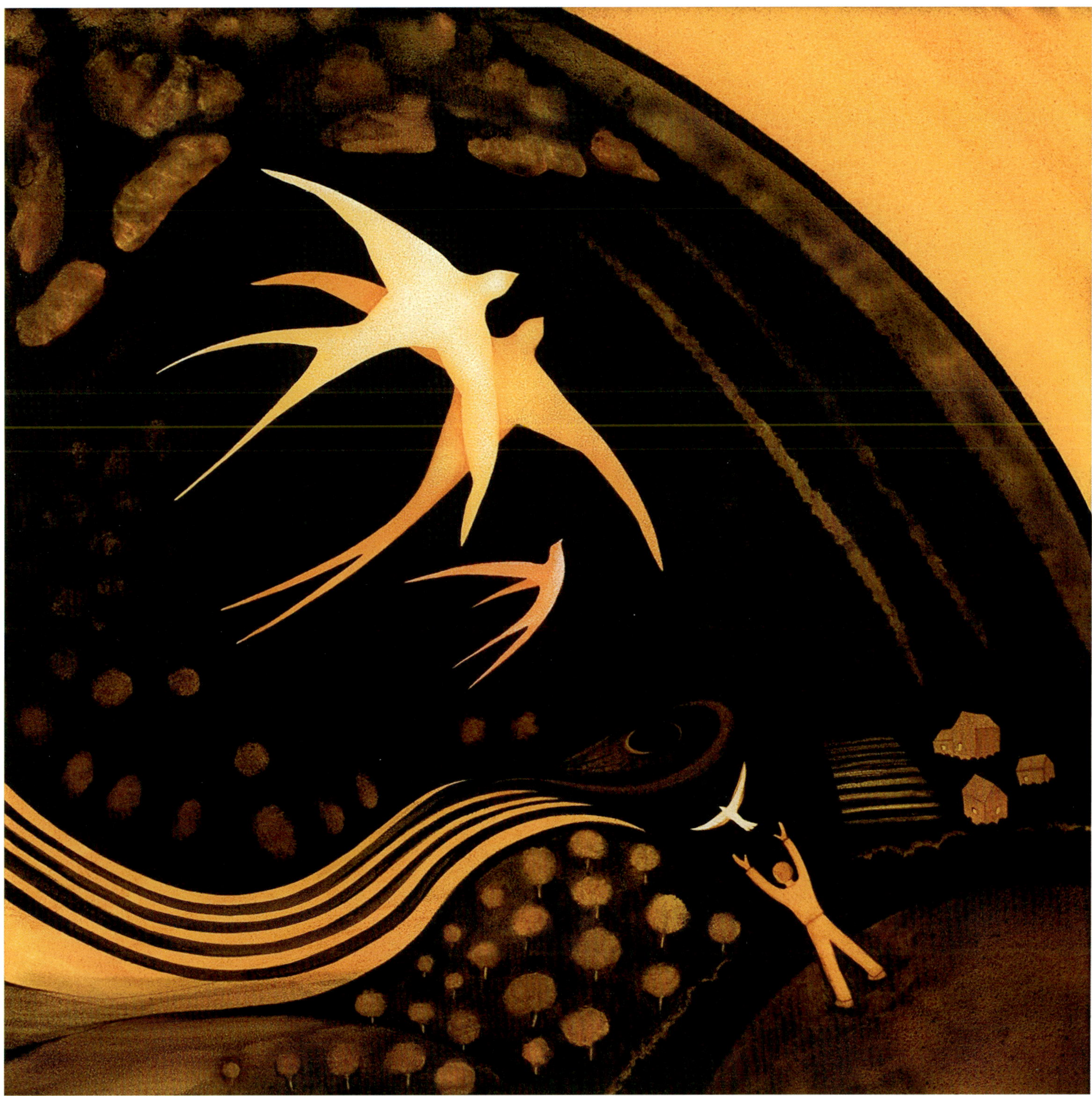

Transcendence, 2001, 24 inches by 24 inches

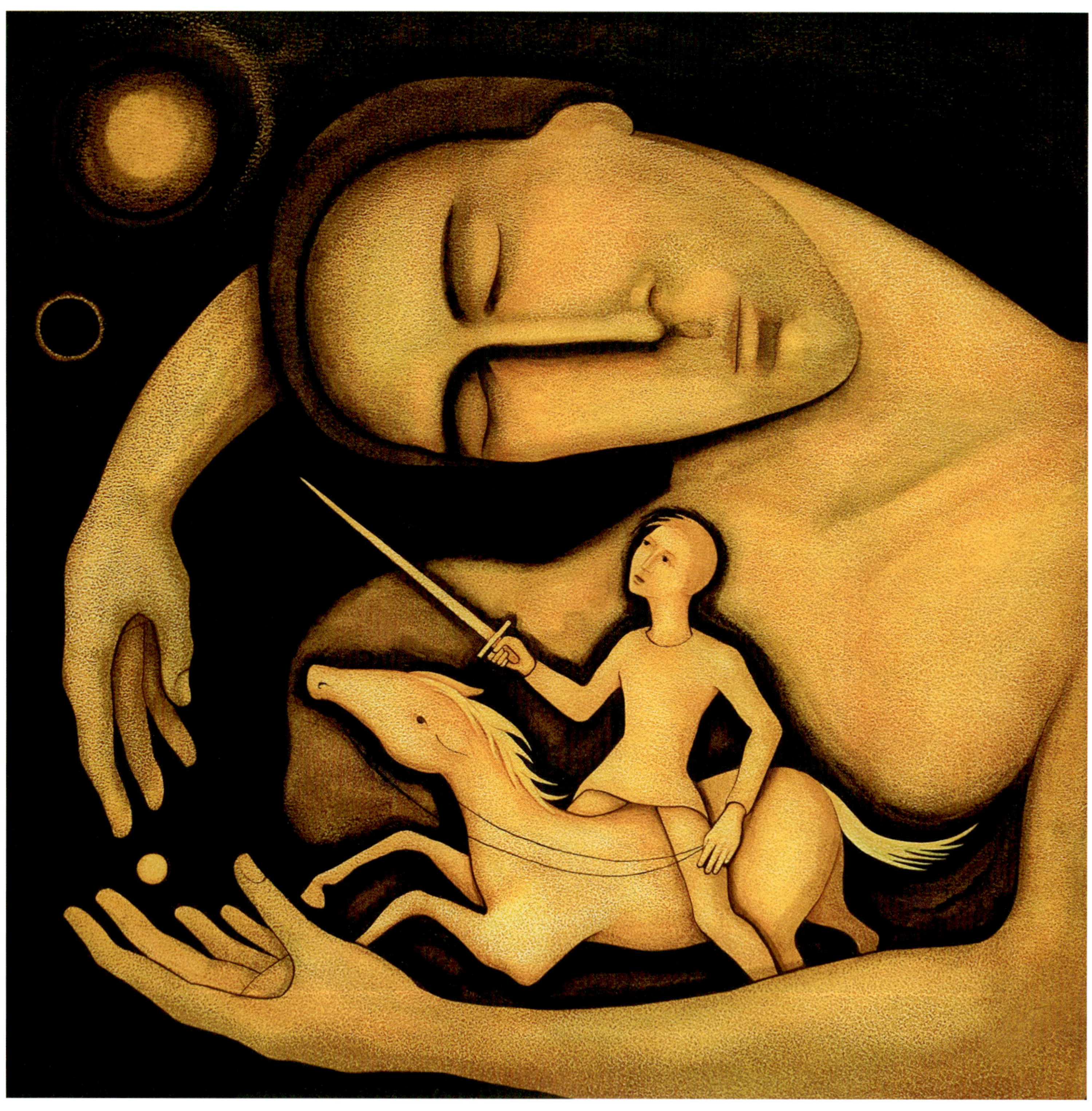

The Dream, late 1990s

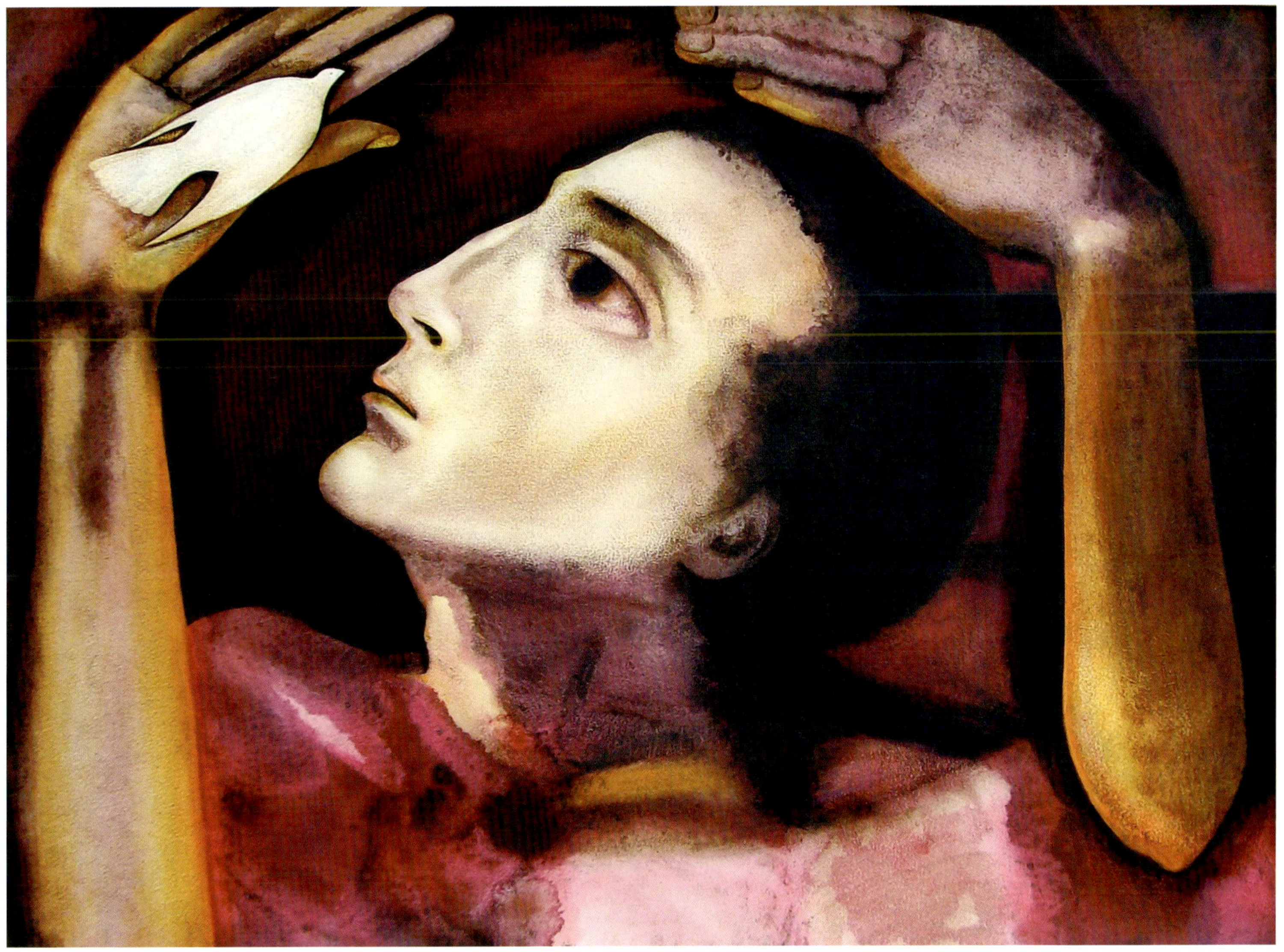

Freedom, 2003

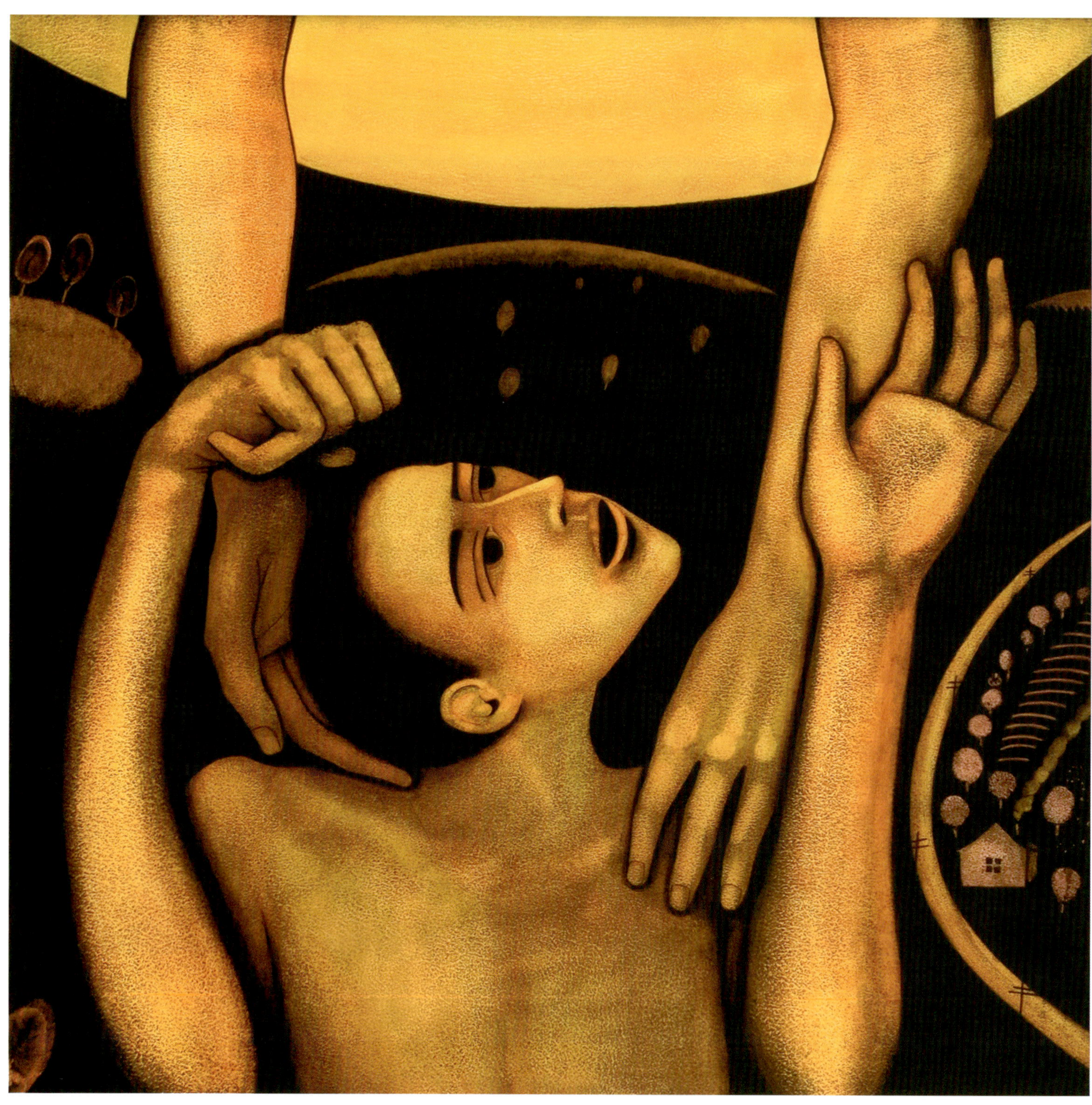

Birth-Death, late 1990s

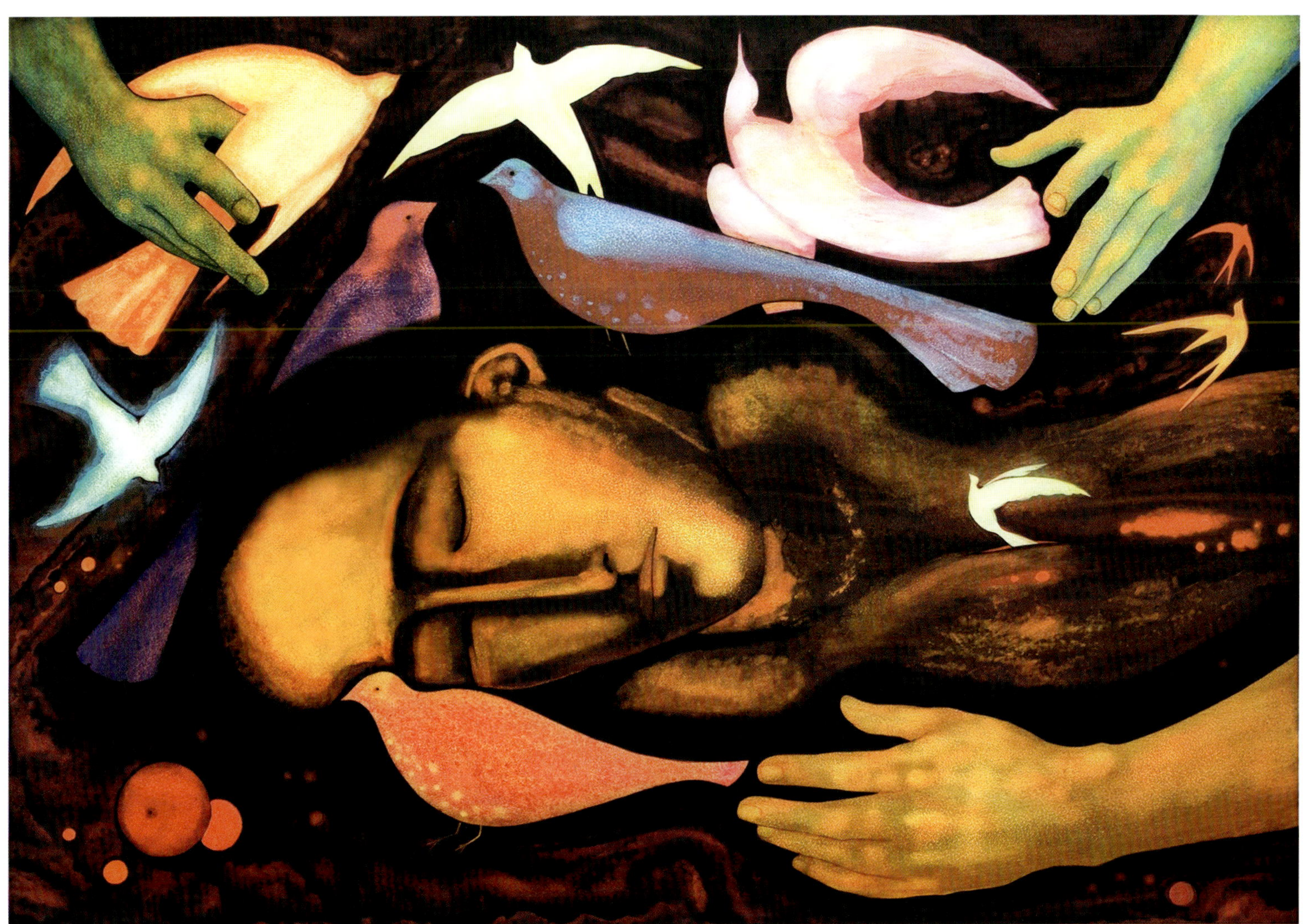

Creation of the Birds, 2002

Reflections

The Kingdom of God is vast and deep, overflowing with marvels and ever revealing new understandings. I have often painted images of truths of the faith that do not fit into precise categories, sometimes explicitly religious, sometimes implicitly. Here is a collection of such works, which range widely in themes and styles—devotional portraits of Christ, landscapes, metaphors, spiritual insights, and purely human scenes.

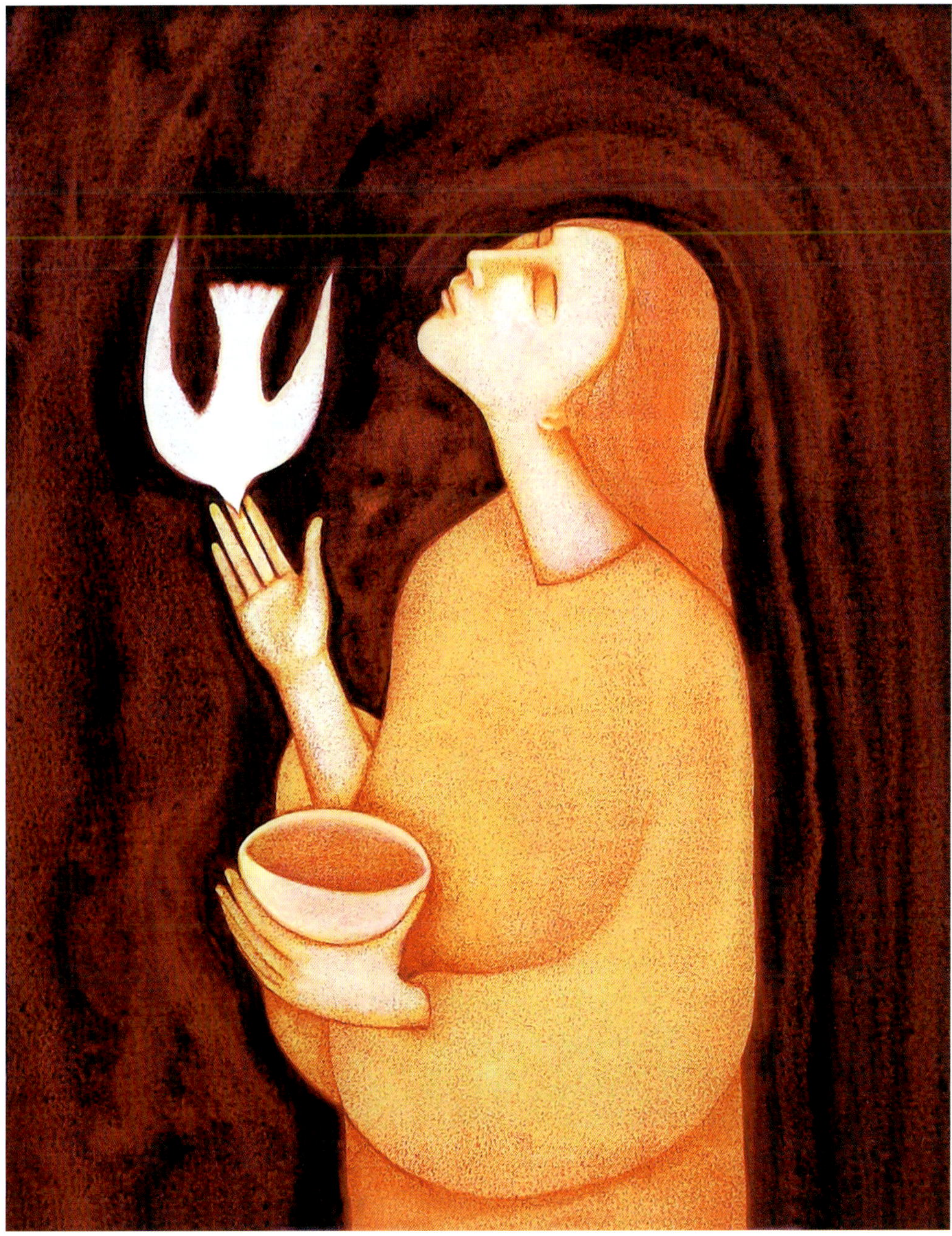

Prayer, 2003–2005, 11 inches by 14 inches

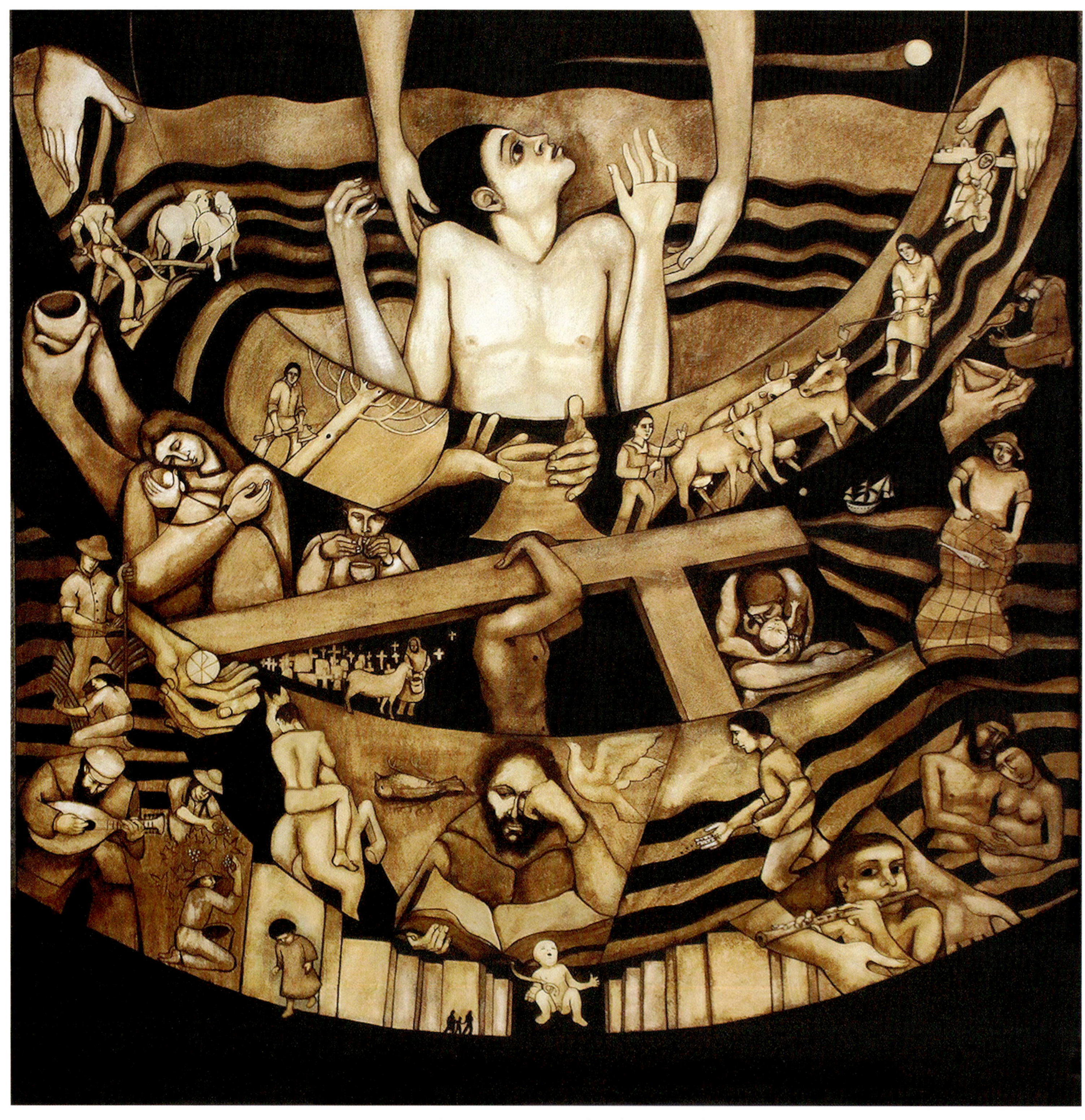

Ora et Labora, 1982, 48 inches by 48 inches

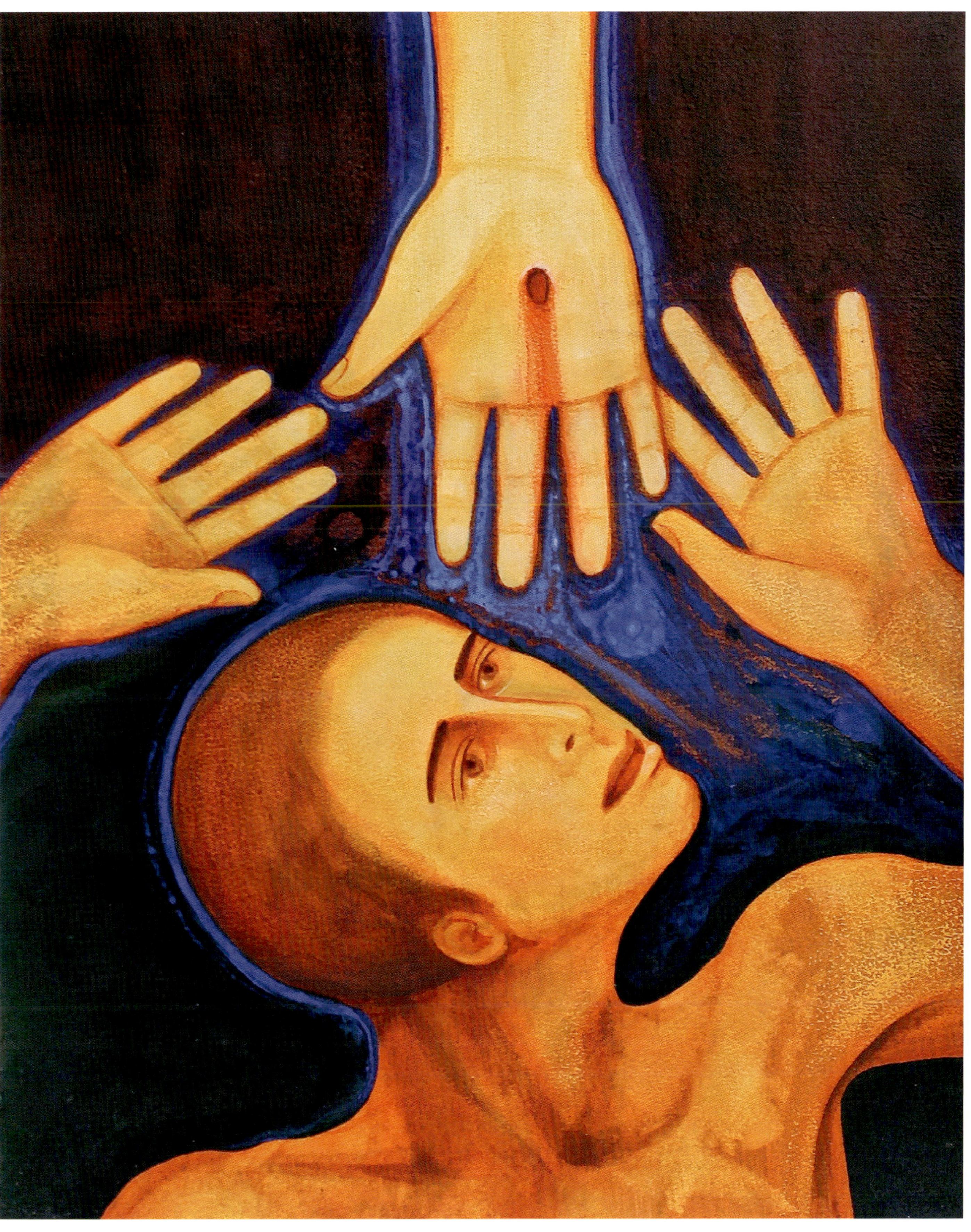

Mercy, 2013

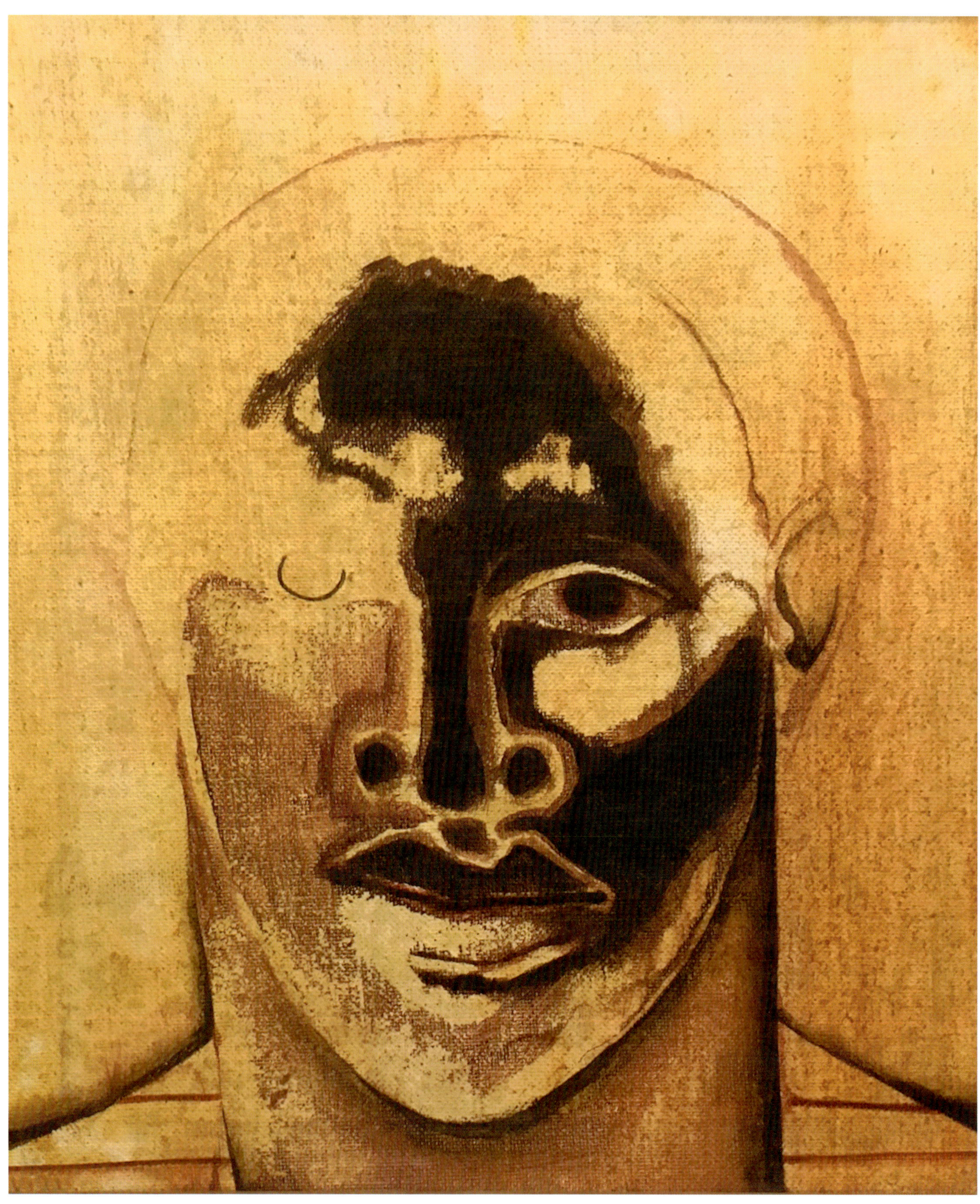

Africa, painted sketch on canvas, 1980

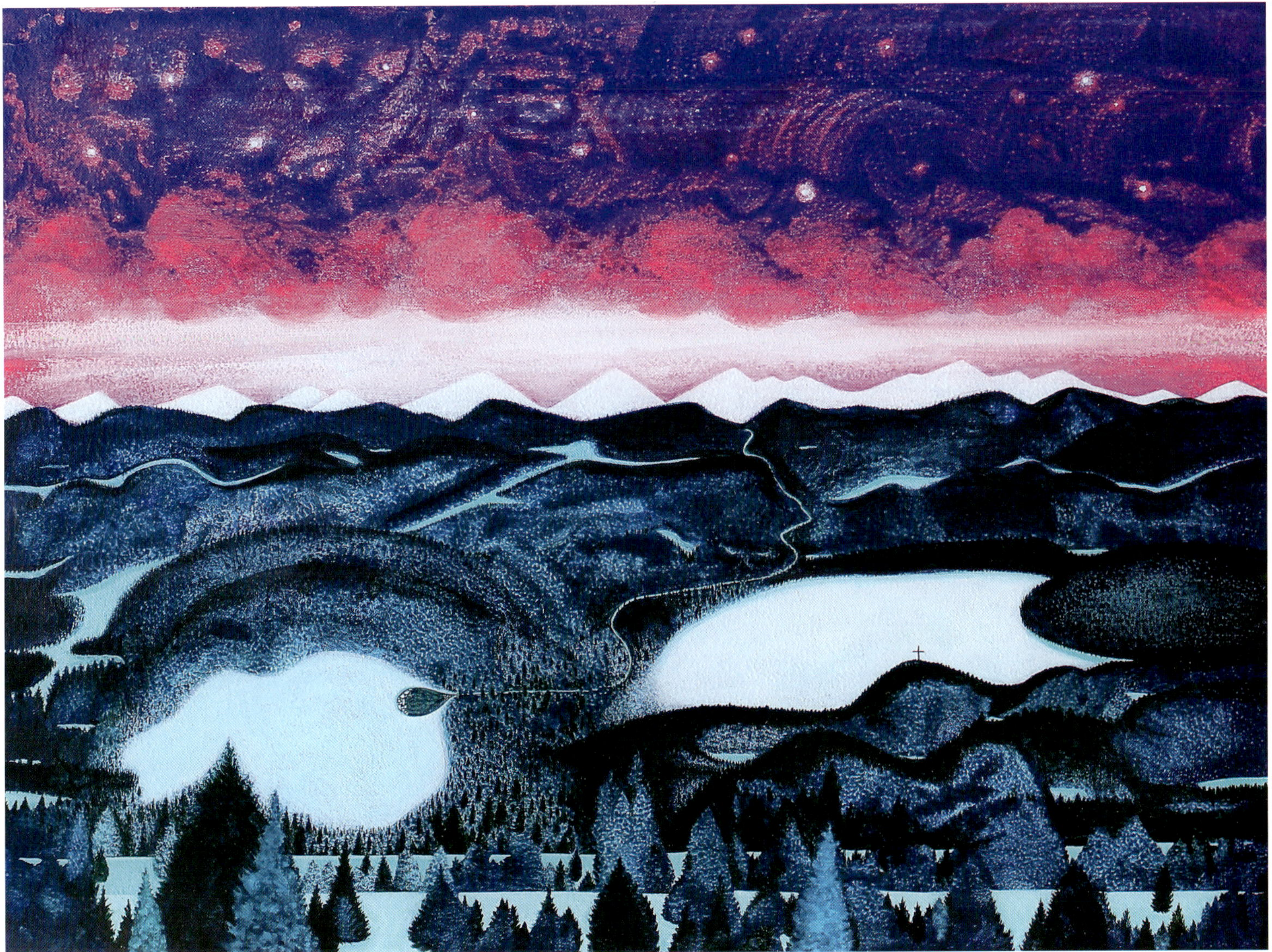

The Cross in the Wilderness, 2016

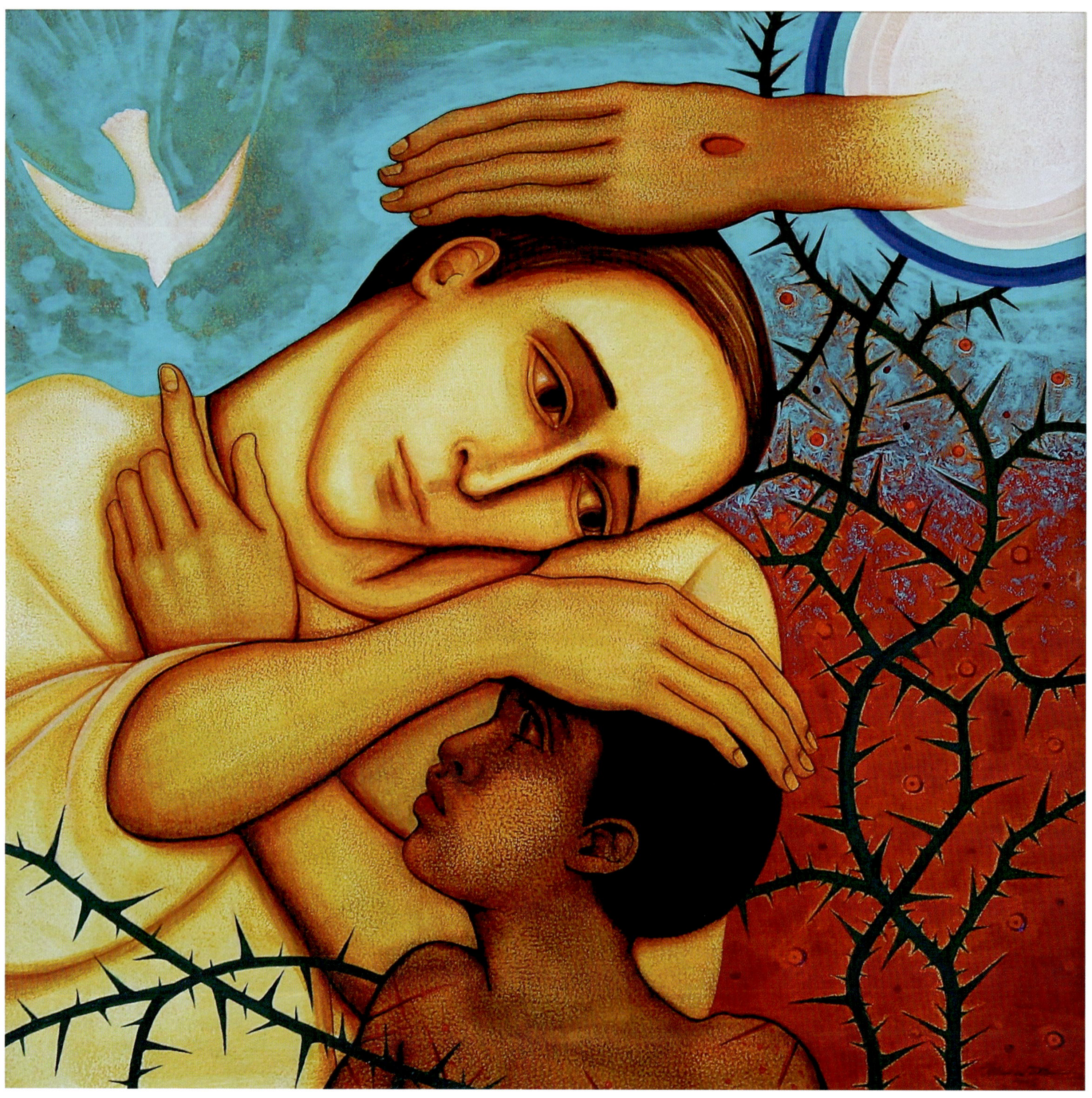

The Healer, 2015, 24 inches by 24 inches

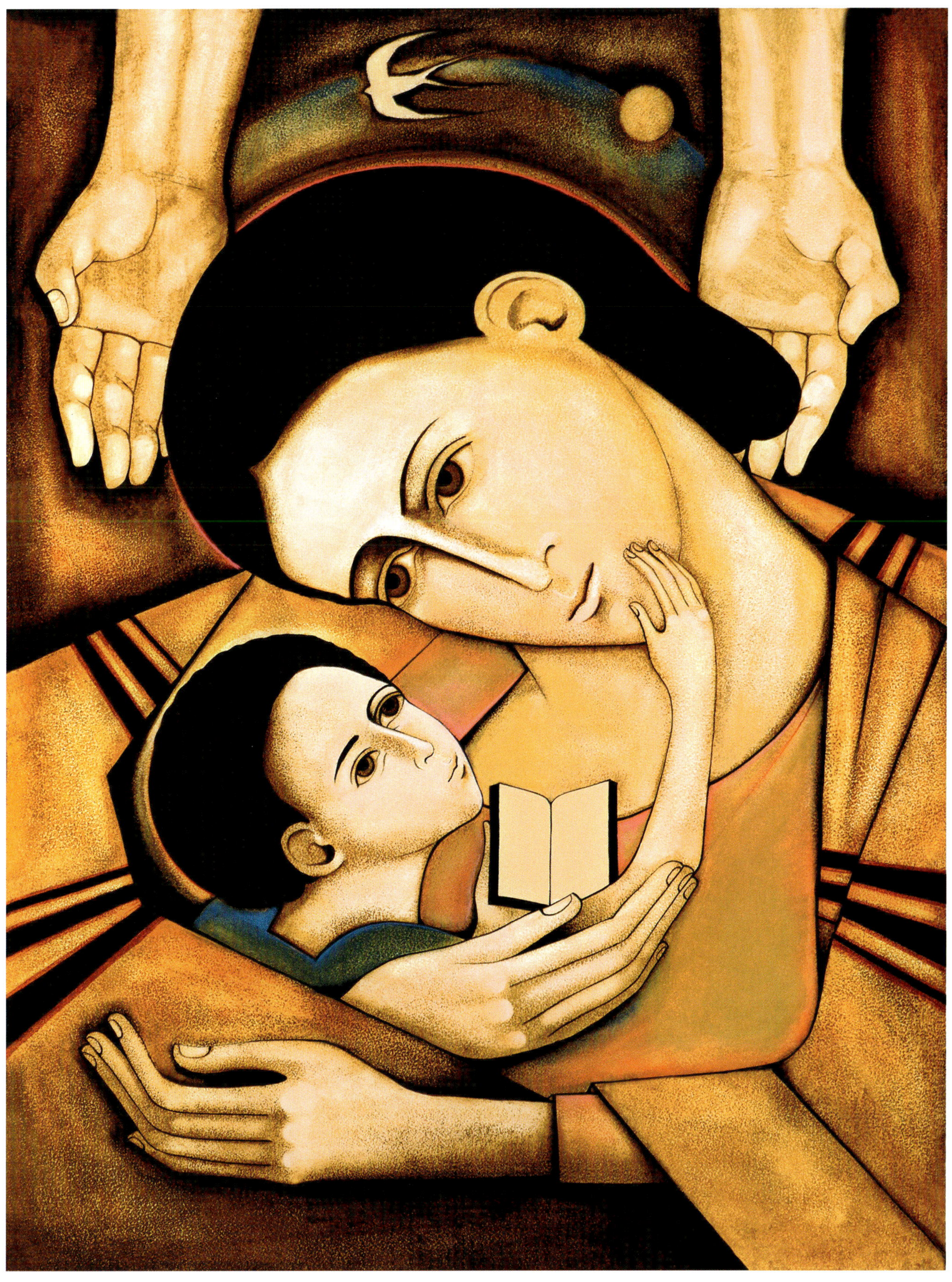

Mother and Child Reading the Word, early 1990s

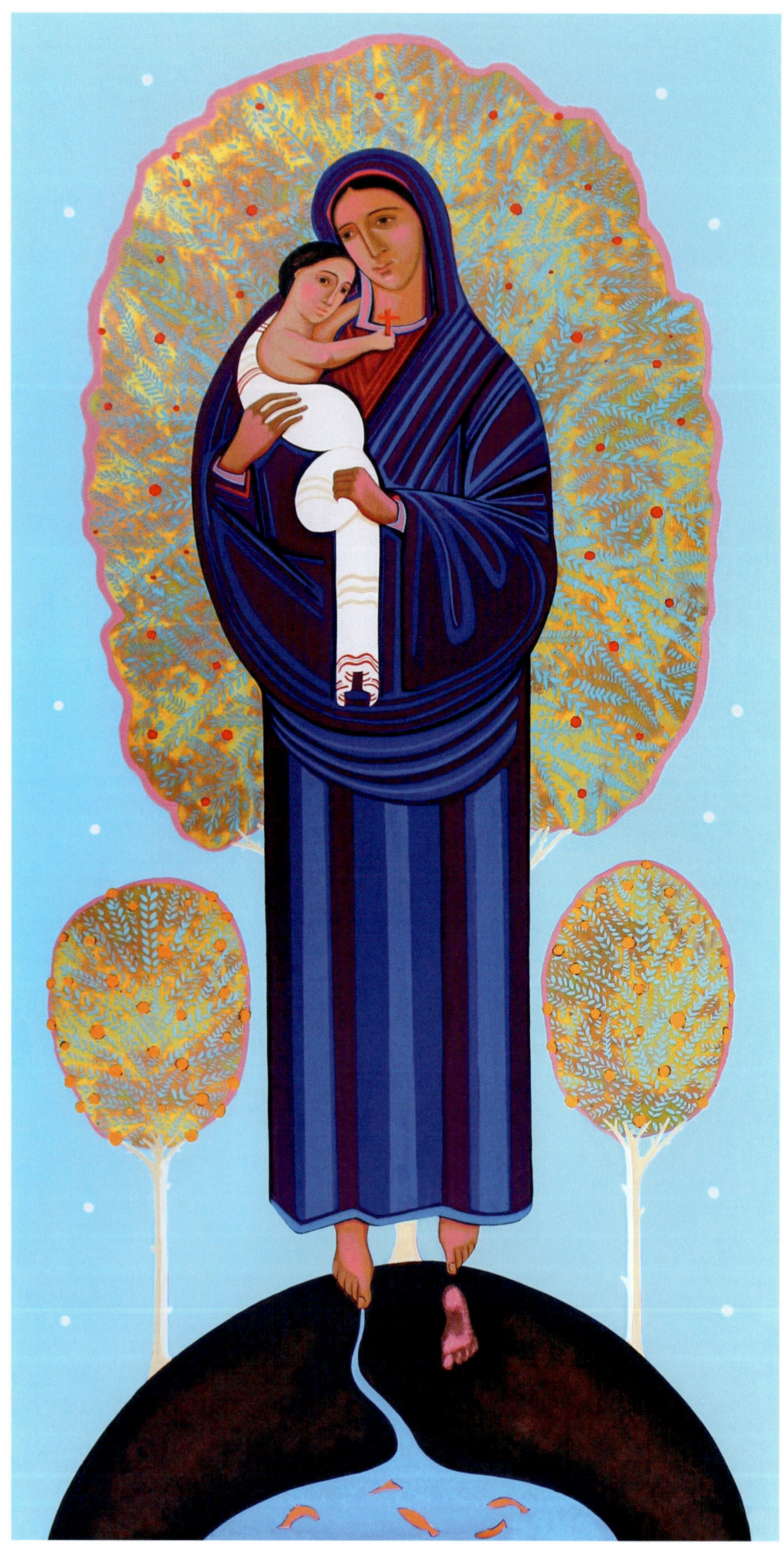

Our Lady of Pochaiv, 1986

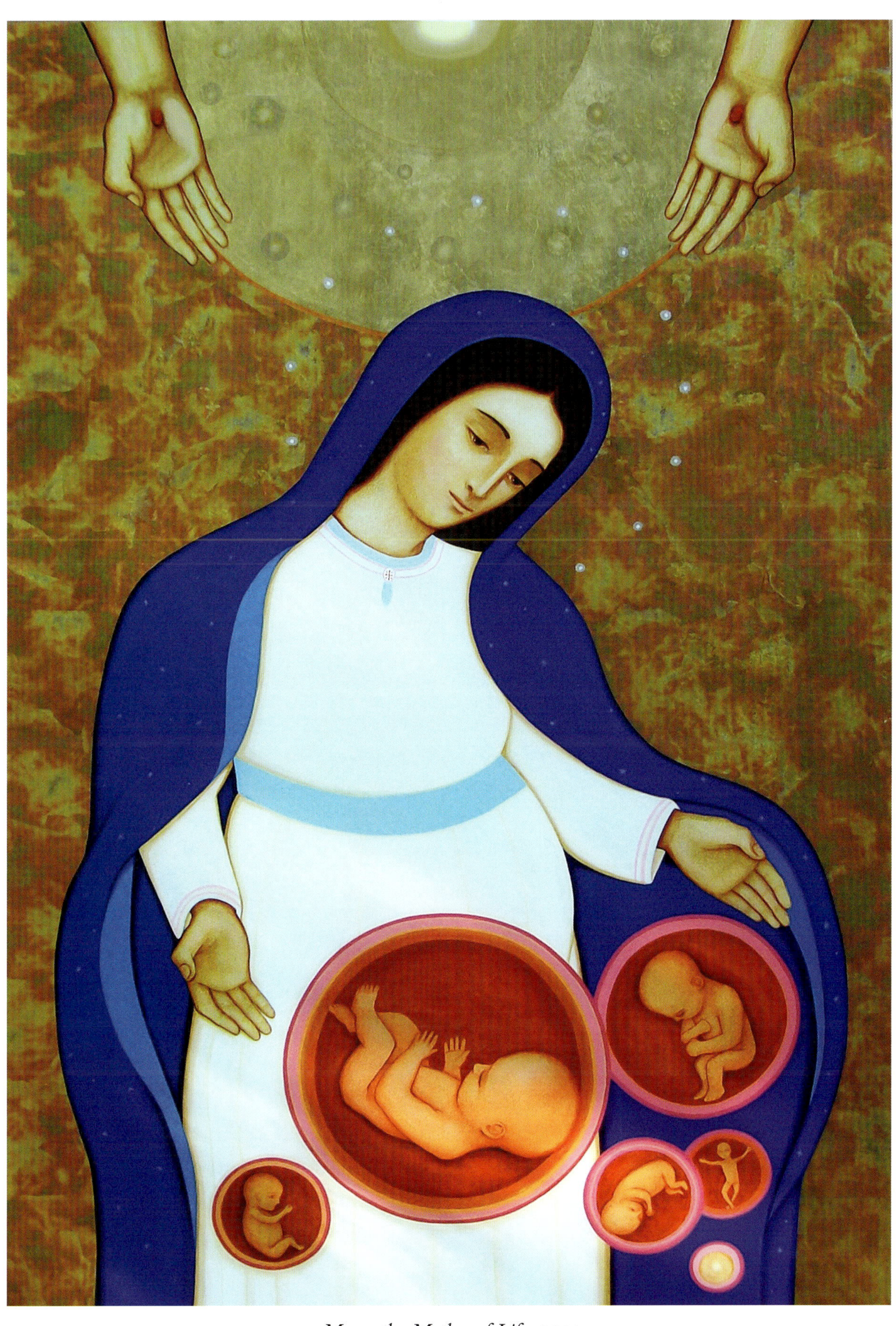

Mary, the Mother of Life, 2013

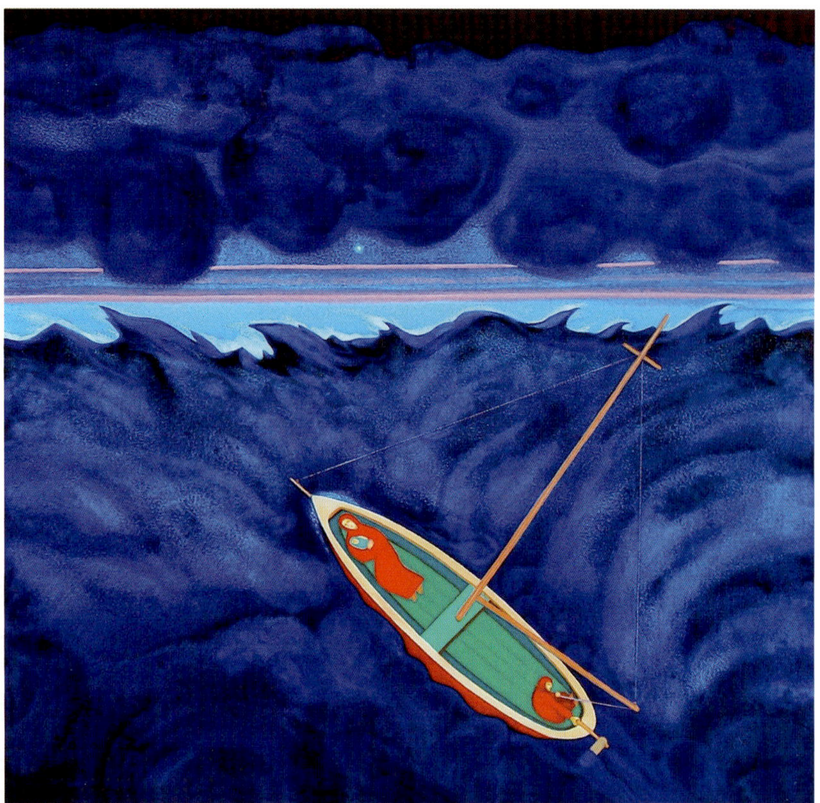

Christmas at Sea, 2012

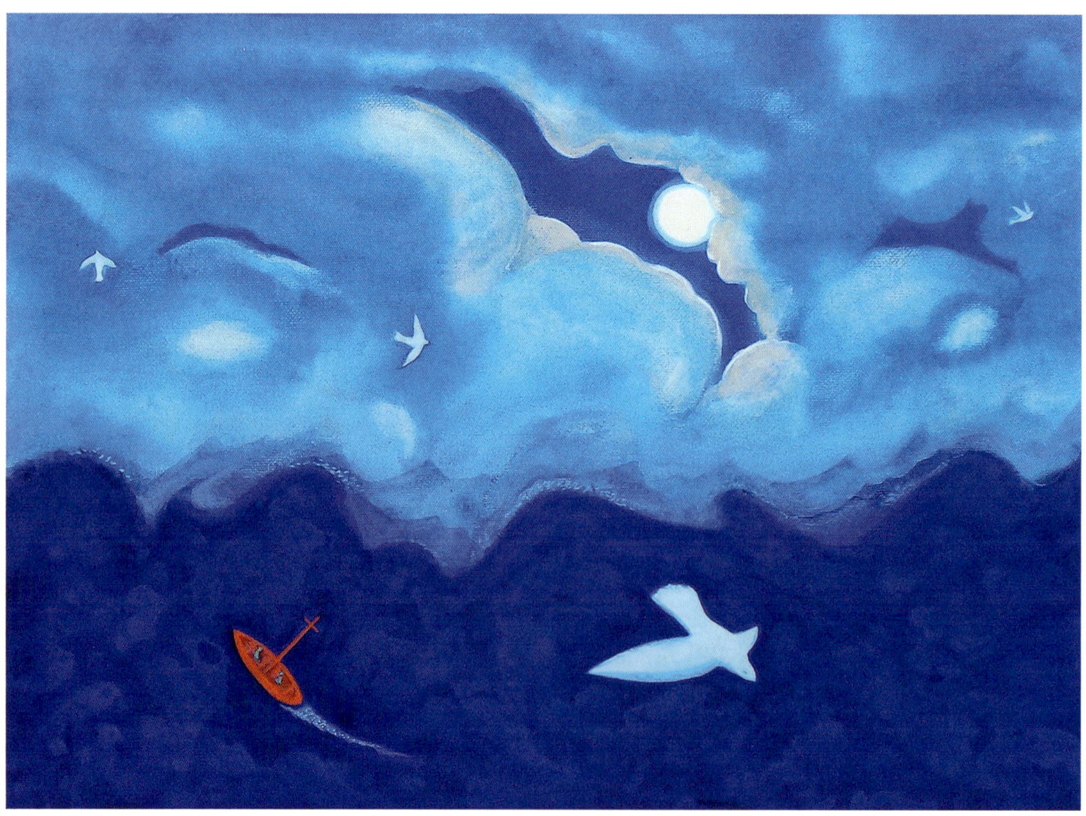

My Little Boat, 2012

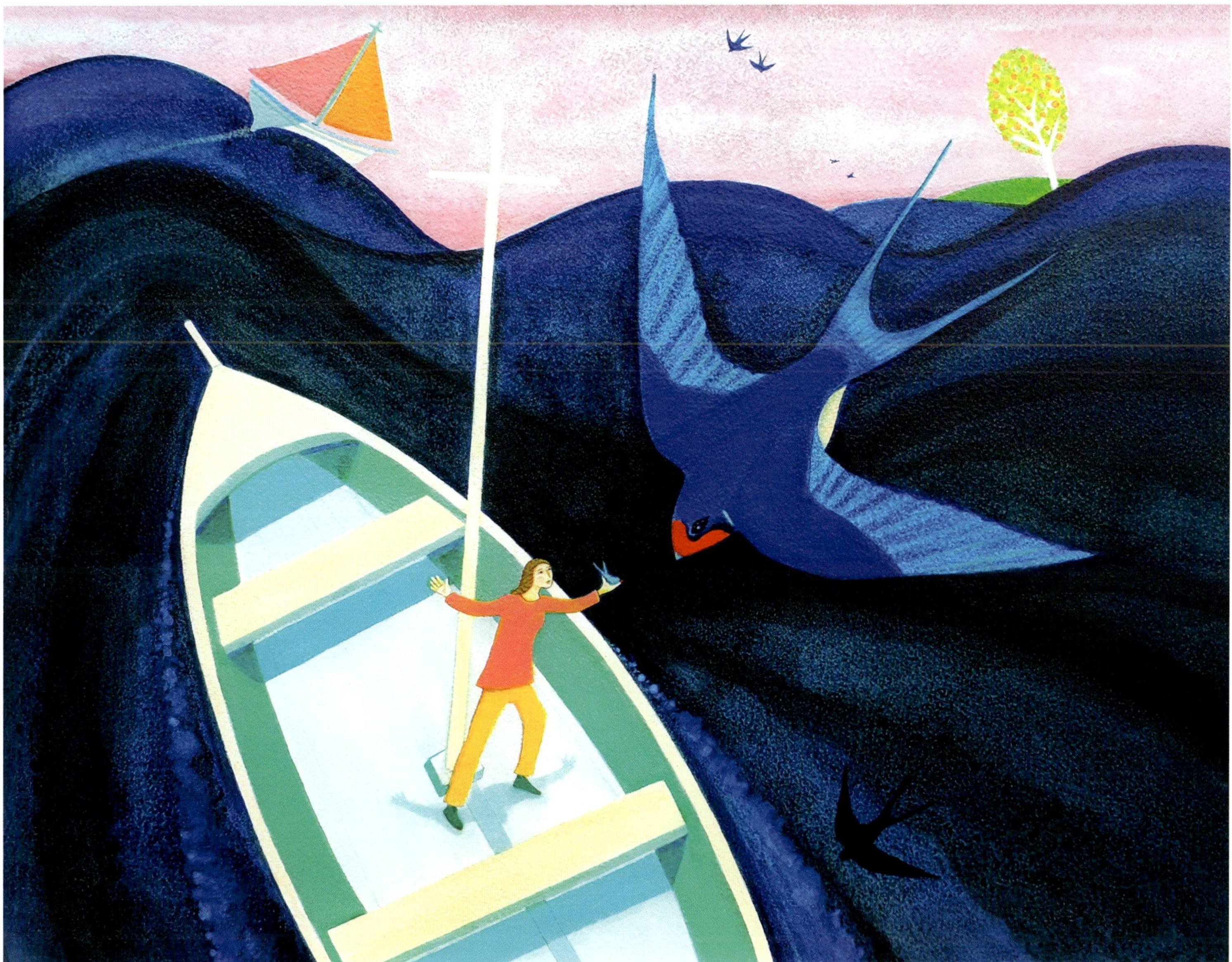

The Swallow, 2016

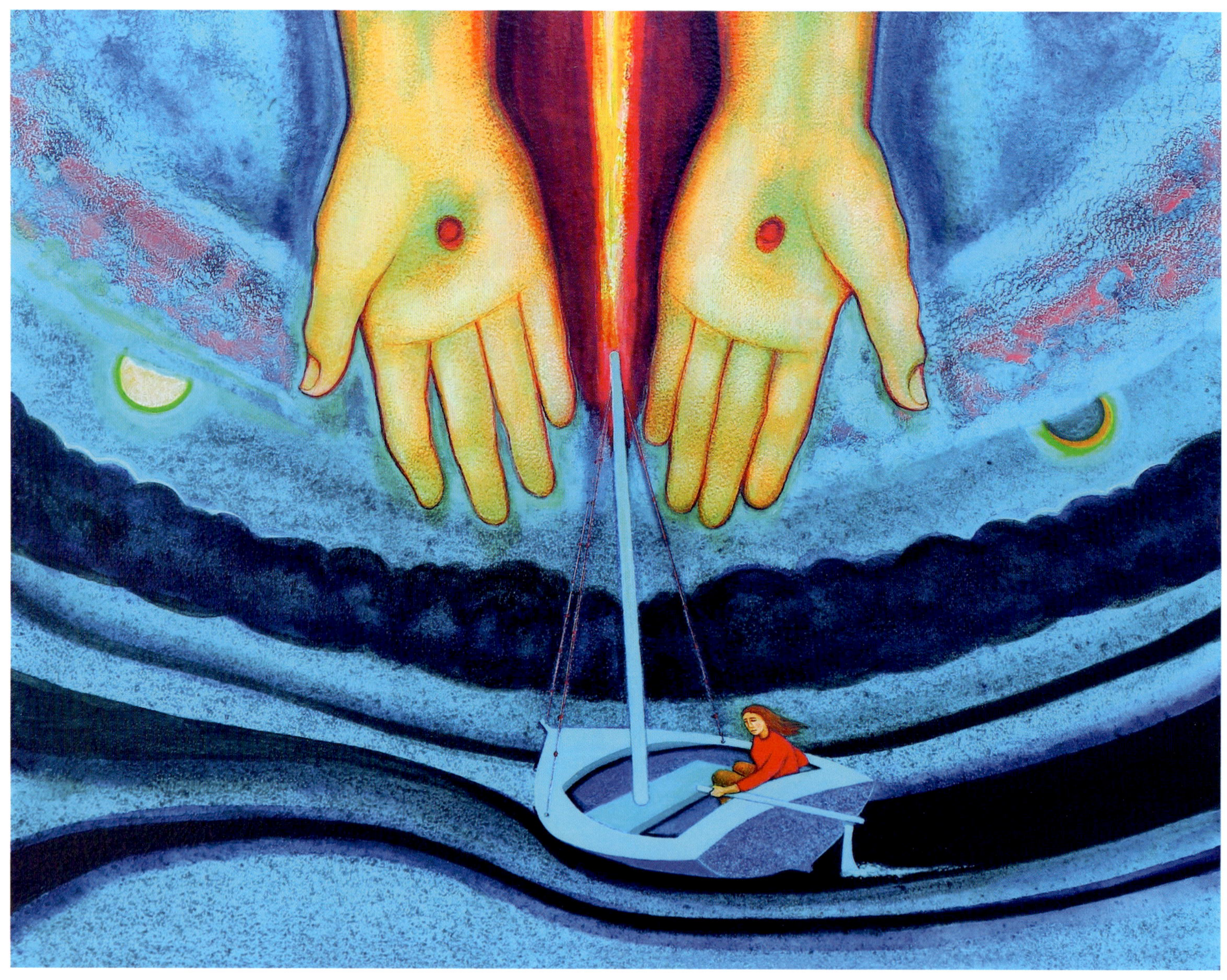

The Voyage, 2017, 16 inches by 20 inches

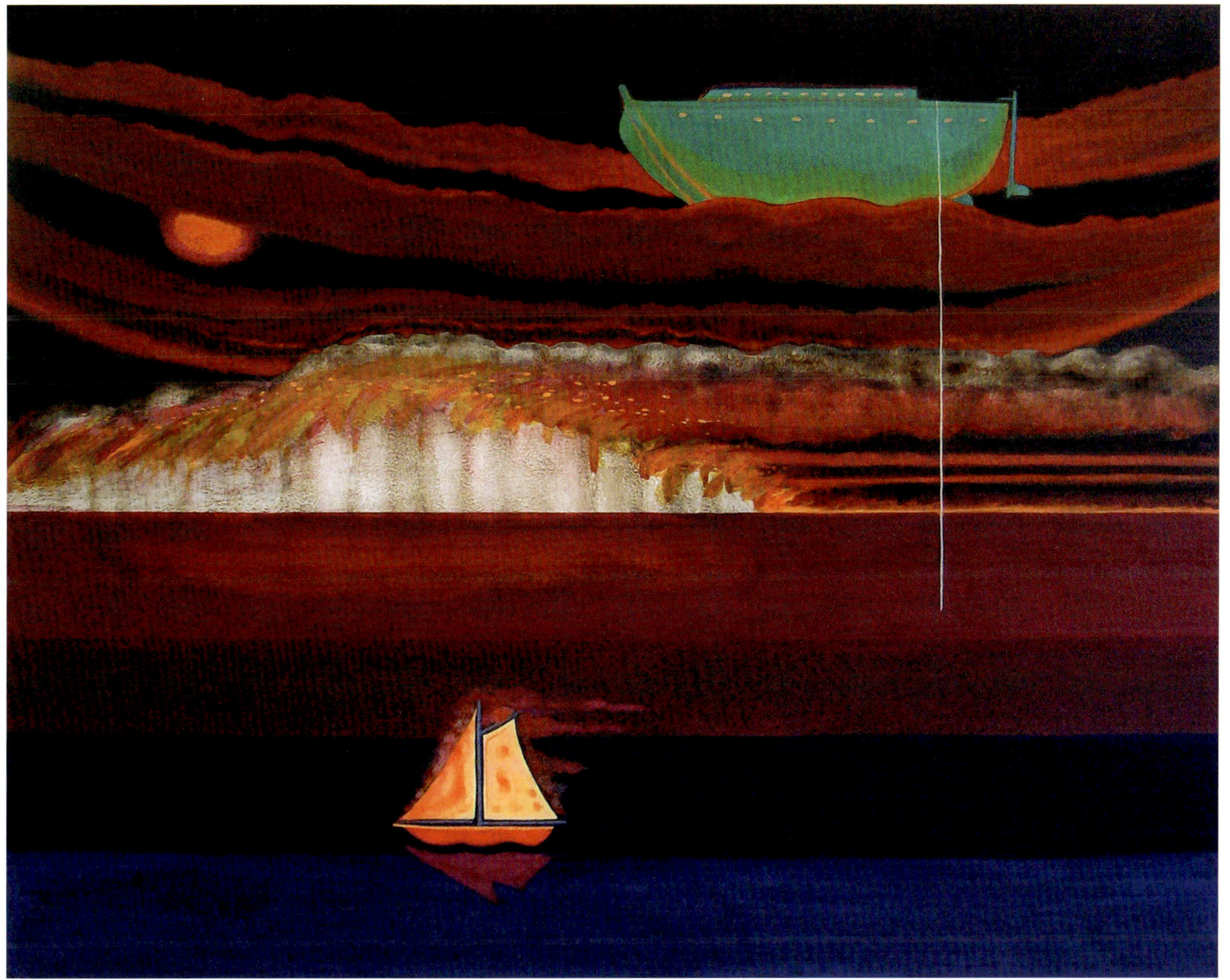

Look Up!, 2008

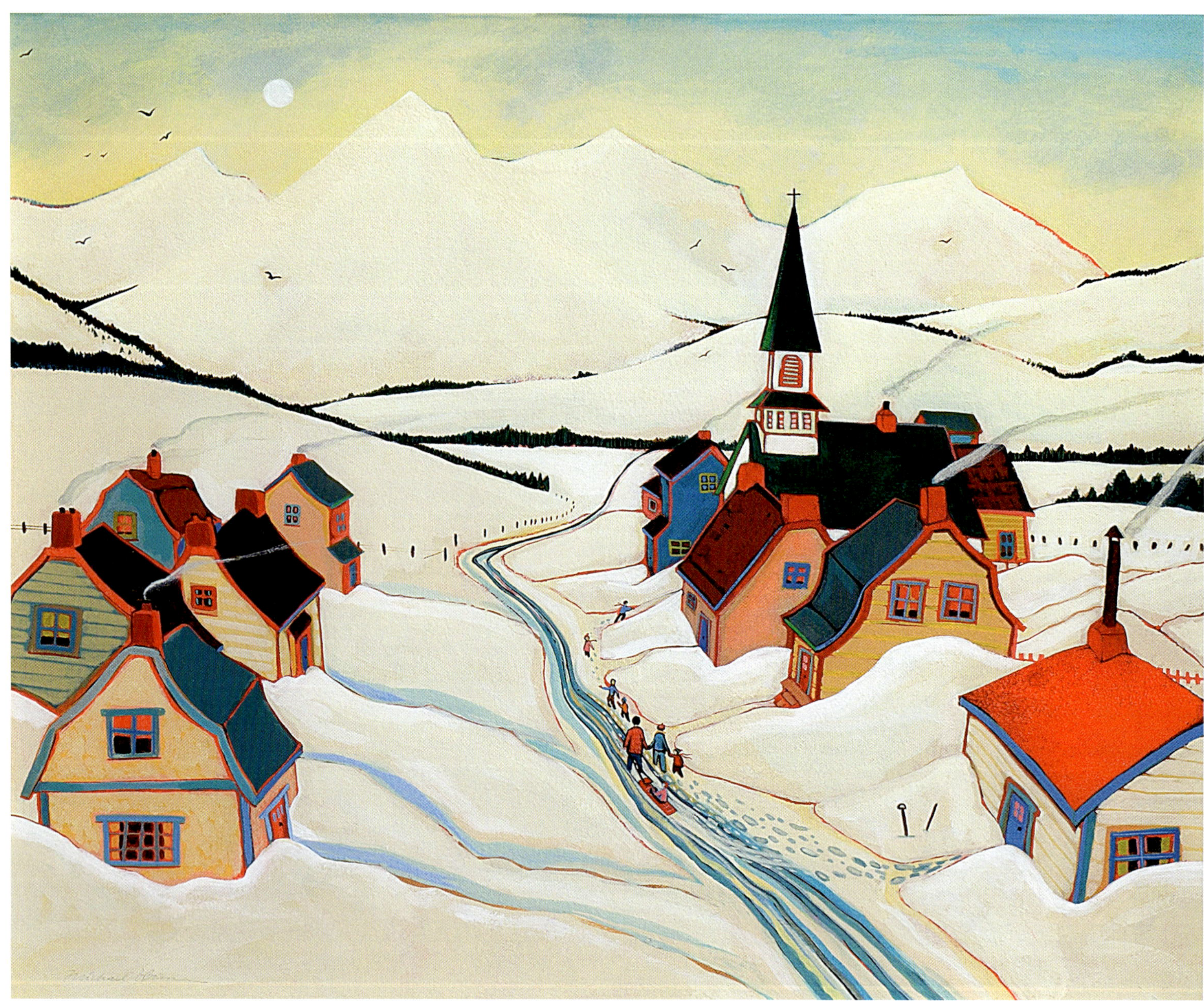

A Place Where We All Could Live, 1986, 20 inches by 24 inches

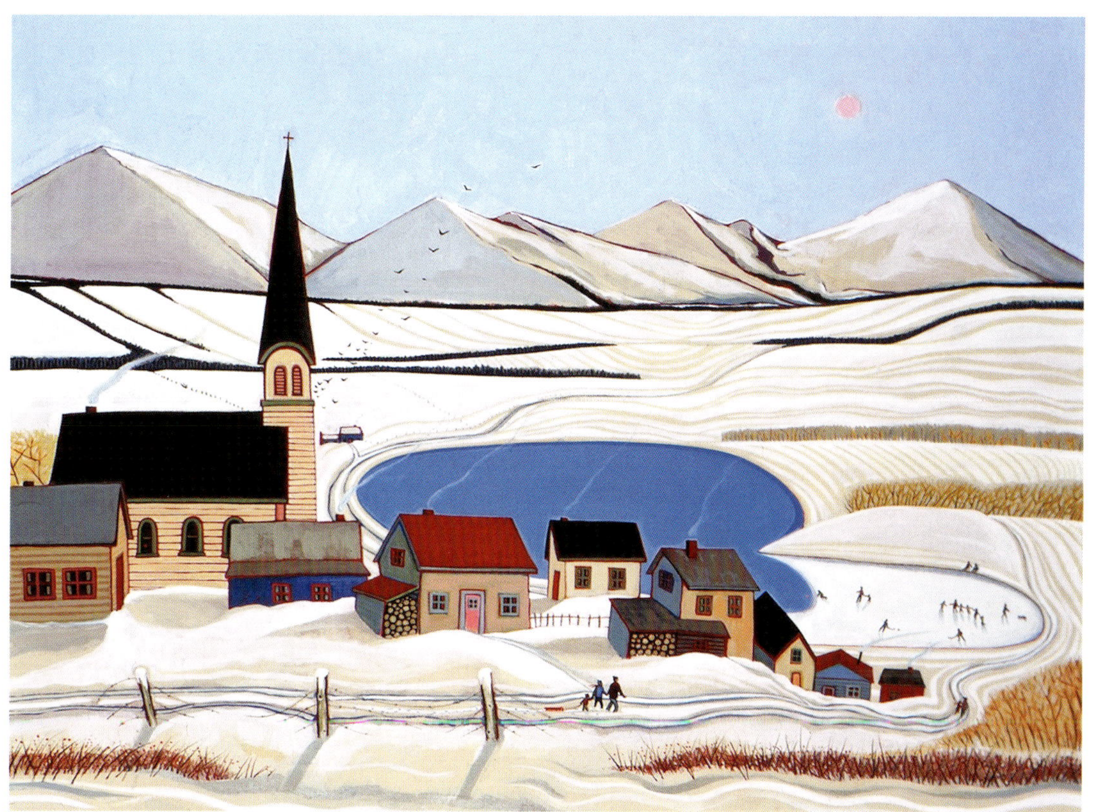

A Place Where We All Could Live, 1987, 20 inches by 24 inches

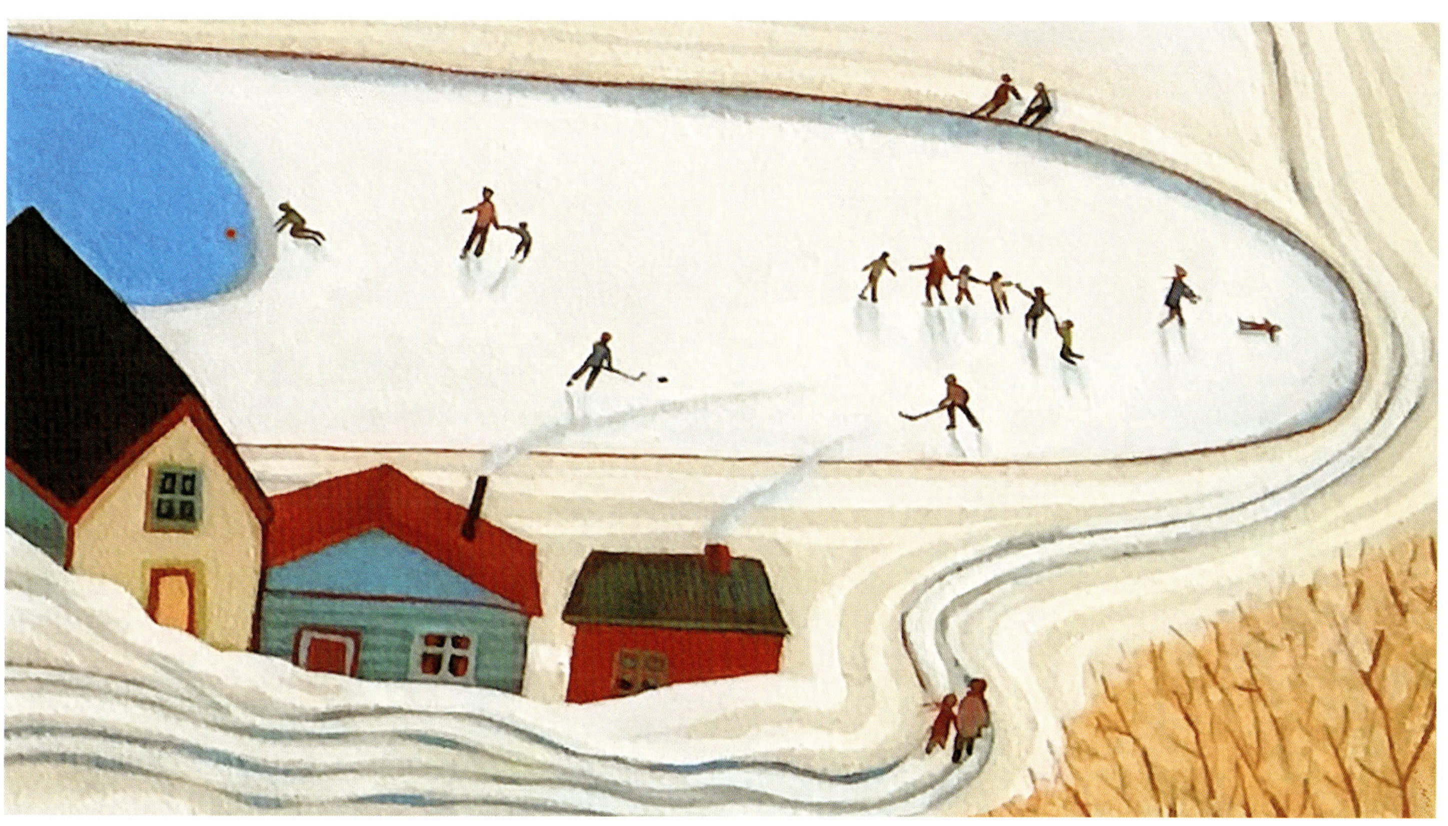

A Place Where We All Could Live, detail

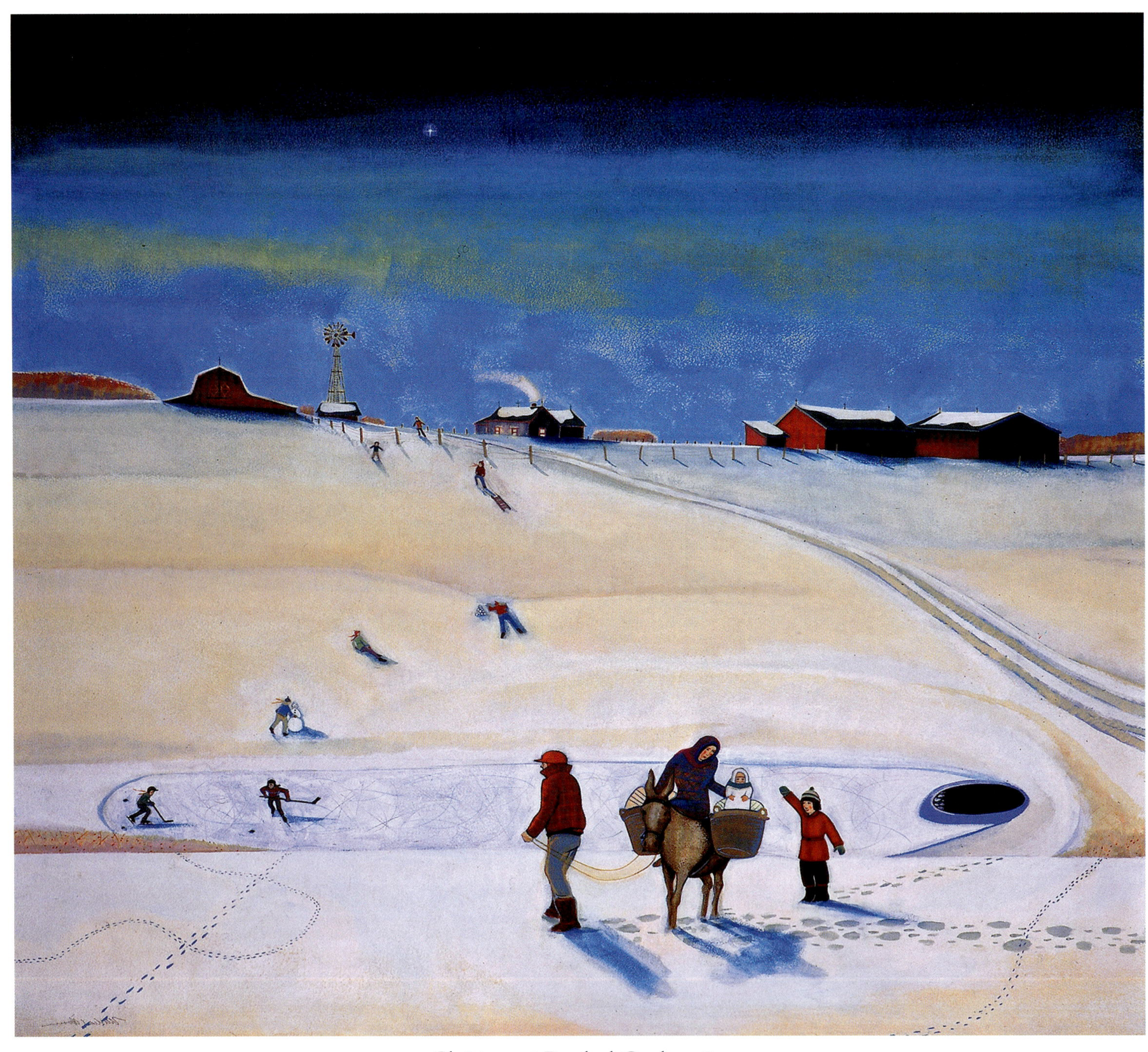

Christmas at Rosebud Creek, 1989

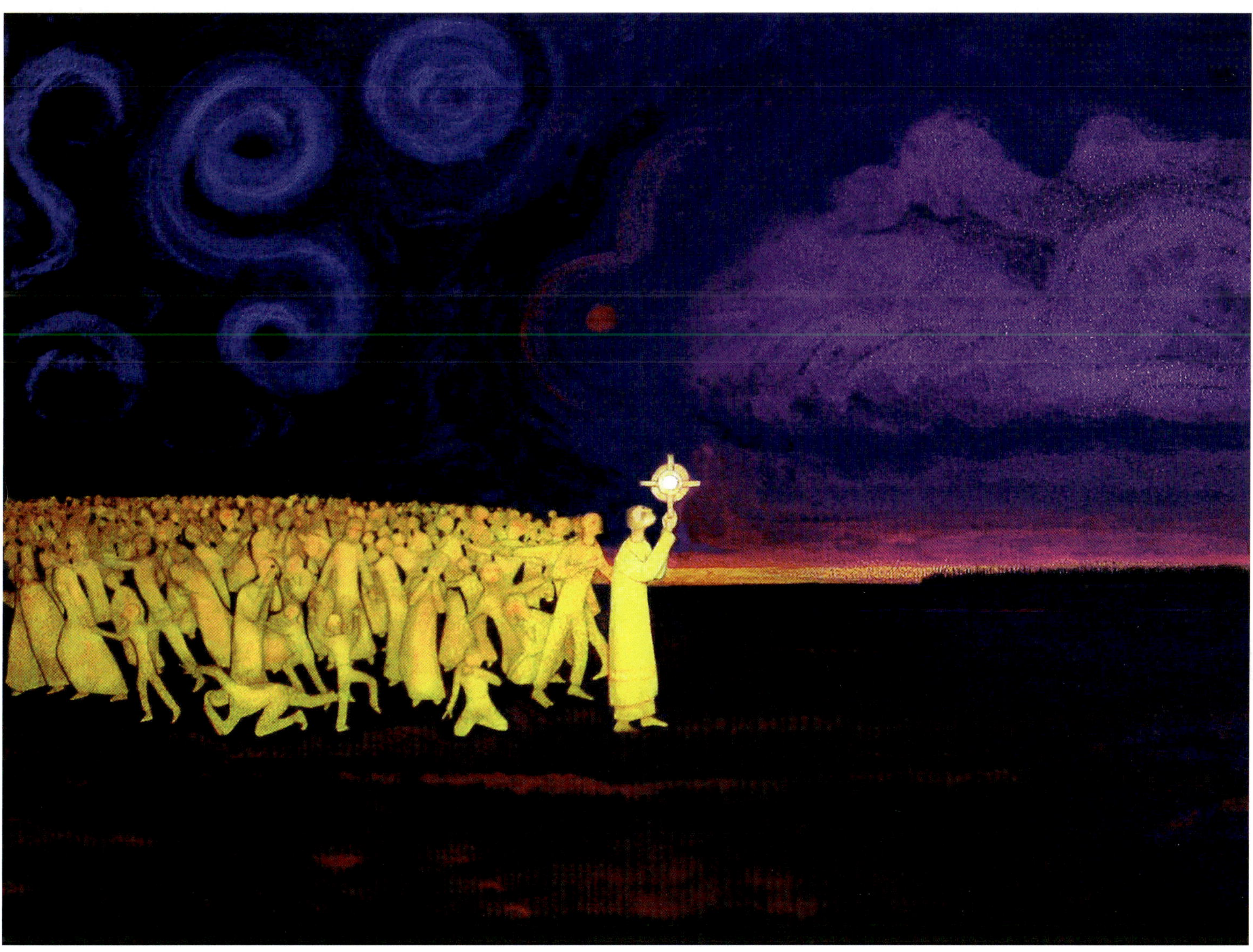

The New Exodus, 2000–2005

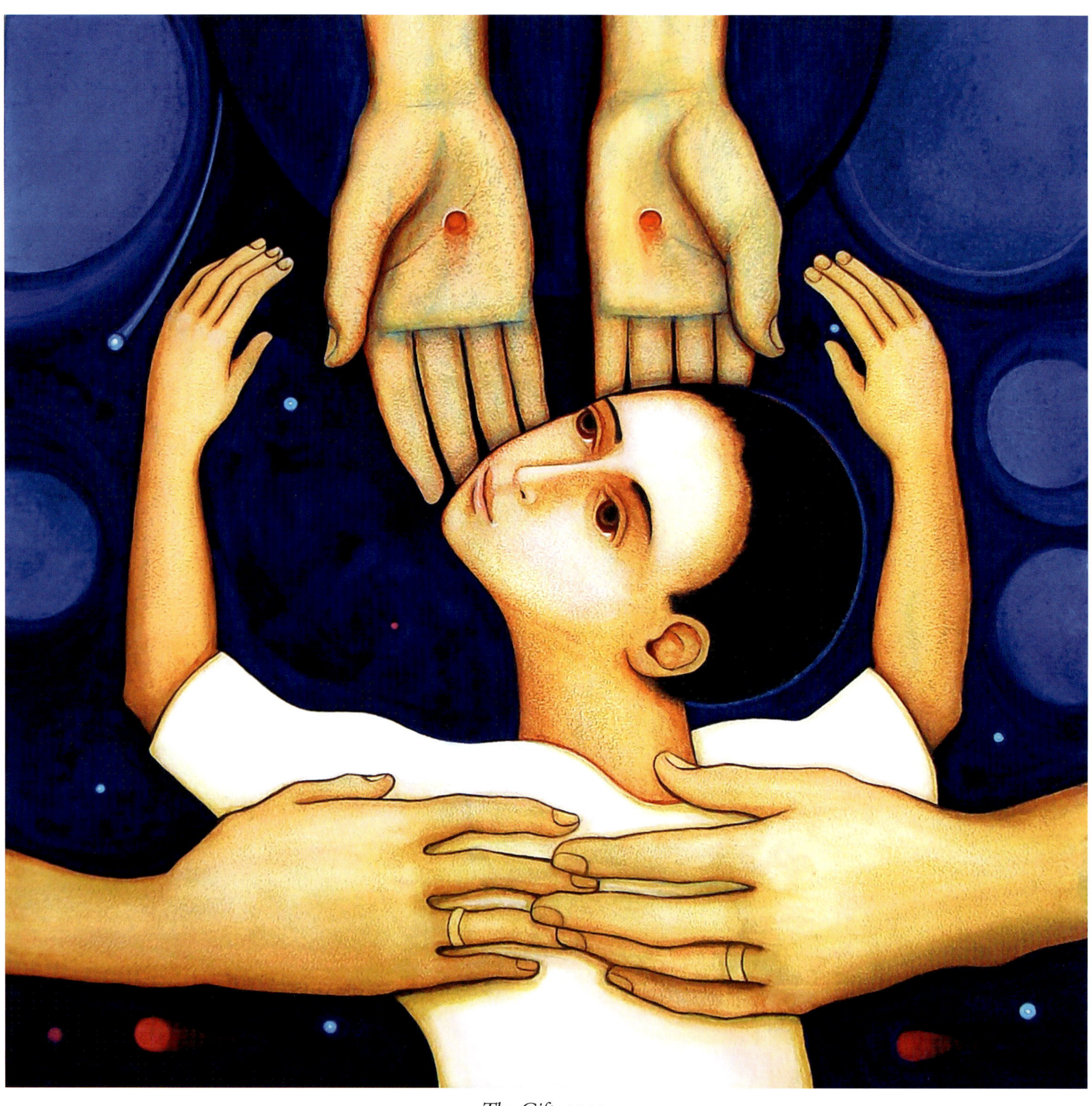

The Gift, 2012

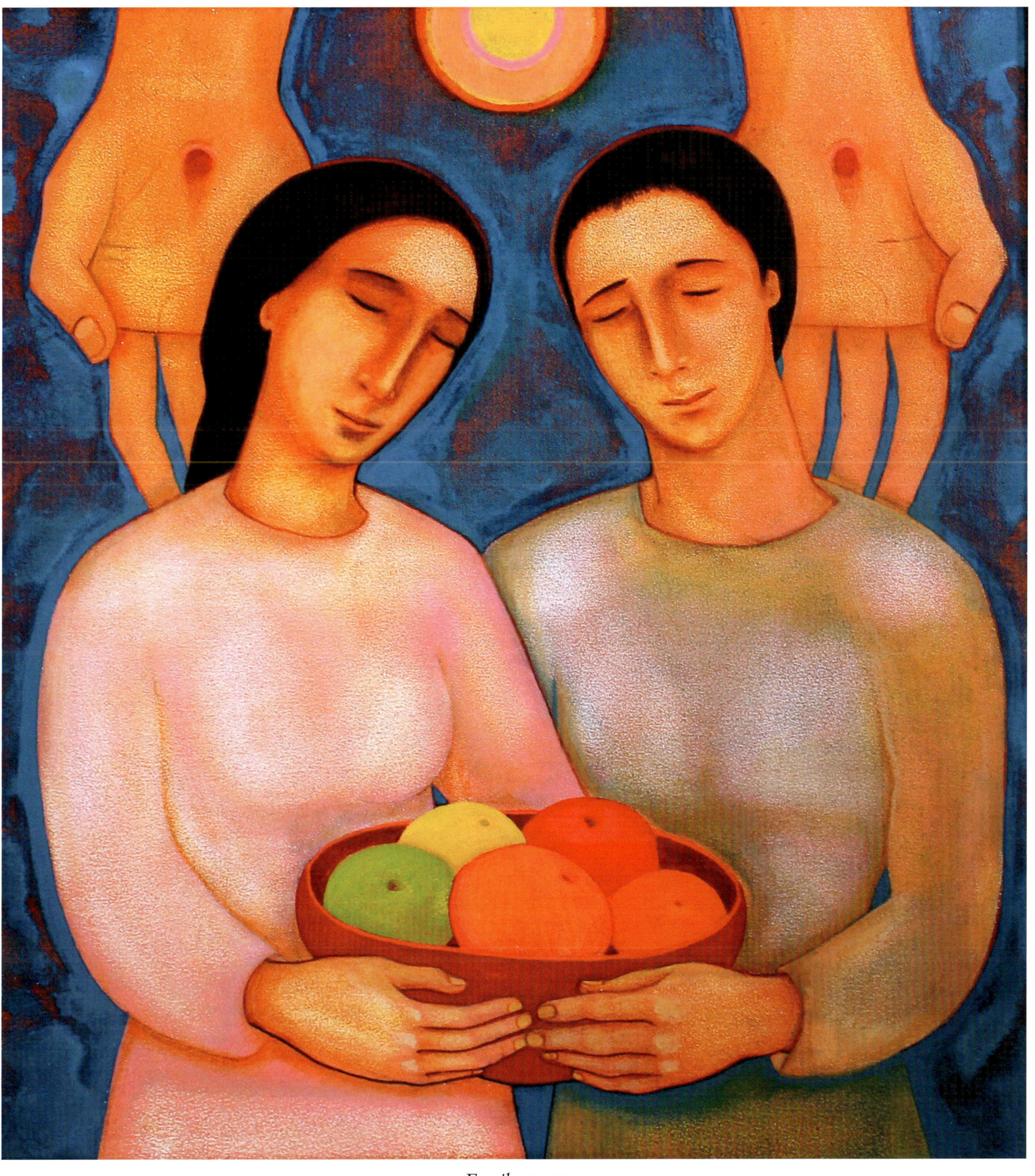

Family, 2014

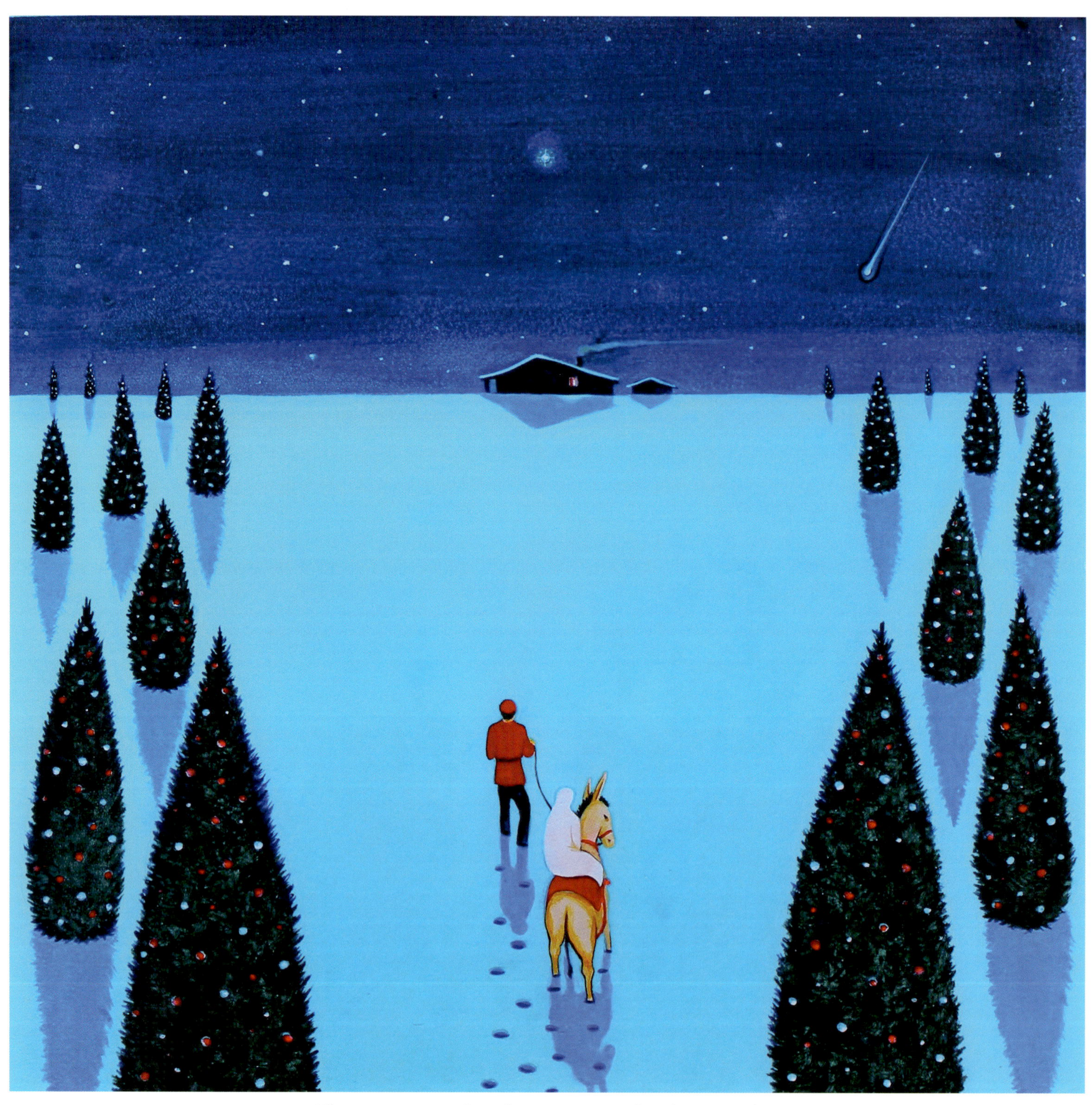

Christmas Eve in Canada, 2014, 15 inches by 15 inches

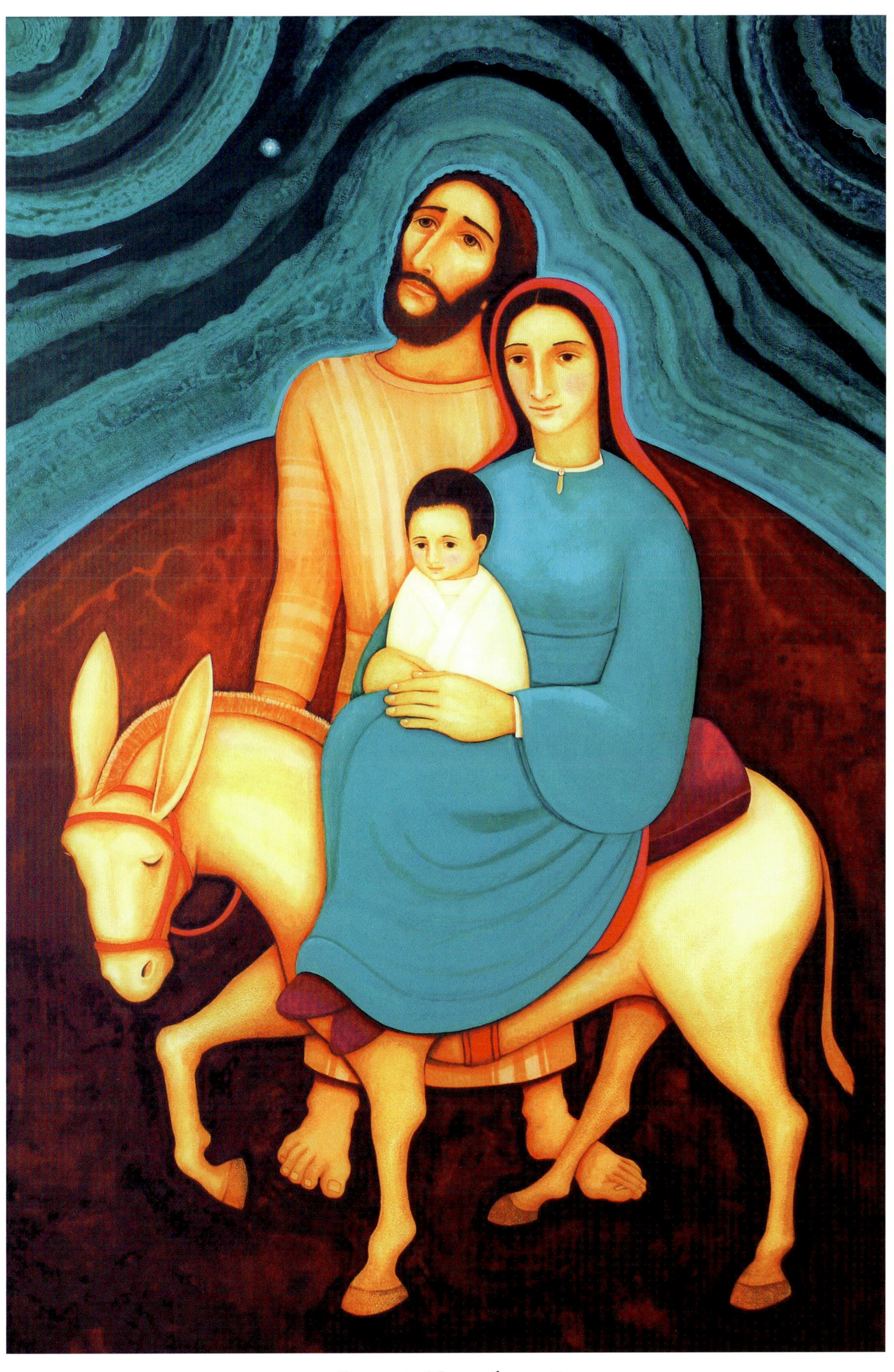

Return to Nazareth, 2016

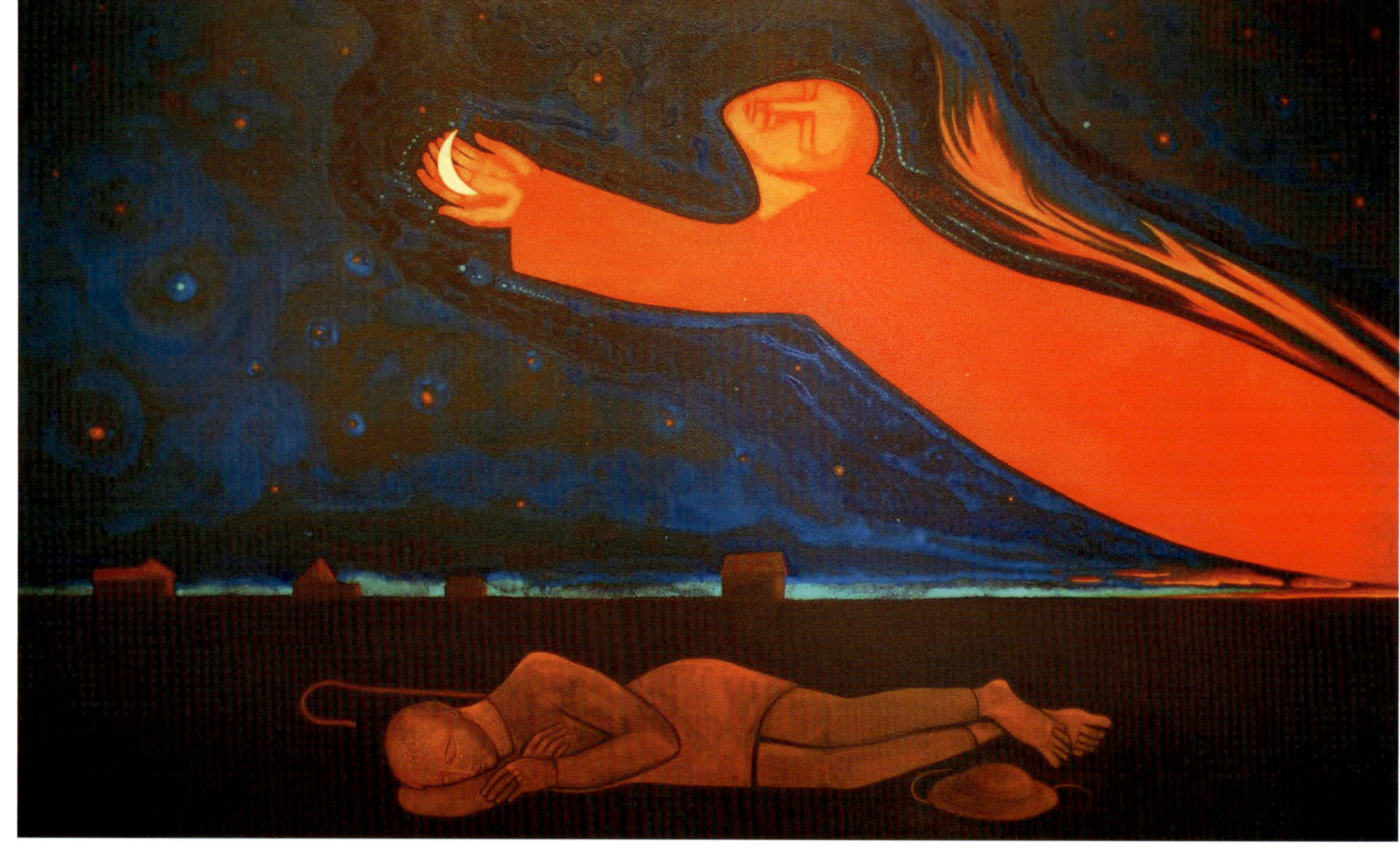

Angel of the Dawn, 2001

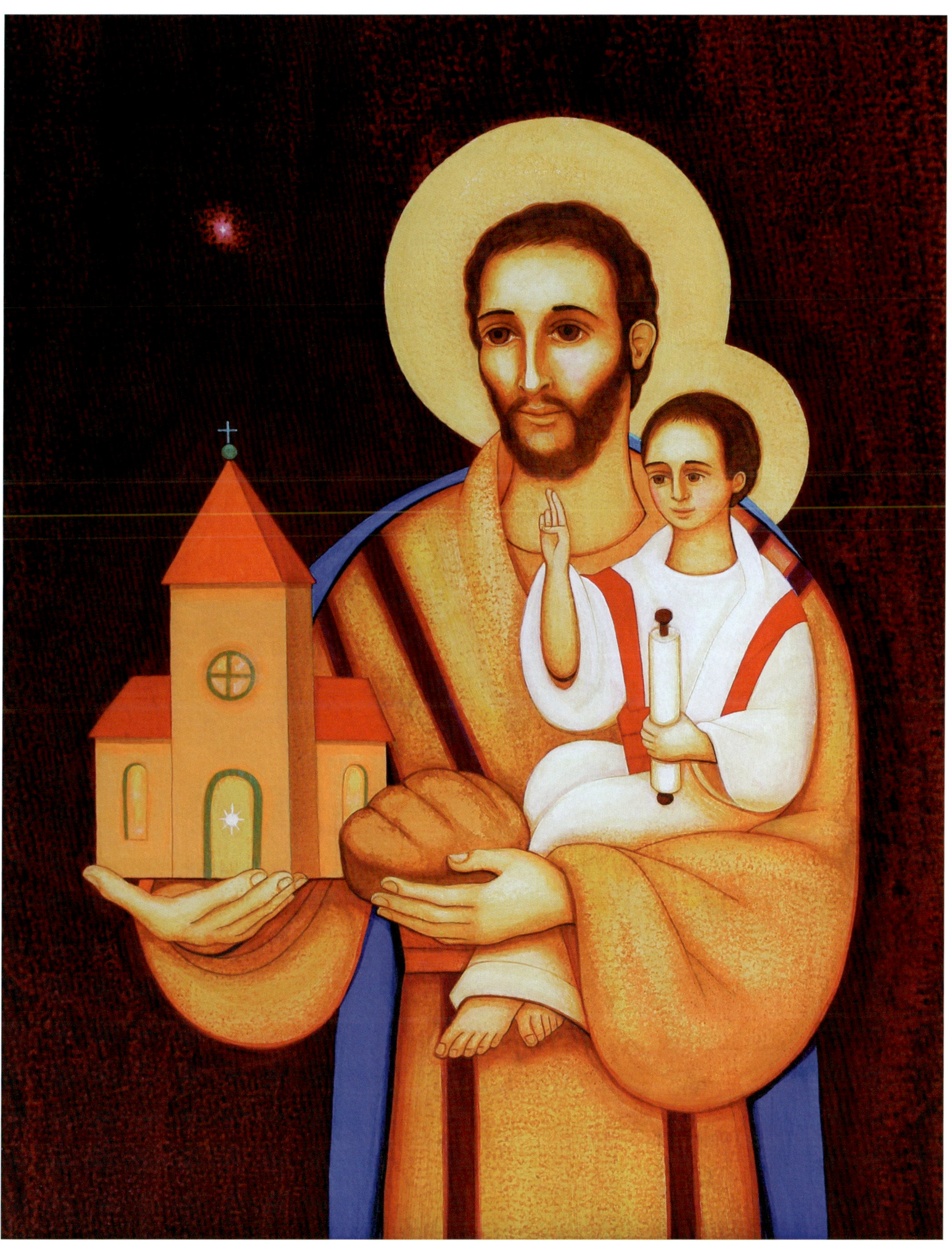

St. Joseph the Provider, 2017, 22 inches by 30 inches

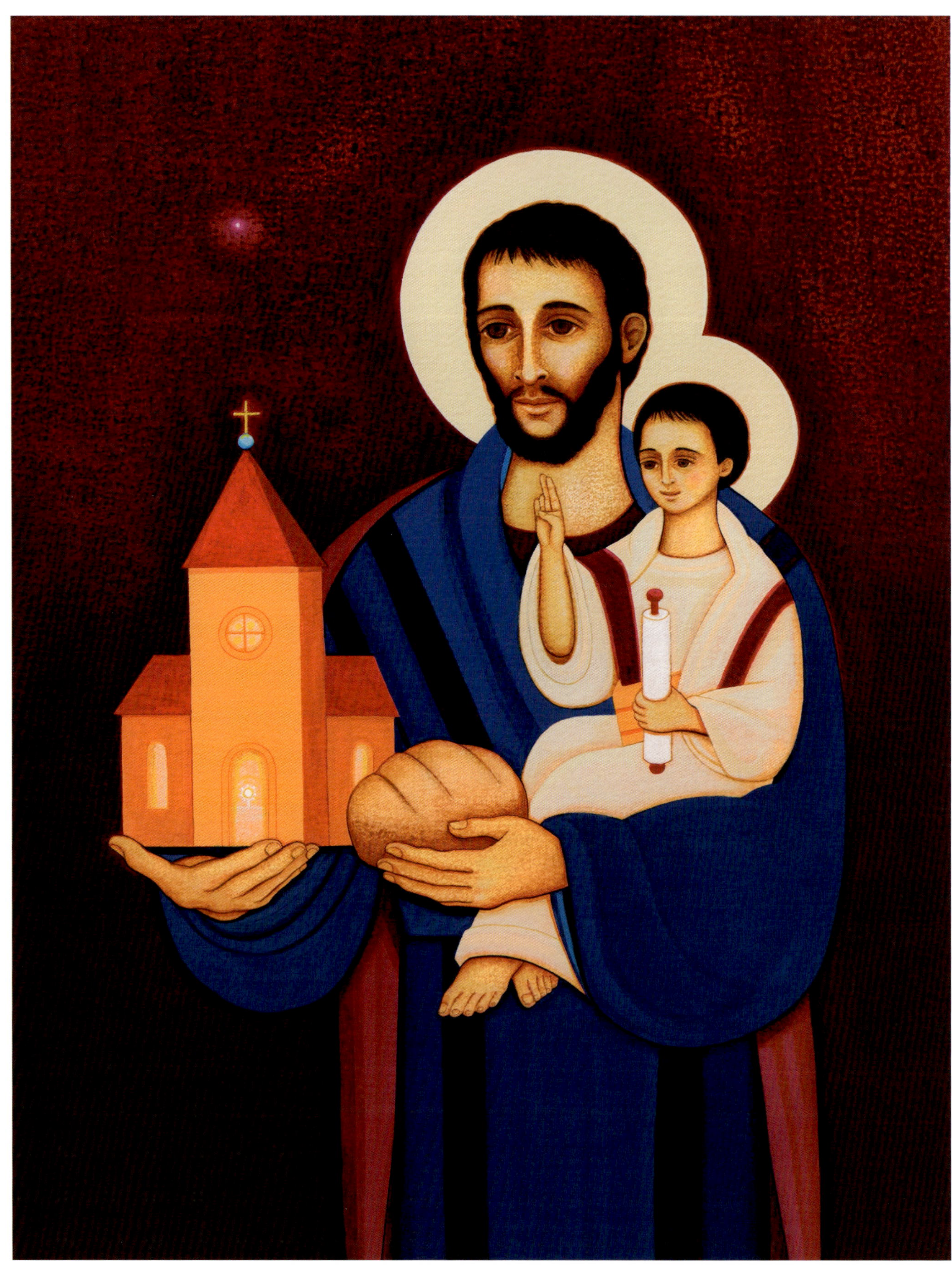

St. Joseph the Provider, 2018, 22 inches by 30 inches

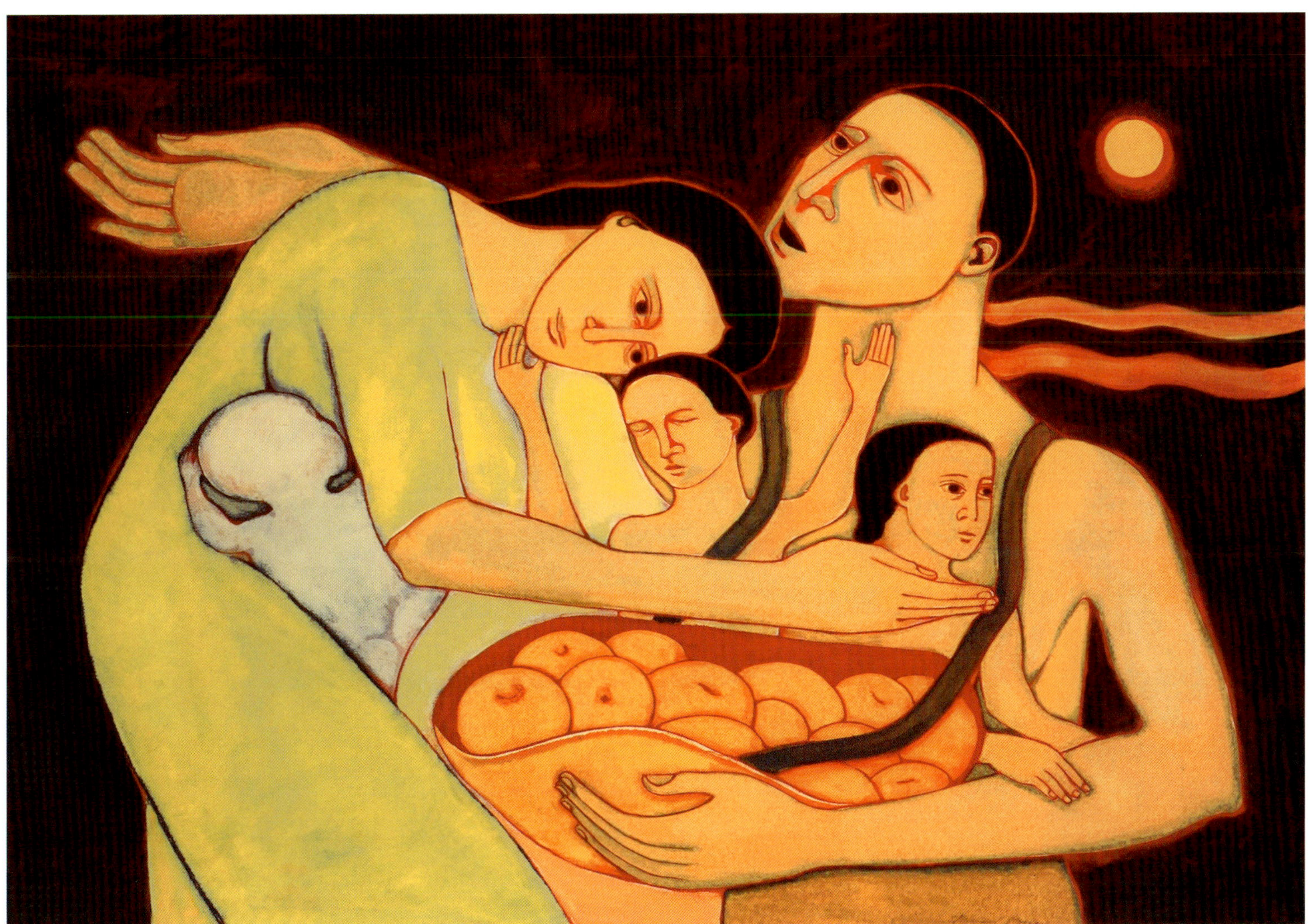

Where Are the Missing Children?, 1984

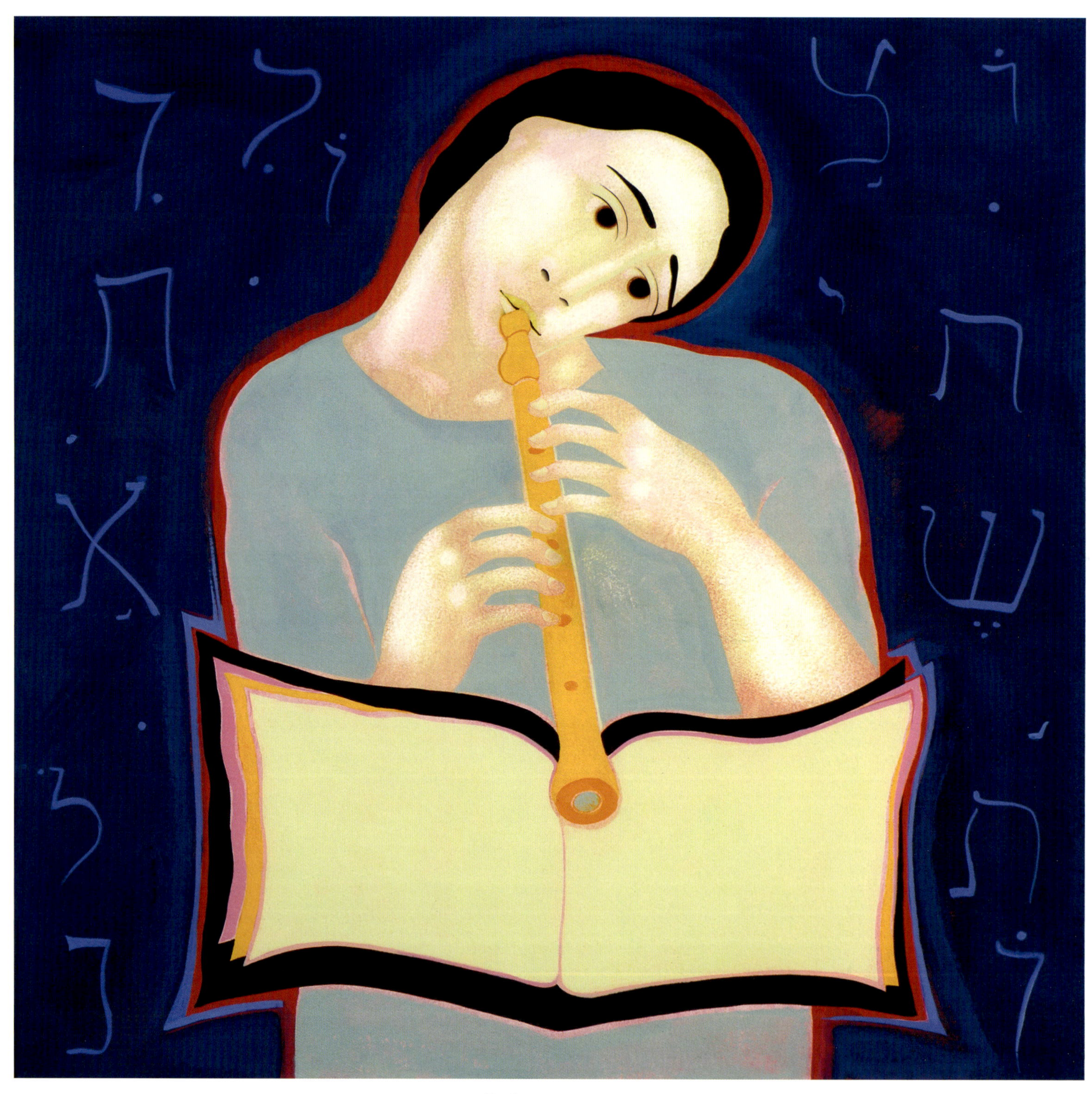

Psalm 23, 1993

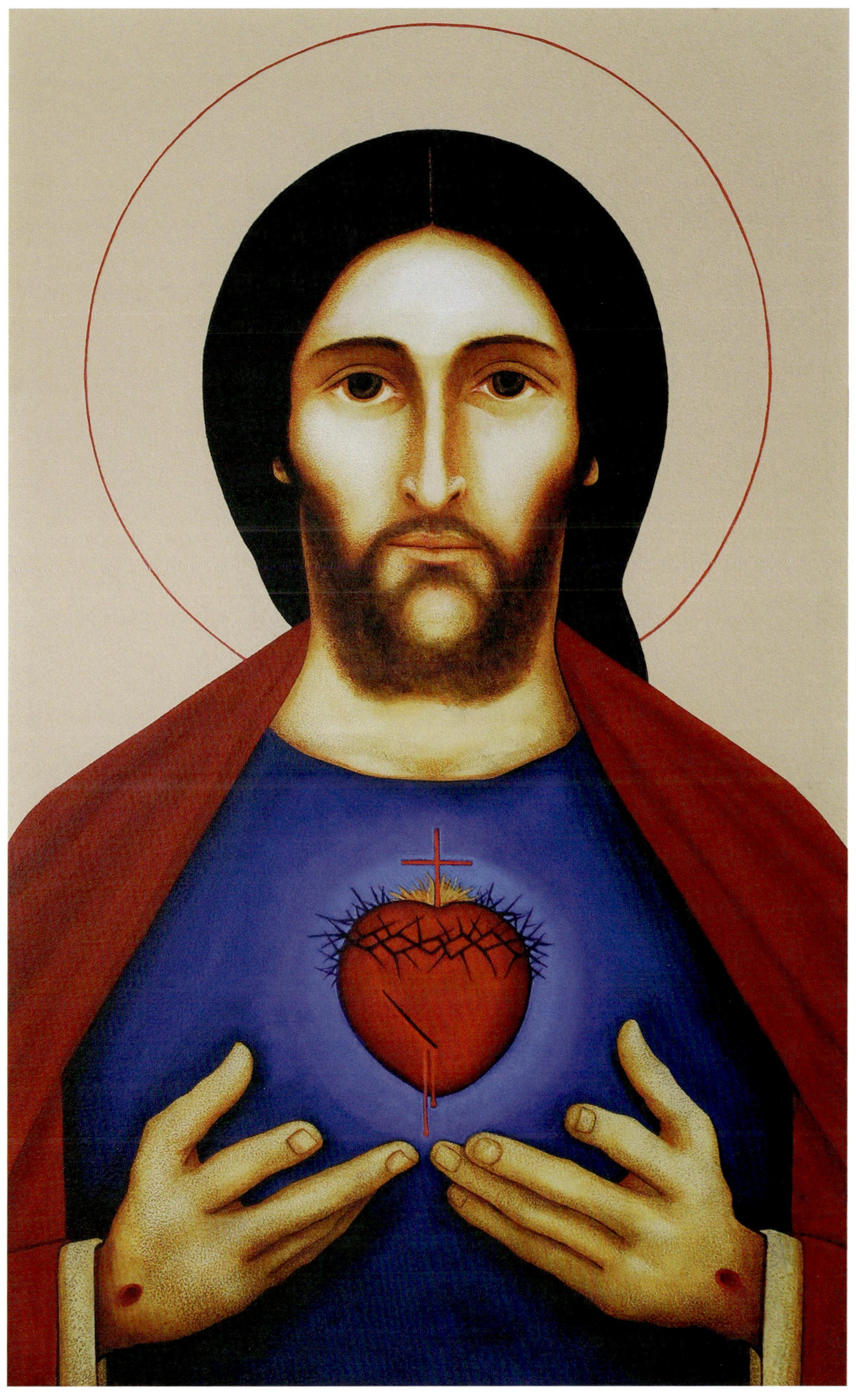

The Sacred Heart of Jesus, 2005, 16 inches by 28 inches

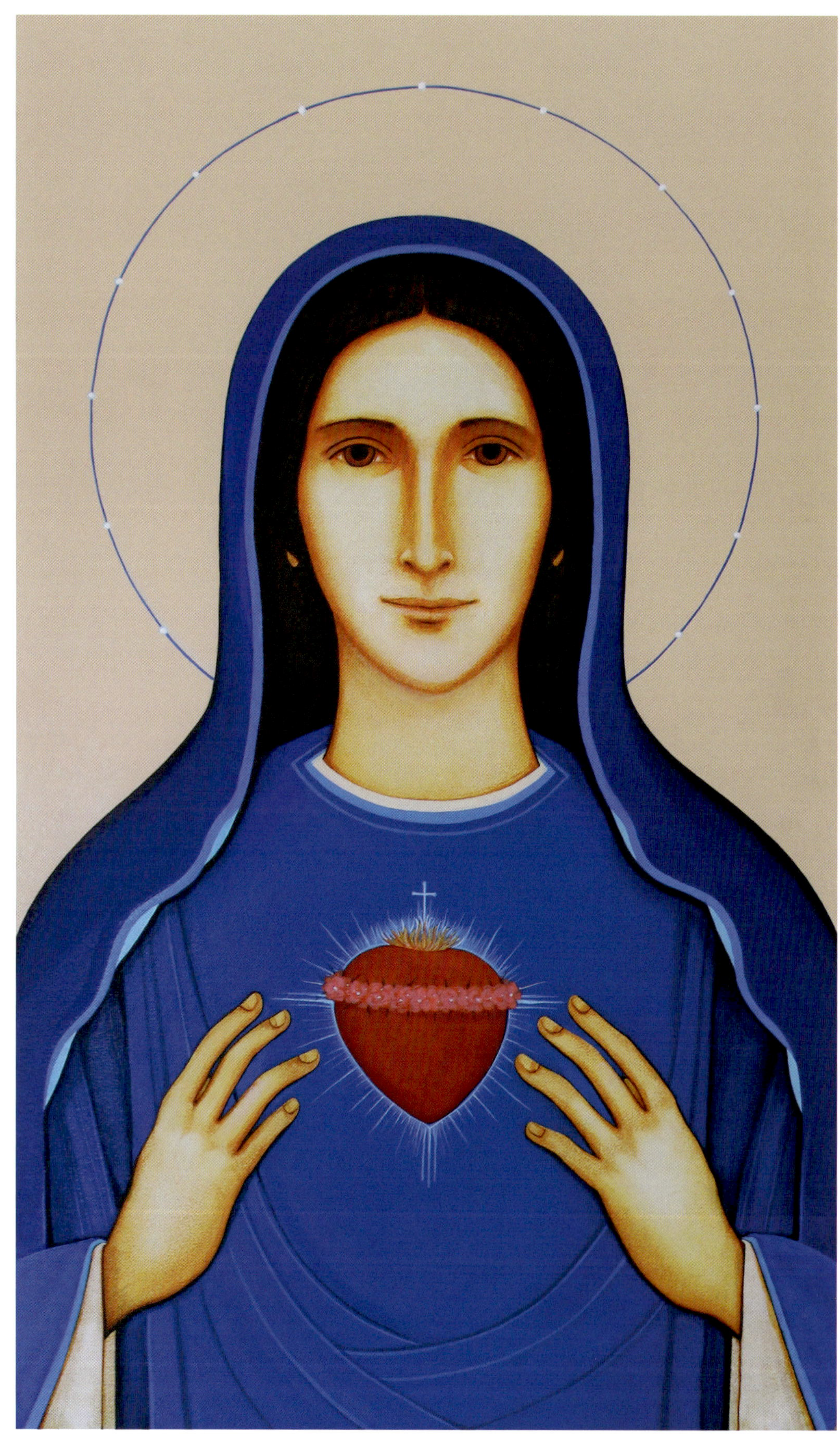

The Immaculate Heart of Mary, 2005, 16 inches by 28 inches

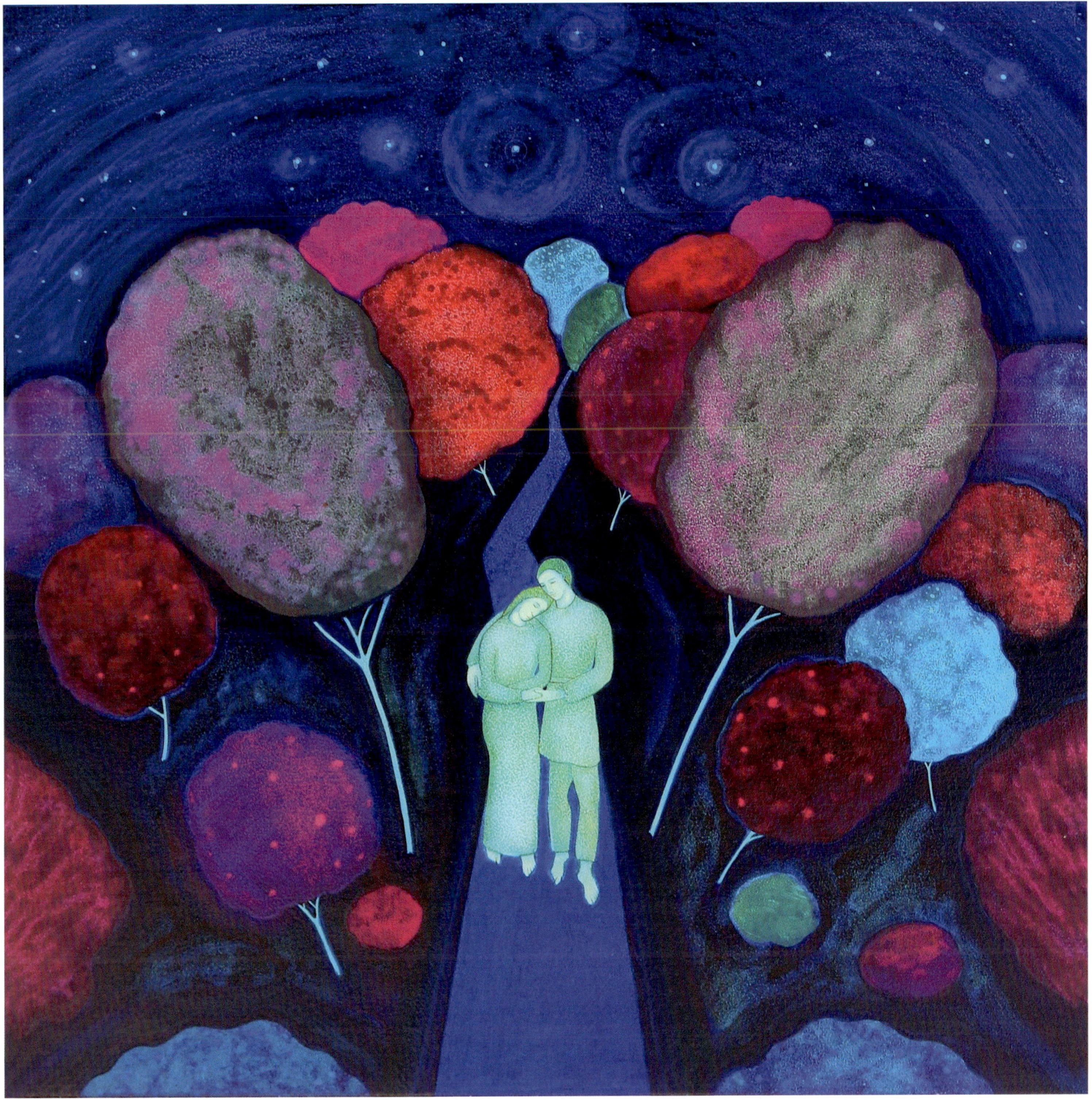

Love Makes the Darkness Light, 2004, 24 inches by 24 inches

166

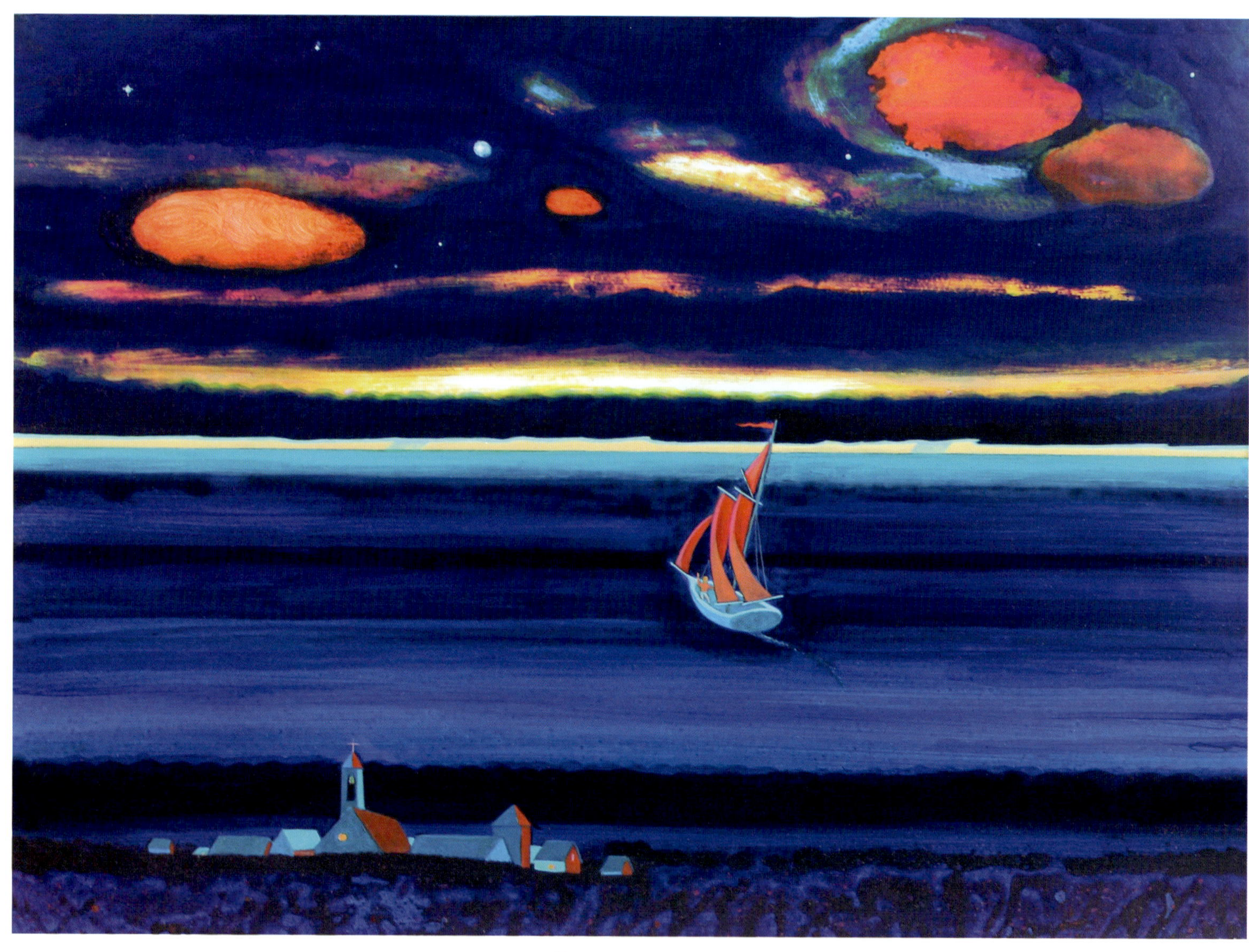

Departure, 2017

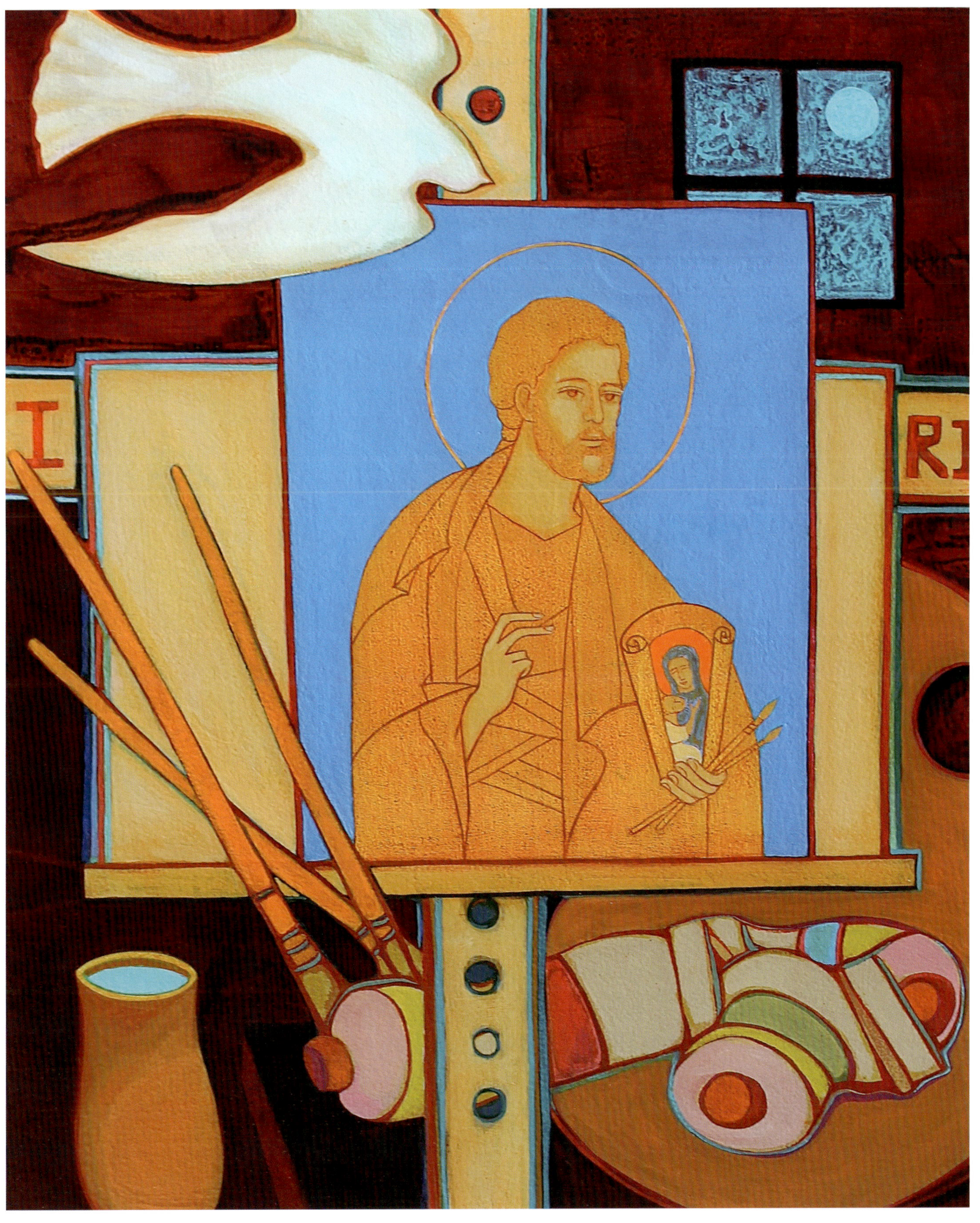

The Studio, 2016, 16 inches by 20 inches

APPENDIX

Owners and Curators of Paintings

Mount Angel Benedictine Abbey, St. Benedict, Oregon
Westminster Benedictine Abbey, Mission, British Columbia
Australian Catholic University, Melbourne
Lonergan University College, Montreal
St. Mark's Chapel, Laurentian University, Sudbury, Ontario
Holy Family Parish, Toronto
Dominican Fathers, Kigali, Rwanda
Providence Centre Retreat House, Edmonton
Missionary Oblates of Mary Immaculate Chapel, Ottawa
St. Barnabas Church, Ottawa
St. Michael and All Angels Church, Ottawa
St. Gerard's Parish, Ashcroft, British Columbia
St. Michael's Parish, Burnaby, British Columbia
St. Clare's Monastery, Mission, British Columbia
Most Rev. Adam Exner, Archbishop of Vancouver
Most Rev. Peter Mallon, Archbishop of Regina
Archdiocese of Vancouver, British Columbia, Chancery
Archbishop Terrence Prendergast, Ottawa
Dr. G. Delisle, Pictures Division, National Archives of Canada
Dr. A. Armstrong, Director, Canadian Council of Urban Affairs
The Basilian Fathers, St. Thomas More College, Saskatoon
St. Joseph's Parish, Mission, British Columbia
Liguori House, Redemptorist Fathers, Edmonton
Missionaries of Charity, Bronx, New York
Nazareth Family Apostolate, Combermere, Ontario
Madonna House, Combermere, Ontario
St. Louise de Marillac Parish, Seattle
St. Leo Parish, Tacoma, Washington
Our Lady of the Redwoods Trappistine Abbey, Whitethorn, California
St. Maximilian Kolbe Chapel, Combermere, Ontario
Holy Trinity Ukrainian Catholic Church, Kamloops, British Columbia
Good Shepherd Parish, Valemount, British Columbia
Institute for Christian Communities, Montreal
St. Margaret Mary Parish, Woodbridge, Ontario
Father Bressani High School, Woodbridge, Ontario
St. Peter's Parish, Woodbridge, Ontario
PeaceHealth St. John Medical Center, Longview, Washington
St. Luke's Parish, Maple Ridge, British Columbia

St. Anne's Parish Abbotsford, British Columbia
St. Peter's Parish, Cornwall, Ontario
Blessed Sacrament Parish, Cornwall, Ontario
Archdiocese of Portland, Oregon
St. Joseph Foundation, Steubenville, Ohio
Companions of the Cross, chapels in Ottawa and Combermere, Ontario
Becket Fund, Washington, D.C.
Augustinian Fathers, Klosterneuburg, Austria
Sisters of Life, New York
Contemplatives of St. Joseph, San Francisco

Written Works

Books

Fiction

A Cry of Stone. San Francisco: Ignatius Press, 2003.
Eclipse of the Sun. San Francisco: Ignatius Press, 1998.
Elijah in Jerusalem. San Francisco: Ignatius Press, 2015.
Father Elijah. San Francisco: Ignatius Press, 1996.
The Father's Tale. San Francisco: Ignatius Press, 2011.
The Fool of New York City. San Francisco: Ignatius Press, 2016.
Island of the World. San Francisco: Ignatius Press, 2007.
Plague Journal. San Francisco: Ignatius Press, 1999.
The Small Angel. Brudenell, Ontario: White Horse Press, 1993.
Sophia House. San Francisco: Ignatius Press, 2005.
Strangers and Sojourners. San Francisco: Ignatius Press, 1997.
Theophilos. San Francisco: Ignatius Press, 2010.
Voyage to Alpha Centauri. San Francisco: Ignatius Press, 2013.
Winter Tales. Ottawa: Justin Press, 2011.

Nonfiction

The Apocalypse: Warning, Hope and Consolation. Belmont, N.C.: Wiseblood Books, 2018.
Arriving Where We Started: Faith and Culture in the Postmodernist Age. Ottawa: Justin Press, 2012.
The Donkey Dialogues: Correspondence between Mate Krajina and Michael O'Brien. Ottawa: Justin Press, 2014.
The Family and the New Totalitarianism. Belmont, N.C.: Wiseblood Books–Divine Providence Press, 2019. First published 1995 by White Horse Press (Brudenell, Ontario).
Father at Night. Ottawa: Justin Press, 2011.
Friendly Dragons, Moral Nightmares. Mount Morris, N.Y.: Lamplighter Press, 2009.

Harry Potter and the Paganization of Culture. Rzeszow, Poland: Fides et Traditio Press, 2010.
John Paul II's Biblical Way of the Cross (illustrations). Notre Dame, Ind.: Ave Maria Press, 2009.
A Landscape with Dragons: The Battle for Your Child's Mind. Revised, expanded edition. San Francisco: Ignatius Press, 1998. First published 1994 by Northern River Press (Quebec).
The Mysteries of the Most Holy Rosary (text and illustrations). Brudenell, Ontario: White Horse Press, 1992.
Remembrance of the Future: Reflections on Our Times. Ottawa: Justin Press, 2009.
Stations of the Cross: *Paintings and Meditations*. Ottawa: Justin Press, 2018.
Waiting: Stories for Advent. Ottawa: Justin Press, 2010.
William Kurelek: Painter and Prophet. Ottawa: Justin Press, 2013.

Chapters in Anthologies

"Catechesis and Evangelization" and "Disaster, Rage, Repentance". In *The Wisdom of Nazareth: Stories of Catholic Family Life*. Oxford: Family Publications, 2008.
"Historical Imagination and the Renewal of Culture". In *Eternity in Time: Christopher Dawson and the Catholic Idea of History*. Edinburgh: T and T Clark, 1997.
"In Search of the Father". In *Either Protagonists or Nobodies*. Milan: Mondadori, 2009.
"Subsidiary in Art: The Flow of Celestial Language". In *Logos et Musica: In Honorem Summi Romanum Pontificis Benedicti XVI*. Frankfurt am Main: Peter Lang Intenationaler Verlag der Wissenschaften, 2012.

Essays and Articles in Periodicals

Nazareth Journal, editor in chief from 1989 to 1996, with editorial and articles in each issue.
Essays, reviews, and articles for the following periodicals: *Communio*, *Inside the Vatican*, *Catholic Insight*, *Chesterton Review*, *Catholic Dossier*, *Canadian Catholic Review*, *Lay Witness, Restoration*, *Second Spring*, *National Catholic Register*, *Traces*, *Our Sunday Visitor*, and others.
Interviews and translated articles in foreign-language journals published in France, Spain, Italy, Poland, Croatia, and Bosnia-Herzegovina.

Awards

Canadian Christian Writing Award, from the Evangelical Fellowship of Canada: First Place, for *Eclipse of the Sun*; awarded 1999.
Andrija Buvina Award from the Church in Croatia, for accomplishments in Faith and Culture; awarded 2005.
Servant of the Word Award, from the Archdiocese of Denver, Colorado; awarded 2006.

Archbishop Adam Exner Award for Catholic Excellence in Public Life, from the Catholic Civil Rights League, Canada; awarded 2012.

Logos Book Award, "Best 2012 Book—Fiction", for *The Father's Tale*, from the Logos Bookstore Association, USA; awarded 2013.

Catholic Culture Award, from Our Lady Seat of Wisdom College, Barry's Bay, Ontario; awarded 2014.

Aquinas Award, from Aquinas College, Nashville, Tennessee, for *Elijah in Jerusalem*; awarded 2016.

Feniks Award (Phoenix Award), from the Association of Catholic Publishers, Poland, for *Elijah in Jerusalem;* awarded 2017.

St. Katharine Drexel Award, from the Catholic Library Association, Baton Rouge, Louisiana; awarded 2019.

John Cardinal O'Connor Award, from The Sisters of Life, New York City; awarded 2019.

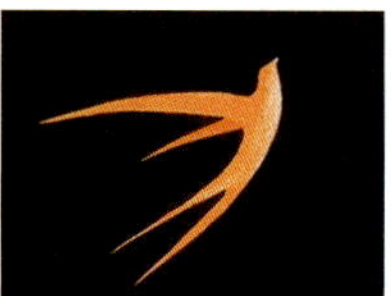